The Digital Art Book

Imagine Publishing Ltd
Richmond House
33 Richmond Hill
Bournemouth
Dorset BH2 6EZ
☎ +44 (0) 1202 586200
Website: www.imagine-publishing.co.uk
Twitter: @Books_Imagine
Facebook: www.facebook.com/ImagineBookazines

Head of Publishing
Aaron Asadi

Head of Design
Ross Andrews

Production Editor
Sarah Harrison

Senior Art Editor
Greg Whitaker

Designer
Abbi Denney

Photographer
James Sheppard

Printed by
William Gibbons, 26 Planetary Road, Willenhall, West Midlands, WV13 3XT

Distributed in the UK & Eire by
Imagine Publishing Ltd, www.imagineshop.co.uk. Tel 01202 586200

Distributed in Australia by
Gordon & Gotch, Equinox Centre, 18 Rodborough Road, Frenchs Forest,
NSW 2086. Tel + 61 2 9972 8800

Distributed in the Rest of the World by
Marketforce, Blue Fin Building, 110 Southwark Street, London, SE1 0SU

The Digital Art Book Volume 1 © 2014 Imagine Publishing Ltd

ISBN 978 1909 758 476

Part of the

Photoshop®
creative
bookazine series

IMAGINE
PUBLISHING

CONTENTS

DISCOVER THE VERY
BEST TECHNIQUES FOR
CREATING DIGITAL ART
AND ENHANCING YOUR
PROJECTS THROUGH
STEP-BY-STEP GUIDES

8
The
ultimate
guide
to digital art

42

62

18

52

The Digital Art Book

The world of digital art is vast, with programs such as Photoshop and Illustrator dominating the market, alongside 3D software such as Maya, MODO and CINEMA 4D to name a few. Knowing where to start can be challenging, but having an initial concept is half the battle. Whether your area of interest lies in editing photos, painting digital masterpieces or creating eye-catching typography, or perhaps you prefer building characters, experimenting with mixed media or using 3D software, The Digital Art Book explores each of these areas, demonstrating what you can do to take your projects to the next level. With expert guides on essential techniques, the book is packed full of step-by-step tutorials so you can follow along or simply take inspiration for your own work. And if that wasn't enough, we have included a free disc full of tutorial files, so you can use the same images we used, as well as video tuition and resources such as brushes, textures and models. Enjoy the book.

98

112

90

108

82

134

144

166

170

150

THE ULTIMATE GUIDE TO DIGITAL ART

GET INSPIRED BY THE MANY WAYS TO CRAFT VISUALS DIGITALLY

The ultimate guide to digital art

Digital art is a fascinating movement bristling with many exciting visual forms. Computer-aided painting, 3D worlds and dynamic effects all help define this digital Renaissance. Most historic and traditional styles can be replicated digitally, while the ever-expanding toolsets and capabilities of modern creative software empower techno-savvy artists, animators and graphic designers to formulate new breeds of art that enthral viewers.

3D programs such as Maya, CINEMA 4D and 3ds Max enable the creation of models that can be used in stunning animations, 3D visualisations, or mixed with 2D assets for intricate compositions.

Illustrator is the go-to program for crisp shapes and typographic expressions. You can create full-blown vector artwork that scales as large as you want, or export your creations to other programs for additional work or integration into incredibly pixel-heavy concoctions.

Photoshop is the hub of many visual workflows and you can create artwork inside this powerful software using both 2D and basic 3D tools, and bring in various elements such as scanned-in textures or assets from other software packages. Numerous plug-ins augment Photoshop's already formidable toolset, such as ArtWork from AKVIS, which helps jumpstart your painting process by converting photos into real-media works.

Painter is a potent alternative to Photoshop's paint game, providing a whole range of brushes, paint styles, and paper textures, along with a highly realistic brush engine. You can even edit Photoshop files directly in Painter!

So, read on, get inspired, and create your own amazing digital artwork!

" Beginners can explore photo painting with filters, while pros can take advantage of evolved brush engines and access to millions of colours "

DIGITAL PAINTING

USE SOFTWARE TO TURN YOUR COMPUTER INTO THE ULTIMATE CANVAS

So, are you ready to take your painting into the digital realm? The numerous tools and features of software such as Photoshop and Painter enable artists of all skill levels to create art appropriate for their experience. Beginners can explore photo painting with filters and guide layers, while professionals can take advantage of evolved brush engines and instantaneous access to millions of colours.

Layers and history states grant digital painters the full freedom to explore their creativity without fear of failure, so if you make an artistic wrong turn, you can delete or rearrange your layers, or simply go back through your history.

FOUR WAYS TO PAINT DIGITALLY

JUST A FEW OF THE BEST WAYS YOU CAN GET CREATIVE WITH A COMPUTER

01 MERGE TOGETHER PAINT AND TEXTURES
One of the big advantages of painting digitally is the ability to create your work across multiple layers. This gives you the flexibility to move and edit your composition's elements at will. You can also intersperse various textures and grit.

02 USE PLUG-INS
Plug-ins such as AKVIS's ArtWork turbocharge Photoshop's already rich artistic capabilities. This image was created using a variety of ArtWork's filters, which mimic traditional media. Layer masks, blend modes and Photoshop's Mixer brush were employed to meld everything together.

03 GO ABSTRACT
Without the need to purchase a canvas for every artistic endeavor, you're free to let loose and experiment! Go abstract and let your feelings flow out from your stylus or mouse. Mix in random scraps for added mixed-media fun.

04 COMPOSITE AND PAINT
You can mix together compositing, filters and painting for a complex masterpiece. Here, a lot of hand-painting was done throughout, but the more-intricate techno details were first composited, processed with artistic filters, then painted over for a final macabre glaze.

CHARACTER

CREATING AN APPEALING CHARACTER STARTS WITH DEVELOPING A PERSONALITY

When it comes to creating characters, there are currently a multitude of digital options available. Photoshop can offer simple paint and sketch possibilities and also has a great community. Illustrator can also provide a fantastic toolset, if vector artwork is your flavour. Let's not forget the 3D players such as 3ds Max and Maya. But before you turn to your chosen application, don't forget the important goal, which is to create a character with appeal. You need to go deeper than just technique and tools – you need to create a personality, a background story, a purpose and, above all, an attitude.

> **Executing good technique and using the right tools is a great place to start, but these will never replace a great concept**

INJECT SOME CHARACTER
SOME IMPORTANT TIPS TO REMEMBER FOR BRINGING OUT PERSONALITY IN YOUR CREATIONS

01 TEXTURE USING SOME BLENDING MODES

Adding texture to your character can bring a greater level of realism. Simply import a texture image into Photoshop, then copy and paste it onto a new layer over your character. Change the blending mode until you have the required look.

02 EYES REVEAL THE SOUL

Don't ever underestimate the importance of eyes in your character designs. The eyes are a window to the soul and if executed correctly, can relate an incredible amount of information about your character's motivation, attitude and personality. Remember: study your reference.

03 PRODUCE A STRONG SILHOUETTE

Dynamic posing is a technique used by character illustrators and comic book masters alike. It simply means silhouette character posing. The viewer needs to immediately know what is happening. Check your poses by filling the character with black on a white background.

04 DON'T FORGET THE ENVIRONMENT

A successful character illustration has to relate information about the character and about a greater narrative. By focusing on the character alone, this can be quite a challenge. Many accomplished artists rely on using background elements to relate important information.

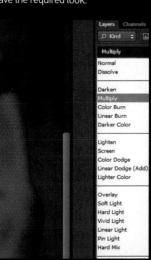

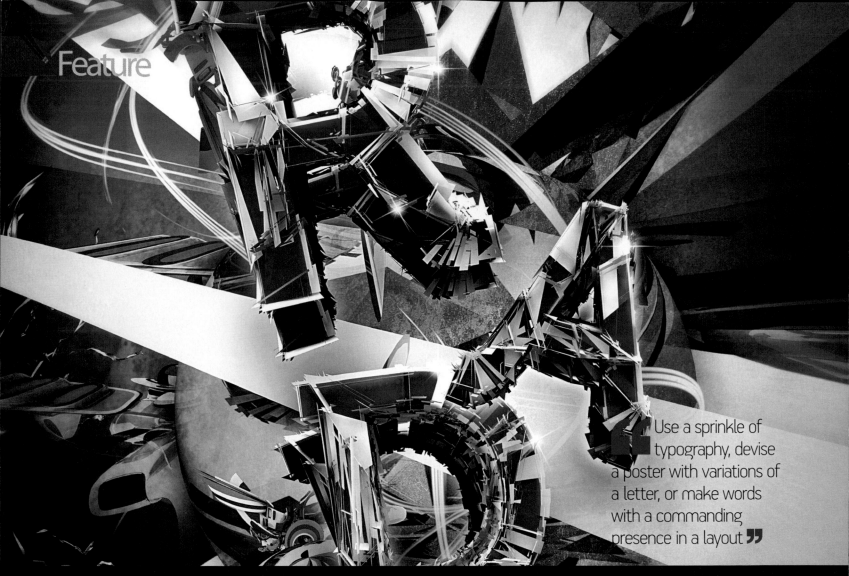

> Use a sprinkle of typography, devise a poster with variations of a letter, or make words with a commanding presence in a layout "

TYPOGRAPHY

LOOK AT TYPE IN A DIFFERENT WAY AND WIELD IT TO UNLEASH THE BEAUTY OF LETTERFORMS

Have you ever noticed the artistry behind a well-designed font? Yes? Well, why not add words and letterforms to your artistic arsenal? You can use a light sprinkle of typography, devise a poster with just variations of a single letter, or make words a commanding presence in a layout.

Different font families add different types of flavour. Calligraphic and script fonts can lend looping, swirling elegance, while blocky Sans Serif fonts can add no-nonsense rigidity to chaotic spreads. Illustrator is the perfect typographic environment, enabling you to hone each detail. You can also combine primitive shapes to form your own unique lettering.

BUILD UNIQUE TYPOGRAPHY
FOUR INSPIRING WAYS TO TURN ORDINARY TYPE INTO EXCITING ARTWORK

01 CREATE YOUR OWN LETTERFORMS

Illustrator is the ultimate playground for creating and combining shapes that can scale freely. Start with a simple array of geometric shapes, combine them to create your own letterforms, then bring it all into Photoshop and apply texture and various adjustments.

02 WEATHER AND GRUNGE

Photoshop can aid you in removing the sheen of perfection inherent in digital works with a nice helping of grunge. Blend old paper scans, cut and paste newspaper scraps, or desaturate and alter colours and tones using one of the many adjustment layers.

03 KEEP IT SIMPLE

This stripped-down layout was started with a few smoke shots merged together. FontFabric.com is a great place to go for elegant fonts, a great deal of which are free. Here Code was used to complete the typographic composition.

04 PLAY WITH 3D

With Photoshop CC, it's easier than ever to play with 3D. Quickly add dimensional oomph to your text and shapes with just one click, then use the intuitive 3D tools and on-canvas controls to arrange them in 3D space.

"There really are no mistakes when working digitally; if you hit a snag, you can undo your steps or rearrange your layers"

MIXED MEDIA

BLUR THE LINES BETWEEN DIGITAL AND TRADITIONAL FORMATS FOR TRULY UNIQUE RESULTS

Digital mixed media can be one of the most liberating artistic undertakings. Scan images, textures and drawings, then blend them with digital assets for spectacular unions. There really are no mistakes when working digitally; if you hit a snag, simply back-track your steps or rearrange your layers. Sometimes the process of jumbling layers can lead to pleasantly unexpected variations.

Photoshop is the main program to use when constructing mixed media, but since most creative software use a layer-based approach, you could try using Illustrator or even a page-layout program like InDesign to blend media. So, without any further ado, let's get mixing.

MIX UP YOUR ARTWORK
LET YOUR IMAGINATION TAKE CONTROL BY UTILISING MULTIPLE FORMATS

01 COPY AND PASTE
Create a collage without the paper cuts! Gather your photos and paper scans, then use Photoshop's Polygonal Lasso or Pen tool to make imperfect selections. You can simply copy and paste these into your main document to build up your composition until complete.

02 MIX WITH ILLUSTRATION
Illustration and mixed media have always been good teammates. Start with an illustration, or dust off one that you began but could never quite finish. Cut up and scan some random bits of paper, then arrange them within your illustration.

03 COMBINE WITH 3D
By taking a sci-fi slant to the canvas, you can jumble brush explorations with digital shapes and 3D renders to create an exciting fusion that will really stand out. See what other combinations of styles and genres you can come up with.

04 GO STREET STYLE
Hit the streets (from the safety of your studio). Harness the chaotic energy of street art and create a masterpiece fit for the back alley. Use various spatter brushes, images and street textures to produce beautifully chaotic creations.

> "3D digital art is one of the easiest mediums to learn and master. After all, we do live in a 3D world"

3D ART

CREATING A 3D MASTERPIECE HAS NEVER BEEN MORE POSSIBLE THAN TODAY

Once upon a time the art world was a master and apprentice affair, where most people could only aspire to become an artist. However, with the advent of digital hardware, software and more importantly the internet, being artistically creative has never been so easy. Not only is it more accessible than ever, the planet seems to be full of people itching to share their creative knowledge. This is especially true in the world of 3D. Whether you're interested in 3D architectural visualisation, modelling, character animation, abstract artwork or even cinematic matte painting, both the tools and a vibrant community are just waiting to be explored.

ENTER THE WORLD OF CG
FOUR WAYS YOU CAN TAKE YOUR WORK TO THE NEXT DIMENSION

01 BRING A NEW SPIN
There are many traditional art forms which, when brought into the 3D world, offer a whole new spin. For instance, graffiti, which has always been restricted to a 2D surface. Mix in a little 3D and the possibilities are quite striking.

02 TRY CONTRASTING LIGHT AND SHADOW
A difficult challenge has always been balancing light areas with shadow. In other mediums, the ability to create convincing and consistent lighting is quite hard to master. However, in a true 3D environment, lighting and shadows are both accurate and easy to manage.

03 BRING LIFE TO YOUR CHARACTER CREATIONS
Once a character has been modelled in 3D, adding an animation rig will enable you to play with poses. This, coupled with varying the camera angle, can add a certain attitude or personality, without the need to redraw the character.

04 EXPERIMENT WITH FANTASTICAL WORLDS
By using good reference, lighting, modelling, texturing and rendering, you can explore worlds that are not readily accessible. These can include the microscopic, outer space, the deepest oceans, the past, the future or even hostile environments, just to name a few.

> Apply intense effects and use eye-catching techniques to promote your photos beyond dusty albums and into cutting-edge advertisements and murals

PHOTO EDITING

ELEVATE YOUR PHOTOS INTO BEAUTIFUL WORKS WITH CREATIVE PHOTO EDITING

The rise of digital cameras has led to a photo-editing revolution. Anyone who has ever taken a digital snapshot has seen the results on-screen and wondered how it could be improved. Tone and colour can be corrected, red-eye can be abolished and extraneous detail can be cropped away.

Sure, that's all helpful. A focused and tonally sound photo can be a beautiful thing. How about we take it even further? Blend disparate photos, apply intense and exotic effects and use eye-catching techniques to promote your photos beyond dusty albums and into cutting-edge advertisements and exciting murals.

TAKE YOUR DIGITAL PHOTOS FURTHER
INCORPORATE YOUR OWN PICTURES INTO YOUR CANVAS

01 GET CREATIVE WITH PHOTOSHOP MASKS

Photoshop's clipping masks let you create windows of visibility. For example, you can use a word as a mask and clip a picture inside. Here multiple masks were used to create a lively sprawl of windows using the same photo.

02 SPLIT TONE IT

Experimenting with juxtapositions of photos can produce some impressive results. Case in point, the wild diver here was jumbled with an almost random roster of textures and flora, then split-toned to get a moody blend that borders on abstraction.

03 MAKE A STATEMENT

Is your photo lacking something? Try giving it a hand by creating a bold declaration manually, or use a nice handwritten font (or even combine both). You could end up with a print-worthy addition to your portfolio with minimal sweat.

04 USE BLEND MODES

Photoshop's exquisite library of blend modes is the secret weapon for photographers and graphic designers who love to experiment and mix their photos together. This image was constructed using a picture of a woman, a bokeh shot and various textures.

DIGITAL PAINTING

TURN YOUR FAVOURITE
PHOTOGRAPHS INTO
PAINTINGS OR LEARN
TO PAINT ARTWORK
FROM SCRATCH

Sketch it out
Use a small, hard brush, or pick the Pencil tool to create a rough sketch. Don't worry about being too precise; a few rough lines will help your image look all the more realistic

SOURCE FILES ✓
AVAILABLE ON THE FREE DISC

PHOTOSHOP

TURN PHOTOS INTO PAINTINGS

TRANSFORM PHOTOSHOP INTO A DIGITAL CANVAS USING THESE FAIL-SAFE TECHNIQUES FOR REALISTIC MEDIA EFFECTS

Digital art is a fantastic avenue for creatives to explore, with a host of techniques and tools to help you make something to be proud of. But there can be an issue with digital artwork. Unless a concerted effort is made, the results can lack the texture and tactile nature of real media. Now we said that an effort needs to be made. The good news is that even a small amount of effort can give a fantastic result. By getting clever with a combination of techniques, you can make amazing art.

Over the following pages, you will discover all of the tricks needed for emulating traditional art media. In researching these, we deliberately limited the equipment and tools used.

This means that whatever version of Photoshop you are using, you will be able to follow along. Yes, CS5 and above have a bunch of shiny, real-media brushes all ready and raring to go, however, if you have a different version, you will not be left behind. Everything is created with a mouse, and photographs are used as the basis, so you do not even have to be able to draw.

In addition to a general look at the best painting tools, we have four projects that create digital versions of popular mediums; namely oil, charcoal, watercolour and pencil sketch. We will share our tricks for re-creating them in Photoshop, helping ensure you get the best results every time.

Scatter the brush
If you increase the Scattering value from the Brush palette, you can rough up the edges of your brush and make it look more realistic. Uniform strokes are the hallmark of digital – real media is more random

Mixed media with blend modes
To add the final flourish to your painting, scan in some real brush marks and use the blend modes to make them merge with your image. Adjust the colour with Hue/Saturation to make things just so

Introduce texture
Once you have sorted the main image, be bold with large, sweeping textured strokes. Use the Texture setting from the Brush palette to make a defined pattern and ensure the Opacity slider in Transfer is low for maximum effect

Know your tools
You have different ways of applying paint in Photoshop, but all will use brush tips to give the final effect. Here the Smudge tool was used to smear and blend splots of colour, with an oil brush tip for the buttery, smooth finish

GETTING STARTED
A FEW PREPARATION TRICKS TO GET YOUR ARTWORK UNDERWAY

Just as a traditional artist might make some preliminary sketches or colour studies before creating a main image, there are a few tasks the digital artist can do to set themselves up for a more successful result. All of these can be followed whatever style you are working in, and will help ensure that you give your work the best start possible.

QUICK TIP
FIX MESSY SCANS

If you have scanned in a sketch and find that the Levels command is picking up unwanted detail, use the Black and White command instead. Sometimes your scanner will pick up texture in the background, which the Levels adjustment accentuates. A quick whack of Black and White, however, and you can proceed with the Levels as normal.

SCAN IN ELEMENTS

  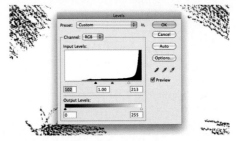

01 CREATE YOUR ELEMENTS
We're going to scan in some charcoal marks to turn into brushes. The first task is obviously to make the marks, in this case charcoal on white paper. Use a pale background if possible. You can also use this technique to scan your sketches.

02 INPUT SCANNER SETTINGS
Although scanning software differs, there is one thing you absolutely have to do. Look for the setting to dictate the resolution of the object you are scanning – put this to 600. That way you have a bit more flexibility in terms of editing and use.

03 EDIT FOR USE
Open your scan and use Image> Adjustments>Levels in Photoshop or Enhance> Adjust Lighting>Levels in Elements to whiten the background and darken the sketch. Drag the white slider to the left, and the black slider to the right.

CORRECT COLOUR

Part of the joy of painting with Photoshop is that you can play with colour in a way that is out of reach to traditional artists. Let's say you have a daytime shot but you want to paint a sunset scene. Open up the Photo Filter command and apply a deep yellow or red filter. Job done! Maybe you are going to paint a portrait, but aren't keen on the colour clothes the subject is wearing. Make a selection of the area and use Hue/Saturation to alter the colour. Once you have finished the painting, you might find that it looks a little drab. Use the Vibrance command to inject some zing, or use Brightness/Contrast to strengthen the highlights or shadows.

CONSTRUCT SCENES

Even if you are solely relying on a photo for reference, you don't have to put up with what reality serves. Use the selection tools, copy and paste, plus some transform magic to construct the precise scene you want. In our example, the starting photo was okay but it lacked foreground interest. This was fixed by selecting trees and flowers from another image, and copying and pasting them. The Free Transform tool was used to get these pasted objects to the right size. Another sky was also added. It doesn't matter if the selections aren't perfect or the objects a bit pixellated, as this will all be hidden with a layer of digital paint!

THE ESSENTIALS
BECOME ACCUSTOMED TO THE BEST TOOLS

Obviously there is a high amount of creative freedom when it comes to you actually making your painting, but there are also a few set skills and elements that you will call upon whatever type of image you are dabbling with. All of these will make an appearance in your work. You may only use one or two at a time, but keep them in mind and you can rest assured your work will shine.

BRUSHES

The key to a realistic effect is picking the correct brush. Photoshop and Elements ship with a raft of brush tips' some tailored to media effects such as oil, watercolour and pastel. These, coupled with the tweaks that can be made should be all you need. If not, you can pick up free brushes online, or if you have a specific need, make your own.

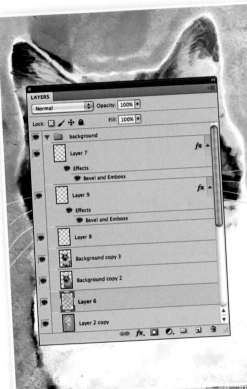

FRAMES

Create a mount by cutting out an area on a doc and applying a small bevel. For a simple frame, use a big brush on a new layer over the painting, click on a corner, hold Shift and click in the opposite corner. Repeat for all edges.

FILTERS

Although Photoshop hasn't got a filter that will instantly create a great work of art (we have looked!), they work well for prepping a photo. The Artistic filters are a treasure trove for this, with Cutout and Palette Knife being the best.

SPECIAL TOOLS

The Smudge tool and the Art History tool (the Impressionist brush in Elements) can take colour and shape information from a photo and then translate the information into the effect of whatever brush is chosen.

SET UP THE CANVAS

A lot of artists will roughly block in a canvas with colour to avoid staring at a blank space, and you can do the same when setting up your document. Pick a colour that complements the overall tone of your image (red for warm scenes, blue for cool) and brush over at low opacity. Also use the Texturizer filter or Texture layer style to add a texture.

LAYERS

An artist has to wait for paint to dry if they want to add paint on top of paint, but we get to do it instantly thanks to the Layers palette. In addition to isolating different areas on layers so they can be edited without affecting the rest of the image, layers also offer blend modes to incorporate texture and layer styles for special effects.

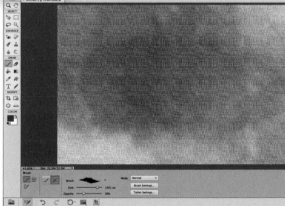

MAKING SELECTIONS

Selections are great for building a start photo, or isolating areas for specific brushwork, colour tweaks or deletion (things don't always go right!). And you don't have to be too precise, because you can paint over any stray pixels.

APPLY AND ADAPT BRUSHES
THE BRUSHES ARE ESSENTIAL TOOLS IN YOUR DIGITAL PAINTING QUEST, SO LEARN HOW TO BLEND THEM TO YOUR WILL

The brushes in Photoshop would be pretty smart on their own, but combined with the customisation options in the Brush palette, you have all you need to get the precise look you want. In addition to the obvious size and opacity options, you can play with texture, wetness, angles and more. If you have a graphics tablet, ensure you enable pressure sensitivity so you can adapt settings by pushing harder or lighter. For everyone else, get used to using the [and] keys to change brush size and keep the Brush palette open to make changes on the fly.

CONTROL BRUSHES IN ELEMENTS

Select the Brush tool in Elements and hit the Brush Settings button. Here you have sliders to control Fade, Hue Jitter, Scattering, Hardness and Roundness. You also have an Angle setting for adjusting the angle of a brush and enabling you to squish it. If you have a tablet, use the Tablet Settings area to decide how it is controlled. In addition to these, you can also adjust size, opacity and blend mode from Brush Tool Options.

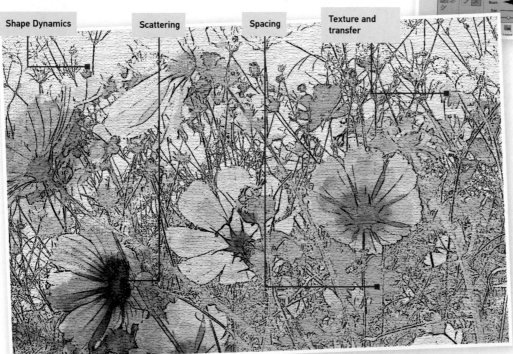

Shape Dynamics | Scattering | Spacing | Texture and transfer

Without texture

With texture

TEXTURE AND TRANSFER

Use the Texture option to add texture to brushstrokes. You can pick the type of texture used as well as how visible it is. This is controlled with the Opacity Jitter slider in Transfer.

Without Scattering

With Scattering

SCATTERING

This option is very important if you are emulating a charcoal, chalk or pastel effect, as by whacking the Scatter slider up, you can give the effect of using the charcoal or pastel on its side. Artists do this to quickly block in large areas.

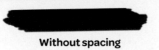

Without spacing

With spacing

SPACING

The Brush Tip Shape option holds the Spacing slider. This compresses or separates the elements that make up a brush. If you want a light, random dab of a brush, whack this slider up. For a more intense brush stroke, bring it down.

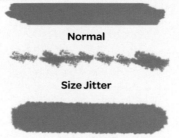

Normal

Size Jitter

Angle Jitter

SHAPE DYNAMICS

Two sliders really stand out in this set – Size Jitter and Angle Jitter. The first alters the size of the brush as you use it. Angle Jitter alters the direction of the brush at the edges and is great for mimicking a splayed brush.

LAYERS AND SPECIAL EFFECTS
USE LAYERS FOR THE ULTIMATE REAL MEDIA EFFECTS

Although the vast majority of your time will revolve around the brushes you pick and how you use them, layers and layer styles will help take your work over the finishing line. Adding the look of texture and depth is the easiest way to trick the eye into thinking it is seeing a real, physical painting.

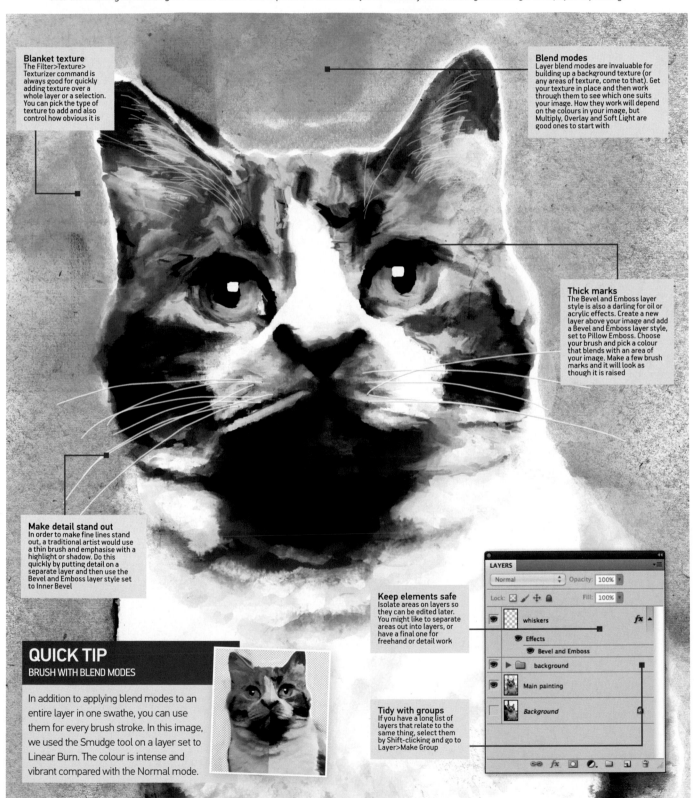

Blanket texture
The Filter>Texture>Texturizer command is always good for quickly adding texture over a whole layer or a selection. You can pick the type of texture to add and also control how obvious it is

Blend modes
Layer blend modes are invaluable for building up a background texture (or any areas of texture, come to that). Get your texture in place and then work through them to see which one suits your image. How they work will depend on the colours in your image, but Multiply, Overlay and Soft Light are good ones to start with

Thick marks
The Bevel and Emboss layer style is also a darling for oil or acrylic effects. Create a new layer above your image and add a Bevel and Emboss layer style, set to Pillow Emboss. Choose your brush and pick a colour that blends with an area of your image. Make a few brush marks and it will look as though it is raised

Make detail stand out
In order to make fine lines stand out, a traditional artist would use a thin brush and emphasise with a highlight or shadow. Do this quickly by putting detail on a separate layer and then use the Bevel and Emboss layer style set to Inner Bevel

Keep elements safe
Isolate areas on layers so they can be edited later. You might like to separate areas out into layers, or have a final one for freehand or detail work

Tidy with groups
If you have a long list of layers that relate to the same thing, select them by Shift-clicking and go to Layer>Make Group

QUICK TIP
BRUSH WITH BLEND MODES

In addition to applying blend modes to an entire layer in one swathe, you can use them for every brush stroke. In this image, we used the Smudge tool on a layer set to Linear Burn. The colour is intense and vibrant compared with the Normal mode.

Digital painting

OIL LANDSCAPE
CREATE JUICY, OPAQUE, TEXTURED WORKS OF WONDER

Traditional oil painting is a lot of fun that offers artists a range of possibilities. Oil paints can be diluted with turps to give a washy feel, but they are generally used opaquely. Oil paintings tend to be bumpy terrains, with layers of paint forming to give a crusty feel. You can mimic this look in Photoshop, but for a great project, print your digital oil onto inkjet canvas and embellish with real paint. Sticking digitally, though, the Wet Media Brushes set houses good oil options. Angle Jitter in Shape Dynamics will emulate the choppy brush movement artists favour. Use the Brush Tip Shape for the oval shape of a filbert brush. Texture-wise, oils are known for being on canvas. Make sure you have bits of canvas showing, but only in some areas. Oddly, the less texture, the more realistic it is.

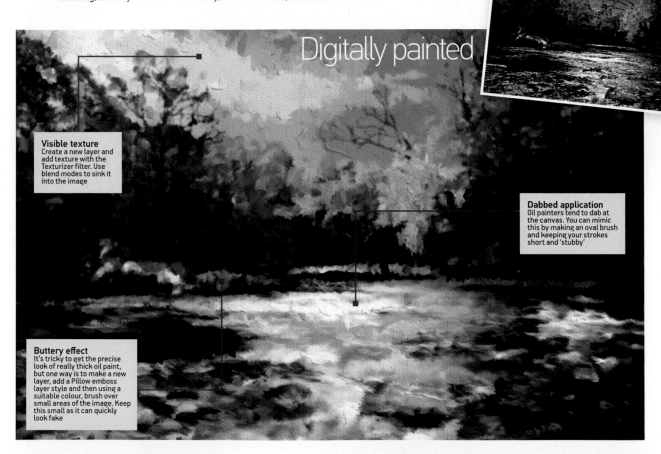

Digitally painted

Original

Visible texture
Create a new layer and add texture with the Texturizer filter. Use blend modes to sink it into the image

Dabbed application
Oil painters tend to dab at the canvas. You can mimic this by making an oval brush and keeping your strokes short and 'stubby'

Buttery effect
It's tricky to get the precise look of really thick oil paint, but one way is to make a new layer, add a Pillow emboss layer style and then using a suitable colour, brush over small areas of the image. Keep this small as it can quickly look fake

ALL HAIL CUTOUT

The Cutout filter is perfect for simplifying photos to get them ready for over-painting with oil effects. Because oils are so wet, an artist has to wait for them to dry slightly

before progressing. A usual workflow is a roughing in stage with very weak oil to block in tonal values, and then overlaying this with a thicker layer for more detail. The final touch is to bring in the detail.

The Cutout filter is a good way to replicate this process, as you can set up your photo for each stage. Then, by forcing yourself to paint in separate layers in your document, you will find that detail from lower layers show through where you have missed parts on the layer you are currently working on (and you will miss bits!). This helps give a feeling of depth.

FAKE REAL BRUSHES

Amazingly, the brushes used by oil artists can all be faked in Photoshop. The Filbert brush (sometimes called a Cat's Tongue brush) is great for building up texture with dabs and can also be used on its side for a thick and thin effect. Use the Light Oil Flat Tip brush from Wet Media, and select the Brush Tip Shape Angle device to squeeze into an oval. An artist's flat brush is used for blocking in large areas and can be replicated in Photoshop with the Square Brush set. Pick any of them, increase the Scatter slider from Scattering slightly, add Texture and turn Wet Edges on.

Use round brushes for detailed areas and fine lines. Go for the Basic Brushes set for this and pick a hard, round brush. In Shape Dynamics increase Size, Angle and Roundness Jitter.

CHARCOAL PORTRAIT
GET THE DARK AND DRAMATIC EFFECT OF CHARCOAL WITHOUT THE MUCKY HANDS

Charcoal is a lovely medium but man-oh-man is it messy! It is therefore good to know that a very realistic charcoal effect can be achieved in Photoshop. Because charcoal is so soft, any photo you are working from needs to be heavily simplified. Then it is a case of setting up a strong texture for the canvas and getting the brushes ready. The Natural Brush set offers a good range of tips; drop Spacing, increase Scattering for blocking in areas, set Texture and play with Transfer for how light or dark you want the effect to be. Artists hold charcoal on it side for big blocks of colour, which can be handled by the Scatter option.

Charcoal images usually have areas of smudging, either deliberately or because a hand has inadvertently smudged something. Simply scan in real charcoal marks and incorporate using blend modes for the ultimate realistic touch.

> Charcoal images usually have areas of smudging, either deliberately or because a hand has inadvertently smudged something

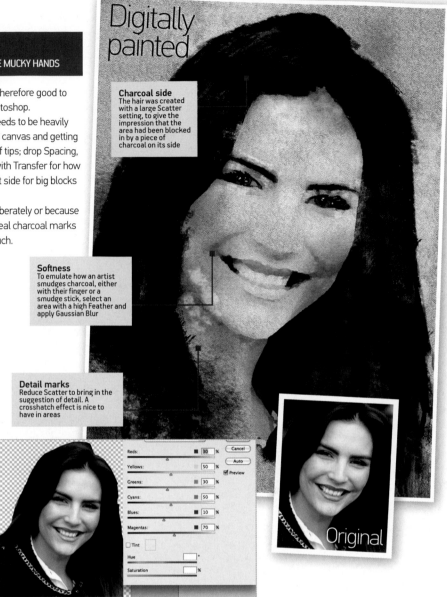

Digitally painted

Charcoal side
The hair was created with a large Scatter setting, to give the impression that the area had been blocked in by a piece of charcoal on its side

Softness
To emulate how an artist smudges charcoal, either with their finger or a smudge stick, select an area with a high Feather and apply Gaussian Blur

Detail marks
Reduce Scatter to bring in the suggestion of detail. A crosshatch effect is nice to have in areas

Original

PREPARE YOUR PHOTO

01 ISOLATE YOUR SUBJECT
Charcoal portraits are usually on a plain background, so make a rough selection of the subject. A simple Lasso will suffice. Copy and paste onto a new layer and turn off the Background layer.

02 QUICK TIDY
If any areas were missed, pick the Eraser tool to get rid of them. This can be quite rudimentary because any mistakes can be sorted. Convert the image to black and white.

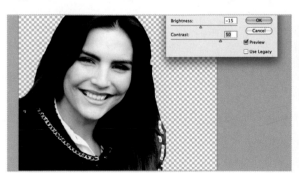

03 BUMP UP THE CONTRAST
Most filters work best with a decent amount of contrast. Either use the Brightness/Contrast command or pick Vibrance. Keep tones, but aim for deep shadows and bright highlights.

04 THE FILTER
Duplicate and go to Filter>Artistic>Palette Knife. This softens the edges. As a general rule, go for a Stroke Size: 45%, Stroke Detail: 3 and Softness: 8. Transfer to the canvas.

WATERCOLOUR EFFECTS
COMBINE REAL BRUSH MARKS WITH DIGITAL FOR A WATERCOLOUR MARRIAGE MADE IN HEAVEN

Achieving a realistic watercolour effect in Photoshop is like chasing the Holy Grail, and while we would love to say we cracked the code, it didn't happen. To achieve the whole gamut of watercolour effects, you have to use brushes created with a real brush and real watercolours. Most watercolour paintings start with water being brushed over the paper and then colour being added. This results in softer colours, with more intense colour in some places where the paint has pooled. Watercolour can also be used with a drier brush, and because the paper is usually rough, the paint skims the top, giving wonderful texture. Most watercolours are simple in their shapes, so don't get caught up with trying to capture minute detail.

Real and digital
Most of the colours here were added with a digital brush, but we also used scanned in elements from real watercolour

Erase for white
For highlights, artists will either use acrylic or more often, leave parts of the paper unpainted. Use the Eraser with one of your brushes to erase back to the canvas

Soft colours
Watercolour paints dry pale. Achieve the same effect by using a brush with low opacity

No hard black
You rarely see deep, dark black in watercolour paintings. Instead artists mix blue, red and brown to get a dark colour. You can just pick a dark blue or red

Digitally painted

Original

> " To achieve the whole gamut of watercolour effects, you have to use brushes created with a real brush and real watercolours "

QUICK TIP
START WITH FILTERS

Don't be tempted by the Watercolor filter. Your best bet is the Sumi-e filter from Artistic. This softens a photo and adds subtle bleed. Now couple with some enhanced Watercolor brushes for a killer real media combination.

CREATE BRUSHES FOR WATERCOLOUR

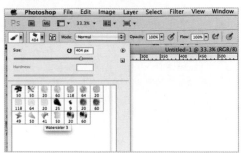

01 PICK YOUR BRUSH
A good hive of watercolour brushes is the Natural Brush 2 set. Pick a watercolour one, open the Brush palette.

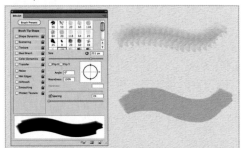

02 BRUSH SHAPE
Click on Brush Tip Shape. Drag the Spacing slider to 0, to avoid drag in the brush strokes.

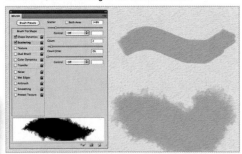

03 SPREAD OUT
Watercolour paint spreads, so go to Shape Dynamics and increase Size Jitter. Go to Scattering and increase Scatter.

04 LOVELY TEXTURE
Pick a texture in Texture, go to Transfer and increase Opacity. Finally turn Wet Edges on.

SKETCH STUDIES
COMBINE AUTO COMMANDS AND FILTERS FOR GRAPHITE ART

We've all created a pencil sketch of some sorts at one stage in our lives, so this is an easy one to get to grips with. You don't have to worry about texture, and a lot of the effect can be handled by Photoshop; you just have to control sliders. But for the best results, you need to roll up your sleeves and go freestyle. A pencil sketch has clear characteristics. If a large area is to be covered, you need to mimic a pencil being used on its side, or get that darker colour caused by marks overlapping. Move your mouse or stylus in the same way as you'd use a pencil and you won't go far wrong.

Original

Good brushes
Brush selection is simple for a sketch effect. Either use the Pencil tool (it sits with the Brush tool) or open the Basic Brush set and pick a small Hard Mechanical brush

Two tools is all you need
For a really quick sketch effect, go to Filter>Other and select High Pass and then Image>Adjustments>Threshold. Move the slider to see the detail

Erase and replace
Instead of having lines go all the way to the edge, use the Eraser to cut into the image and then on a blank layer, draw some lines back in. Do not be too accurate – you just need to give the impression of a work in progress

Go black and white
Most sketches are in monochrome, so convert your photo to black and white initially. Choose a setting that offers a lot of contrast

Make them marks
Incorporate traditional marks in your image. Crosshatch is a classic mark made with the pencil

Digitally painted

USE MASKS FOR COLOUR

It's nice to include colour in sketches, and it's easy with a photo. Have your photo layer on the bottom, your sketch in the middle and then a duplicate of the sketch on top. Turn off the original sketch, click the top one and click the Add Layer Mask icon. Pick a small Hard Mechanical brush from the Basic Brushes set. Click on the layer mask and using the movements you'd make with a pencil, scribble over areas to reveal colour.

CREATE EXPERT BRUSH EFFECTS

SOURCE FILES ✓
AVAILABLE ON THE FREE DISC

PHOTOSHOP

PRODUCE A DIGITAL PAINTING USING PHOTOSHOP BRUSHES, BLEND MODES AND MORE

Digital painting is one of the most convenient ways of producing art, especially when done in Photoshop. It offers a wide spectrum of colours, layers, adjustments, transform tools, the History window and more that will save you the trouble when fixing things. Exercising your creative judgement and learning the art itself is still the biggest factor in creating a traditional or digital painting.

In this tutorial we'll tackle different ways to make a digital painting. We'll use a different approach when making the background, which involves working on a black-and-white image and using layer Blend Modes. For the character we will be blocking in colours immediately with the Brush tool. We'll also cover other tools we can use to create the painting faster without sacrificing quality.

This tutorial can actually be completed mainly using Photoshop's default brushes, with a few tweaks to their properties and modes, but we have supplied you with a set of custom brushes. The use of a tablet and stylus is highly recommended for this tutorial. This can be done with a mouse, but it would take more time.

> **"** Exercising your creative judgement and learning the art itself is still the biggest factor in creating a traditional or digital painting **"**

SET THE SCENE
MAKE SURE YOU GET IT RIGHT FROM THE START

01 GET STARTED
Starting up a painting can be quite intimidating, so after opening your canvas apply a gradation or fill of grey using the Gradient or Paint Bucket tool. Create a new layer (Cmd/Ctrl+Shift+N) and start slapping down paint using any kind of brush, just to get you started. Ensure you take your time to build the idea and composition by making rough thumbs.

02 MAKE AN INITIAL PASS
It's advisable to work on the background first to establish the light sources for your main subject or character. Use a hard-edged brush with pressure-sensitive opacity. You can also use the Smudge tool with a dotted brush tip to create interesting texture. If you are using a mouse to apply, try to lower the opacity of your brush to provide greater control.

03 USE PERSPECTIVE LINES
The scene is going to have a city background in order to add a solid foundation, so bringing in perspective lines is a must. To create a perspective line, simply use your Line tool (U) set to Pixels with a weight of 2-5px. Hold Shift, click and drag horizontally, then repeat, duplicate and merge all of the lines. Make sure you use highly saturated colours for readability.

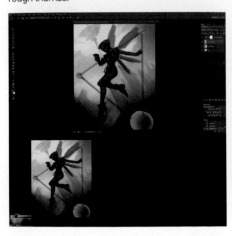

04 BUILD QUICK SHAPES

Now we'll work on the structures of the background. Use the Polygonal Lasso tool (L) or the Pen tool (set to Path) to build shapes of the structures in the background, then fill them with grey. You can bring in more details by using the Line and Brush tools. Remember to hold Shift before clicking, so the outcome will be straight for the Brush tool. At this point it's not that important for the piece to have much detail, a few sets of different structures and shape variations will suffice.

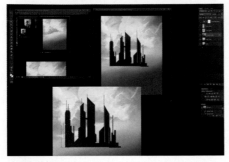

05 LAY OUT THE CITYSCAPE

Make a copy of your perspective lines and use the transform tools (Cmd/Ctrl+T) to position your lines as a guide for the cityscape. While the Transformation box is active, Ctrl/right-click and the other options of the Transform tool will appear. Use Distort and/or Perspective as you see fit. After setting up your perspective lines, drop that layer's Opacity to around 30%. Go back to the structures you made on the previous step and use the transformation tools to lay out the cityscape.

06 ADD SOME COLOUR

To start applying colour, make a new layer, set its mode to Color and use the Gradient tool and brushes. Another method is merging all the layers you want to colour, using Hue/Saturation (Cmd/Ctrl+U) then clicking Colorize, set your preferences then press OK. Pick the Brush tool, change its mode to Color (hold Shift+Ctrl/right-click) and paint directly on the image layer. It's recommended to use Color blending mode as it doesn't require that you merge any image layers below it.

QUICK TIP
CHECK READABILITY AS YOU GO

Go to Window>Arrange>New Window For, to open up a new window for your file. Keep this new window small and in full view, as it automatically updates while you work on the active window. Look at it from time to time so you can quickly view the readability of your painting.

07 REFINE THE RESULTS

To further polish the painting, create a new Normal layer. Since the cityscape is slanted, use the Rotate View tool and position your view to an upright position as it makes painting much easier. Using a hard-edged brush with pressure-sensitive opacity, go to the settings and adjust accordingly. Set the brush tip to look flat in order to make detailing the structures faster. Adjust the spacing to quickly make those windows and bars. You can lower the Hardness of the brush for the atmospheric effects.

08 BLOCK IN THE CHARACTER

Create a new layer and, using the Paint Bucket tool, fill it with any low-saturated colour, setting its Opacity to 90%. This is enough for you to see the background beneath as a reference when you draw the character. Create another layer and use a hard brush to make an outline drawing. Using the Magic Wand tool, click on the area beyond the outline (make sure your outline has no holes), choose the fill layer and hit Delete. Now return the fill layer's Opacity back to 100%.

UNIFY THE IMAGE
POLISH THE PIECE USING BLEND MODES AND ADJUSTMENT LAYERS

09 PAINT THE CHARACTER
Set the outline layer to Multiply and use Hue/Saturation's Colorize option. Adjust it so that the outline will have colour, then click the Lock the Transparent Pixels icon of the fill layer. Block in the colours, preferably using mid-tones, then add in the other colours and values. Once roughly painted, merge the outline with that layer and start blending.

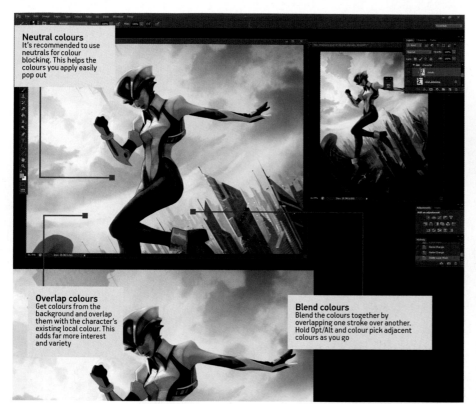

Neutral colours
It's recommended to use neutrals for colour blocking. This helps the colours you apply easily pop out

Overlap colours
Get colours from the background and overlap them with the character's existing local colour. This adds far more interest and variety

Blend colours
Blend the colours together by overlapping one stroke over another. Hold Opt/Alt and colour pick adjacent colours as you go

10 CHOOSE COLOURS CAREFULLY
Choosing colours can be really tough. For this tutorial, to keep it simple, just keep a mindset that the lit areas are warm because of the heat from the sun. The planes that directly face this are a lot brighter, so use the Color Dodge brush mode for the effect, though be careful not to overdo it. For the darker parts we can assume that they receive reflected light from the sky on the opposite side of the sun. Use a blue-violet tone as it serves as a good contrast from the warm background.

QUICK TIP
CHANGE THE PERSPECTIVE

Flip your image to check the balance of the composition. Paint the scene as a whole, never focus only on a single part and desaturate the image to check your values. The nearer an object is to the viewer, the more detail, intensity and colour it has. With that in mind, add adjustment layers like Curves, Hue/Saturation and Color Balance, then clip mask it to the layer.

11 CREATE CYBER WINGS
Use the Pen or Lasso tool to form the shape and the Paint Bucket tool to fill it out with colour. You only need to make half of the image and duplicate the layer (Cmd/Ctrl+J). Transform>Flip Horizontal the duplicate half of the wing to complete it, then merge the two layers (Cmd/Ctrl+E). Make duplicates of the wing layer then Transform>Distort it to properly form it relative to the character. After positioning the wings, merge and set to Multiply.

12 PLACE FURTHER DETAILS
Pick the Ellipse tool to make the shape of the orbs, then apply a hard brush and use a soft brush to blend, using small brushes to add detail. To create the shiny numbers and text you need to use the Type tool, rasterise the text, Distort or Warp, then set to Color Dodge or Overlay. To add a further glow to it you may consider applying a layer style. Double-click on the layer and the Layer Style window will appear, so choose Outer Glow then press OK.

13 FINAL EFFECTS
There are lots of ways to make effects with Blend Modes, such as Screen for the glow. To make the shiny lines and really vivid glows, you can create a new layer, fill it with black and set it to Color Dodge. Make a selection and paint over it with a soft brush using different colours to yield that ray-like effect. Add a Soft Light for subtle atmospheric effects. Feel free to experiment by scrolling down the Blend Modes, as the results can sometimes surprise you.

> It's wise to make sure you have everything defined clearly before moving on. A little spontaneity will prove handy, but not as handy as a solid base

PRODUCE A FANTASY PAINTING

SOURCE FILES ✓
AVAILABLE ON THE FREE DISC

PHOTOSHOP

LEARN ESSENTIAL BRUSH TECHNIQUES TO CREATE DRAMATIC LIGHTING AND VIBRANT COLOUR

With the right skill set and techniques, you can create fantasy concepts for multiple parties within the entertainment industry.

You'll begin here with the sketch phase, drawing out some rough ideas in Photoshop, then you'll discover essential ways to add colour, detail and cohesive lighting to your images. Special effects will breathe further life into these designs, mainly through the use of dramatic lighting effects that enhance atmosphere.

This is all made possible using Photoshop tools and options. Custom brushes have been supplied so you can make the marks seen in this tutorial. You'll also discover ways to layer these new brushes, using the power of blending modes to produce exciting lighting effects.

Brushes are used to paint texture and detail; Lock Layer and clipping mask controls let you shape your design. You'll introduce tonality and colour temperature, too. By the end, you'll be able to tackle your own distinctive fantasy paintings.

GETTING STARTED
SKETCH WITHIN PHOTOSHOP

01 START YOUR SKETCH
Begin sketching the figure very loosely inside Photoshop on a new layer. This is so that you can visualise the proportions and composition you need. A three-quarter view of an owl moving towards the viewer has been chosen here. This example is the best design from a set of thumbnails, as it made sure all of the needs of the piece were met early on.

02 A CLEAR COURSE OF ACTION
Begin tightening up your line work and organise the shadows and lights. Eliminate scribbled brush strokes, as a good, solid direction early on will dictate the difficulty of a piece. It's also wise to make sure you have everything defined clearly before moving on. A little spontaneity will prove handy, but not as handy as a solid base.

03 SEPARATE THE SKETCH
You'll want to make sure that your bird is on a separate layer without any loose or extra strokes. Check for such artefacts by creating a layer beneath the sketch layer and fill it with a pink colour. This reveals any stray white and grey brush strokes in and around the sketch. If there are any in your image, you will need to erase these.

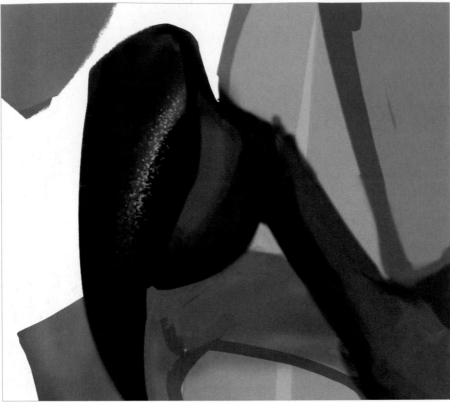

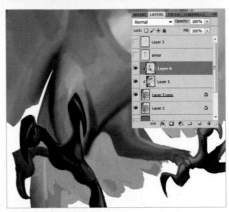

04 ADD TEXTURE

Early on in a painting, it's good to add a little texture to certain areas. Later, these earlier signs of texture may show through and help to pick out subtle shapes, giving the painting a bit more life. Upload the advanced photoshop.abr and select the brush labelled '20'. Paint texture near the light areas of the talon. Be careful to not to paint too brightly this early on, however, as increasing the contrast too soon will make areas seem overly bright or blown out later.

05 COPY AND PASTE

A useful trick when creating similar features like the talons is to use a copy and paste. Since the shapes will be painted over later, you won't run the risk of each talon looking too similar. Select a talon with the Marquee tool (L), then press and hold the Cmd/Ctrl key as you drag the selected area to another location. Doing this creates a duplicate of the selected item.

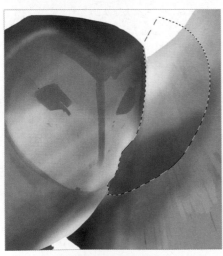

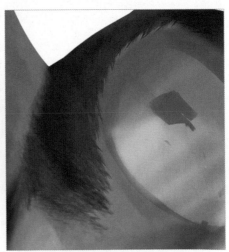

06 CREATE ATMOSPHERE

It was decided that the head would read better if it were in front of the far wing, so you need to add a little bit of atmosphere. Using the Marquee tool once again, select an area outlining the owl's face and a portion of the wing behind it. Select a rounded brush with soft edges and begin stroking in the lighting from the top down, as your light will likely be a top-down lighting.

07 FORM SHADOW

Getting comfortable with the Selection tool? Good, as you're about to practise that same technique here by carefully selecting the legs of your owl. Now press Cmd/Ctrl+Opt/Alt+I to invert your selection. This effectively lets you paint behind the selected area. Use another soft brush in order to paint in some shadow behind the legs. Again, take care not to paint your marks too dark.

08 PAINT FEATHERS

It's time to start painting feathers. To do this, select the brush labelled '700', which closely resembles the hackle you can find in owls and other birds. Take care to not add strokes too wildly. Instead, apply in a uniform manner, tracing the existing contour in your owl's form. This means you'll create a more authentic appearance. Studying a real-world reference to get the right look isn't cheating.

DETAILED BLUEPRINT
LAY THE FOUNDATION FOR FOCAL POINTS, TEXTURE AND FORM

09 ADD BLACKS
Up until this point, the image will be rather grey. But this is fine, as it has allowed you to make sure that the focal point is yet to be decided. Usually, you'll want your focal point to be your subject's face. So it's here that you'll apply your first solid black to create the owl's eyes. Use a Selection tool to draw out a good shape for these, then fill your selection with a solid black. This makes the eyes the darkest point of your piece and therefore your point of focus.

10 HIDE SELECTIONS
You'll have made quite a few of these by now and they can be distracting. With an area of your painting selected, in this case the eyes from the previous step, press Cmd/Ctrl+H to hide your selection. Sometimes doing so will help you see what you're doing more clearly. With your selections hidden, you can begin detailing the eyes, which is done using a soft grey brush on the outer area and a sharper white brush for the reflective highlights.

11 BUILD FEATHER TEXTURES
Continue painting your bird and refining your form and shapes. Uniformly paint the wings, slowly building colour until you create solid-looking results. Try to stay within the appropriate tonal range. Do this on a new layer (Cmd/Ctrl+Opt/Alt+Shift+N). The smoother you keep your forms now, the cleaner your painting will be later. It's not until the very end, when bringing all your painting marks together, that you start to fashion feathers with your strokes.

12 RENDER FEATHERS
It's a good idea to layer your painted feathers. Start with smaller feathers near the top of the wing and paint three rows. Begin with the bottom row, painting in loose feathers. Add a layer on top and paint values that create the shadow from the feathers that will be above that. Then paint those feathers in on a new layer above your shadow layer. Working backwards in this way makes the feathers appear to be casting shadows.

> **"** Begin detailing the eyes, which is done using a soft grey brush on the outer area and a sharper white brush for the reflective highlights **"**

13 PAINT LONG FEATHERS
Now that you're done with the smaller feathers, you need to paint a larger one. First, create a new layer (Cmd/Ctrl+Opt/Alt+N), then use the Marquee tool (L) to create a long, feather-like rectangular shape. Use a soft round brush to paint one side dark and another side a bright grey, manually creating a gradual gradient. This gives the illusion of a single feather, which is longer and thicker than the rest you've just added.

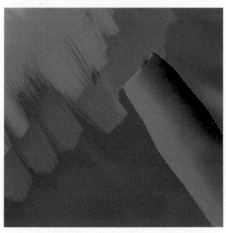

Digital painting

RENDER YOUR LOOK
CREATE DRAMATIC LIGHTING, CONTOUR AND DETAIL IN YOUR IMAGE

14 COPY AND PASTE FEATHERS
Using what you've learnt about the Marquee tool and the duplicate technique, you now implement a combination of the two. Remember the long gradient feather you just painted in the last step? Well, now you're going to copy and paste this into a new layer and slightly enlarge it. Place it so it overlaps the original large feather layer. Continue to copy, paste and place a few dozen times until you have a long row of feathers.

15 BREAK UP REPETITION
Build upon the last steps by repeating their processes, painting and placing feathers in the owl's opposite wing. Make sure you follow the right direction for an authentic look. To break up the monotony of some of these feathers, erase parts of the edges in some of your layers. Also elongate some of them slightly and skew the shape of others a bit. This allows you to create the beginnings of a very interesting wing pattern for your owl.

16 UNIFORM LIGHTING
Now that you've created your feathers, you will need to add larger shadows. First, merge down your owl layers, then make sure that this new layer is locked by clicking on the Lock icon located at the top of the layers tab. Now, apply a large, dark grey, soft round brush and lightly add some shadow to the rounded parts of the top of the wing. This makes sure your wings are being lit by the same light source as the rest of the image.

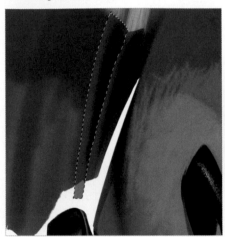

17 START THE BACKGROUND
Since your owl is on its own layer, you can create a layer beneath and begin the background. This image will eventually reveal a bright scene with sparks and cinder flying from a fire. However, to make these effects workable, you need a dark, muted background full of dark purples, dark browns and dark reds. While it seems dark now, adding your effects later will help keep the focus on your owl, rather than spreading the focus around haphazardly.

18 SECONDARY LIGHT
Since the plan is to have your main light source closer to the viewer, a secondary light source can be established – in this case, the moon behind the owl. On a separate layer, draw a circular selection with the Elliptical Marquee tool. Set this layer's blending mode to Color Dodge and paint in the moon with a few large strokes, using a neutral grey colour. This gives the moon its glow effect. Also use the same brush around the moon to give it a halo effect.

QUICK TIP
ADD SPARK EFFECTS

You'll see that spark effects were added to the final image. You can recreate this effect by using several layers and a very easy technique. Create a new layer, set its blending mode to Color Dodge and scatter in some simple sparks with an orange-coloured brush. Now duplicate this layer. Duplicating a Color Dodge layer into itself will make the sparks glow even brighter than before. Now you must copy, paste and place your sparks around the image by selecting the Move tool, holding Opt/Alt and dragging them to other locations. Create depth of field effects, making some seem close up, others further away.

QUICK TIP
CREATE A NATURAL, EVEN GLOW

When painting to a Color Dodge blending mode layer, using a grey colour will create a very natural and even glow. Painting with a saturated colour gives a glow similar to that colour.

QUICK TIP
ADD DETAILS AND KEEP CHECKING

Now that your major elements are completed, go over everything you've done and detail your brush strokes and lighting. Keep taking a step back to check your progress. This will ultimately help push the piece to final completion.

19 CLIP LAYERS

Back with your owl and it's time to add a little colour. At this stage, it's best to keep everything simple – and in this case dark. Create another layer above the owl layer and link the two by hovering your mouse between the layers while holding Cmd/Ctrl. Click and it links the layers. This will ensure that anything painted on this layer will only affect the layer below it, which will be your owl layer and not the background.

20 REFLECTIVE LIGHTING

Using the same method outlined in the last step, create another layer, except this time set its blending mode to Color Dodge. Link the layer again. Even though it appears to be linked to the last layer, they're both actually linked to the owl layer. Use this layer to add both blue rims of light in the edges of the wings and yellow lighting that emulates reflection from the fire. You can also erase lighting and reapply until you're satisfied with the effects.

21 BRING IT BACK

Since the layer below this new light layer is a dark brown colour, it's possible to bring back shadows – just erase areas from the Color Dodge light layer above. Create dramatic shadows in the feathers by using the Marquee tool to make selections like in the example shown, then delete from these. This method is much better than painting with more black because the darkest colour has been established at this point.

22 BACK AND FORTH

At this point in your painting, it's important that you start to flesh out your colouring and continue to tweak your image lighting. You could also add more subtle hints of colour, perhaps some purple or pink hues. Always remember that if you want to add more lighting, then you do this specifically to your Color Dodge blending mode layer. You can take this away by simply erasing it to show the layer beneath.

23 ADD ARMOUR

Now that the hard part is over, you can begin to make some armour that fits with your image lighting. Use a solid colour that outlines the entire shape of the armour on a new layer, then lock it. This allows you to paint evenly over the entire shape, rather than painting each piece individually. Doing the latter has a higher chance of throwing off the balance of the armour. Do the same for the armour's trimming.

24 FINAL DETAILS

In the same way as you've done in previous steps, create another layer and lock it to the armour layer. Set the new layer's blending mode to Color Dodge and choose a saturated orange colour. Paint this on the side of the armour that you feel should receive the most light, with the brightest parts nearest the crease. This gives you a balanced exposure, and good shadow and light separation. Repeat the same process for the trimming. Use the Hair brush (brush 125) to zoom in and add more detail to the face, working your way outward from the focal point and detailing as you go.

PAINT A STEAMPUNK-INSPIRED PORTRAIT

USE LIGHT, SHADOW, COLOUR AND TEXTURE TO CREATE A CAPTIVATING PORTRAIT

The following tutorial is for those who wish to learn the basics of digital painting and discover tips and tricks to add texture, luminescence and mystery to illustrations with simple Photoshop methods.

Learn to sketch non-existent objects using basic perspective and visualise lighting so that you can add any element to your painting regardless of reference. Discover the difference between form shadow and cast shadow and how to effectively render both.

Once you understand how light interacts with your subject matter, the possibilities are limitless.

Learn how to pick compelling colours in order to establish mood, to paint different materials such as cloth, metal, and skin, including how to apply textures and patterns realistically using filters. Finally, discover the secret to creating glow effects and glares using various layer blending modes. From start to finish, you will learn how to employ Photoshop effectively to create a compelling painting.

PHOTOSHOP

SOURCE FILES ✓
AVAILABLE ON THE FREE DISC

BACK TO BASICS
DECIDE THE AIM OF THE PIECE AND CHOOSE YOUR REFERENCE

01 VISUALISE YOUR IMAGE
Before starting, visualise what you want to accomplish. In this case, the goal is to paint a Steampunk piece which integrates portraiture with mechanical elements. It's meant to be a dark, atmospheric image with lush colours to invoke mystery and interest. Remember to download the resources before you start.

02 GATHER REFERENCE
Paintings should be unrecognisable from reference unless the material belongs to you, so take liberties in deviating from online sources. The easiest way to obtain reference is to take photos yourself, but be sure that all of your images have the same light source or be prepared to paint them differently to how they appear.

03 START A NEW DOCUMENT
Begin by creating a new document (Cmd/Ctrl+N). Set the image dimensions to 4800px by 6400px at 300ppi. Decide between RGB or CMYK for your colour mode (RGB can achieve richer colours while CMYK is useful for printing). Fill it with a warm green tone in the middle-range of value (not too light and not too dark).

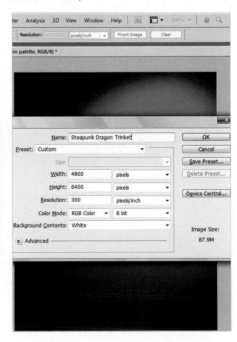

> Once you understand how light interacts with your subject matter, the possibilities are limitless

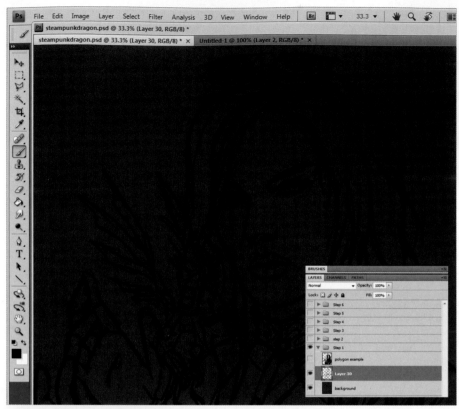

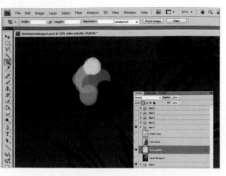

04 SKETCH THE OUTLINE

Create a new layer named 'Sketch' (Layer>New>Layer). When sketching, think about the focal point to keep the eye moving within the image. Use your reference as a rough guide as you freehand the sketch in a dark burgundy colour. Keep in mind perspective as you draw objects without reference, like the dragon and goggles. It helps to sometimes draw boxes in perspective with the rest of the piece and then chisel away at the objects inside to create angular shapes before finally rounding off the details.

05 PICK COLOURS

Colour defines the mood of a piece. The key to having lush colours is finding a balance between rich and dull. Too bright and your image looks contrived and over-the-top. Too dull and your image looks washed out. Lighter colours should be less saturated and darker colours more saturated. On a new layer, pick a basic flesh colour, scribble and repeat, increasing the saturation as you go darker. To help the image pop, add subtle oranges and warm pinks for the eyes and cheeks. Pale cyan works as a highlight colour to contrast against warm shadows.

QUICK TIP
PAINT ON INDIVIDUAL LAYERS

Paint separate elements on their own layers so you can lock the transparency and paint each one without going over the edges. Choose the corresponding layer in the Layers palette and click the checkered square icon at the top.

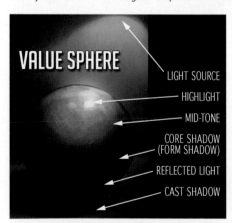

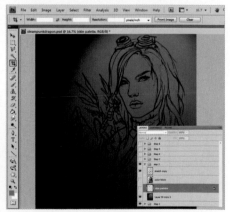

06 UNDERSTANDING LIGHT

Form shadow (or core shadow) creates the illusion of form and gives objects depth. It occurs when light fails to completely wrap around the form of something and is a gradual transition from light to shadow, with softer edges (like the cheekbone, which at first catches the light and then curves downward into shadow). Cast shadow occurs when something (like the nose, for example), blocks the light, throwing areas below into darkness. It tends to have sharper edges.

07 VISUALISE WHERE LIGHT FALLS

When creating an object without reference, it is vital to be able to picture in your mind where the shadow would fall if you could see it. Sometimes it helps to picture the subject matter as if it were made up of several small geometric polygons. Look at each surface plane and ask yourself if the angle would catch the light or not, then translate that into your painting. Don't forget to add in cast shadows of made-up elements to ground the work and give it a cohesive feel.

08 CREATE THE BACKGROUND

Create the illusion of a light source just off canvas using a hard round brush in a pale yellow hue. Sweep the brush downward to emulate the glowing effect of light on a wall. Picking a dark green, sweep the same brush along the edges of the canvas to push the corners into darkness. Blend the colours with a soft round brush as necessary. Note that the light will be brighter and the change between values will be more drastic near the top where the light is closest to the wall.

DOWN TO DETAIL
APPLY PAINT, ADD TEXTURE AND CREATE ATMOSPHERIC EFFECTS

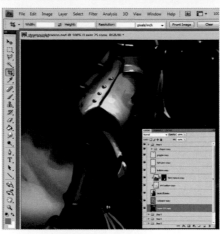

09 START PAINTING
On a layer beneath the sketch, paint the skin using a default round brush. Keep your Opacity and Flow at 100%, and rely on the sensitivity of your tablet to blend the colours. Make a clear delineation between light and shadow. As you continue to refine, add the transitions between the two values using a soft brush when needed. Use your highlights sparingly for the greatest effect. Merge your Sketch layer and your painting layer and gently paint out the sketch until all the lines are gone.

10 SHINY VERSUS DULL
When painting matte surfaces like the cotton vest, do not paint highlights. Only two values are needed for these – mid-tone and shadow – with gradual transitions between the two on occasion. When painting reflective surfaces like silk or brass, however, exaggerate the drastic change in value by using sharp specular highlights in areas where the light would logically fall and by using contrasting strokes. Remember to incorporate surrounding colours, as metal is highly reflective.

11 PAINT SKIN AND HAIR
When painting skin, find a balance between matte and shiny. The skin will have sharper and brighter highlights if the face is wet (like around the eyes) or where oils of the skin reflect light (like on the nose and inner tear duct). If you haven't already, add these specular highlights to create luminescence. When painting hair, start by putting in the darkest values first, and then add the midtones using a chunky round brush. Gradually reduce the size of the brush until you are painting individual strands.

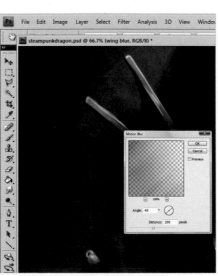

QUICK TIP
MORE ON PATTERN

Pattern should conform to the form beneath. To create the effect of the pattern wrapping around the silk shirt, paste the pattern on a new layer above the painting. Create a quick mask over your painting by clicking between the two layers on the Layers palette and pressing Opt/Alt. Set the layer Blend Mode to Overlay and reduce the Opacity to 30%. Go to the Liquify filter (Filter> Liquify), and with the painting layer visible beneath your pattern, use the Forward Warp tool (W) to push the pattern downward around the edges of the arm. Do the same for the fabric texture above the vest area.

12 ADD TEXTURE AND PATTERN
Texture and pattern add realism to your work when done correctly. To create the illusion of wallpaper, paste a damask pattern on a new layer and set the layer Blend Mode to Overlay from the drop-down menu on the Layers palette. Reduce the opacity of the layer so that the pattern is not overbearing but still present. You don't want your image to be too busy or distract viewers from the figure in the foreground.

13 ADD ATMOSPHERIC EFFECTS
The last step is to add subtle atmospheric effects. Create a glare on the highlight of the goggles using a soft round brush in a pale yellow colour on low opacity. For the blur on the dragon wings, copy the wings onto a new layer underneath and use the Motion Blur filter. Set the angle to 40 degrees and the distance to 200px. Use a smoke brush for the dragon steam. To make it glow, on a new layer use a soft green brush set to Hard Light.

Realistic paint effects
Use a variety of real media paint splatter scans to produce convincing digital watercolour paint effects

Colour blending
Use brush blending modes with layer blending modes to mix vibrant paint colours

Pen and ink
Try your hand at producing line art for the base drawing or feel free to borrow our artwork for your own use!

Hidden brushes
Use Photoshop's Splatter brush set to create drops of far-flung paint and add a sense of energy and excitement to your painting

CREATE STUNNING WATERCOLOURS

PHOTOSHOP

SOURCE FILES ✓
AVAILABLE ON THE FREE DISC

USE A COMBINATION OF CUSTOM BRUSHES, CLEVER TECHNIQUES AND BLEND MODES TO ACHIEVE A REALISTIC DIGITAL WATERCOLOUR EFFECT

Using watercolour in real media can be a creative expression of shape and colour. The water-based properties of the paint allow it to soak into the canvas and then blend with other colours in a way that creates beautiful and vibrant paintings. Splattering the paint can produce particularly enjoyable and unexpected results.

Creating the same effects digitally can be somewhat challenging. The math-ruled world of computer processors prefers order over chaos. This makes the production of the barely controlled watercolour splash effects alien to the perfect lines and rules of digital artwork. Fortunately, Photoshop provides the means to using real paint splashes and splatters as custom brushes to simulate the effect. In this tutorial, we will show you how to harness the power of those custom brushes to create a brilliant and believable watercolour painting that is as vibrant and engaging as any real media piece.

We've included the starter drawing and the required brush sets with your resources for your personal use. So grab those files, launch Photoshop and join us on a wonderful watercolour journey!

Original

MASTER BRUSHES
MIMIC REAL MEDIA USING CUSTOM BRUSHES

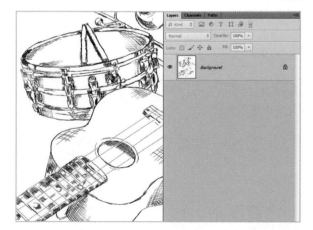

01 STARTER LINE ART
In the supplied resources, we have included the original photos of musical instruments to use to generate your own ink drawing. If you'd rather shortcut this stage, we have also included our own artwork for you to use: 'MusicLineArt.png'.

02 LOAD CUSTOM BRUSHES
Go through the Window menu to open the Brush Presets panel. In the flyout menu at the top-right of the panel, choose the Load Brushes command. On the supplied resources, you will find four sets of brushes to be loaded.

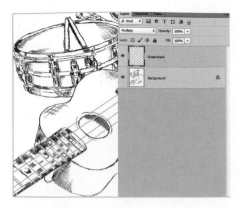

03 PREPARE A BRUSH

Create a new layer for the green wash effect and set the blend mode to Multiply. Select one of the watercolour brushes and open the Brush panel (F5). In the Options Bar, set the Mode to Colour Burn and the Opacity to 60%.

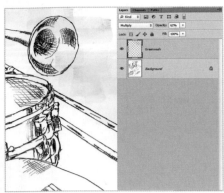

04 APPLY THE WASH

Set the paint colour to a bright green. Don't drag the brush along the canvas, but use single clicks to stamp the brush stroke shape. Use the Brush panel to adjust their size, angle and roundness so that they don't all look the same.

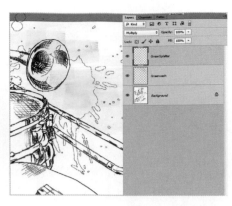

05 SET UP THE SPLATTER

Repeat Step 3, this time selecting one of the CustomSplatter brushes and boosting the brush Opacity up to 100%, but keep the brush Mode at Color Burn. Use the brush outline to help determine the best brush rotation setting.

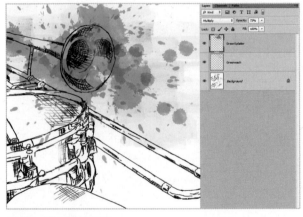

06 ADD SPLATTERS

Use the CustomSplatter brushes in combination with the Splat brushes to add an explosion of colour around the trombone horn. Using the brush Mode at Colour Burn means each stamp reacts to the pixels beneath it, even if these pixels are on the same layer.

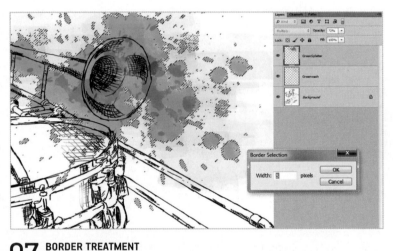

07 BORDER TREATMENT

Cmd/Ctrl-click on the thumbnail for the splatter layer to create a selection around the paint splashes. Then go to Select>Modify> Border. Use a pixel setting of 5. This creates a 5px-wide selection border around the layer.

QUICK TIP
DIY PAINT SPLATTERS

Why not create your own custom brushes to use in projects such as this one? Begin with plain white card with no visible texture, then lightly splash it with some watercolour paint or ink. After it has dried, scan in the splatter and then open the file in Photoshop. Desaturate the image and use a Curves adjustment in order to enhance the contrast. Clean up any stray marks with a regular white brush. Then select the splatter area and go to Edit>Define Brush Preset.

08 REFINE EDGE

Grab any of the Marquee tools to gain access to the Refine Edge dialog box in the Options Bar. In the Adjust Edge area, set Smooth to 50 and tweak Contrast to 40%.

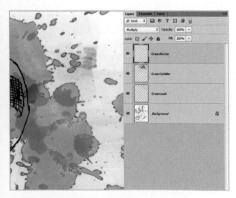

09 CREATE WET EDGES

Press Cmd/Ctrl+J to copy the border selection to a new layer. Keep the blend mode at Multiply but set Opacity to 100%. This will simulate the wet edges of real paint. Reducing the opacity of the splatter layer can enhance the effect.

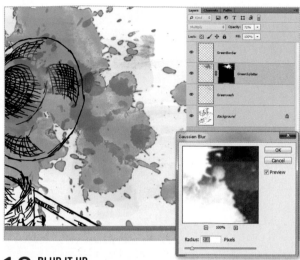

10 BLUR IT UP
Cmd/Ctrl-click the splatter layer thumbnail again to create the selection. Use the Add Layer Mask button to create a mask for the splatter layer. With the mask targeted, go to Filter>Blur>Gaussian Blur and use a setting of 2.0px.

11 HAVE A SPLASH ATTACK
Add another new layer for additional splash, splatter, and splat paint spots. Remember to set the layer blending mode to Multiply and the brush Mode to Color Burn. Now use a variety of different brushes to build up the full painted effect.

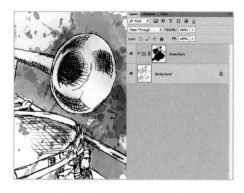

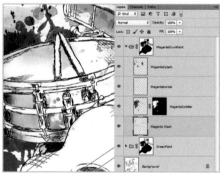

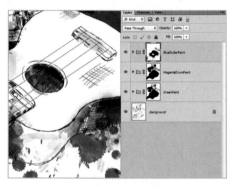

12 GROUP THE LAYERS
Select all the green paint layers and press Cmd/Ctrl+G to group them all together. Then add a layer mask to the group and use a brush with black paint on the mask to remove the green splatter from the trombone shape.

13 REPEAT ON THE DRUM
Go through the same painting process for the drum set using a magenta paint colour. When working the mask on the group, a soft brush with white paint and low opacity can fade the colour into the shaded regions.

14 THE RIGHT LAYER STRUCTURE
Go through the process again with the blue paint splashes on the guitar. Be mindful of how the groups are layered. The blue paint group should be on top and the green should be on the bottom. This agrees with the position of the instruments.

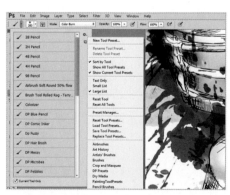

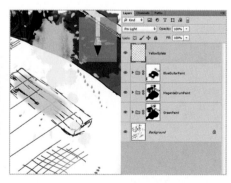

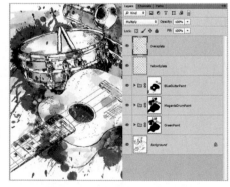

15 OPEN BRUSH TOOL PRESETS
With the Brush tool selected, look at the far left of the Options panel for a drop-down of Tool Presets. Open this and hit the Gear icon to get the flyout menu, then select Splatter Brush Tool Presets.

16 ADD REALISM
These presets give even more options for creating realistic paint splatters. The Spatter Drop brushes are particularly useful for painting small drops of flying paint. Mix these in with the other splatter stamp brush marks on a top layer.

17 FINAL FLOURISH
Use a final paint layer to add in the final few splashes of paint. Set this layer to Multiply and use darker colours on this one. Set the previous layer to Pin Light for brighter colours.

Digital painting

Original

SOURCE FILES ✓
AVAILABLE ON THE FREE DISC

USE BRUSHES FOR GRUNGE ARTWORK

GRAB A DANCER AND CHOREOGRAPH A GRUNGE-TASTIC COMPOSITION COMBINING TEXTURES, CUSTOM BRUSHES AND BLEND MODES

PHOTOSHOP

Grunge music is a gritty movement that gained prominence in the Nineties. Polish took a back seat in this underground brand of rock, with the premium being placed on stripped-down power, unadulterated emotion.

Grunge within an artistic context adheres to a lot of the same tenets. Go for raw energy. Emphasize feeling over exactness. Get a little dirty!

You'll learn easy ways to add grunge to an image. We'll use some custom brushes to paint on some grit and artistic accents and we'll borrow some rough and blurry photos and merge them into our composition with blend modes. We'll lock down the look with adjustment layers and filters.

For Photoshop Elements users who don't have access to the Pen tool, substitute with the various selection tools. If you're lacking the Vibrance adjustment, use Hue/Saturation.

You will be able to try out these great effects on your own photographs, or simply use the one that we have used here. This is just one of the great images from online image library www.ingimage.com – and you can download it free from your supplied resources!

GETTING STARTED
BEGIN BY MAKING INITIAL TWEAKS TO YOUR DANCER

01 OUTLINE THE DANCER
Open 'Dancer.jpg'. Outline the subject with the Pen tool. Refine path with the Direct Selection tool. Hit Cmd/Ctrl+Return/Enter to make a selection. Open 'Start.psd'. From 'Dancer.jpg', with the Move tool click and drag from within the selection into 'Start.psd'.

02 POSITION YOUR FIGURE
Ctrl/Right-click the transplanted layer, Convert to Smart Object. Cmd/Ctrl+T, Shift-drag a corner outward to scale up. Cmd/Ctrl+J to duplicate. Select the lower dancer. Go to Filter>Blur>Radial Blur.

QUICK TIP
A LIGHTER GRUNGE STYLE

Grunge is applicable in a wide range of art and design. You can certainly use a full-blast approach on rock-music packaging, extreme sports advertisements and hip apparel. However, turn back the grunge dial for more understated flavouring. A good way to reduce the digital sheen of pictures is by moving a gritty texture above it, applying a blend mode like Overlay, then reducing the Opacity of the texture layer. Equally effective is a light dusting with a grunge brush on a layer above.

03 THE RADIAL BLUR
Set Amount to 50, Blur Method to Spin, Quality to Good. Click OK. Offset with the Move tool. Add a layer mask with the icon in the Layers palette. Use a soft, round brush at 50% Opacity to paint black into the mask to fade out areas.

04 USE ACCENTED EDGES
Select the upper dancer, hit Cmd/Ctrl+J to duplicate. Go to Filter> Brush Strokes>Accented Edges. Set Width to 1, Edge Brightness to 9, Smoothness to 3. Add a layer mask, fill with black. Paint white with 90% Opacity to add to the effect.

05 PAINT IN SOME SHADOWS
Create a layer below the radial blur. Set foreground to black. Then use a soft, round brush at 80% Opacity to paint in some shadows around the dancer. Next, create a new layer above the radial blur, drop the brush's Opacity to 40% and paint in some more shadows.

06 BRING ON THE GRUNGE
Select the Brush tool. Load 'Grunge.abr' from the supplied resources into your Brush palette menu (Brush Presets in CS5+). Choose Brush 1, set brush Opacity to 100%, foreground colour to #6B1218. On a new layer below the dancer, paint a spurting of colour.

07 CREATE SCRIBBLY STREAKS
Switch to Brush 2 and then change the foreground colour to #9FE840. Create a new layer and then paint several scribbly streaks. These will serve as dynamic accents, suggestive of the zing of urban dancing.

08 GET DOWN AND DIRTY
Change the foreground to #FFFFFF, drop the brush Opacity to 40%, and create a new layer. Using the two grunge brushes (Grunge 1 and Grunge 2), click some texture instead of clicking and dragging.

09 MUCK IT UP
The brushwork for Steps 9-11 will be placed above the dancer. Create a new layer. Set brush Opacity to 100% and choose Brush 1. Using a variety of colours (#6B1218, #B4FFFF, # 79C170, # 745CB3, #A1803D), build up more texture.

10 ADD ILLUSTRATIVE ACCENTS
Switch to Brush 2, drop Size to 10px, and create a new layer. Using #FF1E57 and #FFFFFF, create illustrative accents to add fresh, vibrant energy that'll stand out against the dark atmosphere. For variety, lower the Opacity on some strokes.

11 DRAW CRUMBLY LINES
Switch to Brush 3. Keep the colour at #FFFFFF, set to 100% brush Opacity. On a brand new layer, paint on the dancer's body and make a few trailing lines emanating from her. We are now done with the brushes. Let's now add some texture and adjustments.

12 BUILD UP URBAN BRICKS
Go to File>Place and add 'Bricks.jpg'. Set the blend mode to Color Burn. Add a layer mask and use a soft, round brush at 80% Opacity to remove and lessen the darkening effect.

13 BALANCE COLOURS
Click the Create new adjustment layer button in the Layers palette, choose Color Balance. Set Midtones (from top to bottom): -100, +26, +100. Paint black in all areas apart from the bottom-right and upper-left areas around the dancer.

14 TIME TO BURN, COLOUR, BURN
Click on the Create new fill layer button in the Layers palette, then choose Solid Color. Pick #FFE096. Set the blend mode to Color Burn and then Opacity to 80%. Paint black in the left side and then select areas.

15 LIGHTEN THINGS UP
Click the Create new adjustment layer button in the Layers palette, and then choose Levels. Set the Shadow input level to 5, Midtone level to 1.5, and Highlight level to 245. With black, paint out the periphery in the mask to tone it down.

16 LIMIT THE COLOUR
Go to File>Place and add 'Blur.jpg'. Set the blend mode to Color. This allows us to borrow the restrained palette. Add a layer mask. With black, paint to bring back some of the original colour.

17 MERGE THOSE LAYERS
We'll now merge all layers so we can apply an effect to the whole image. Press Cmd/Ctrl+Option/Alt+Shift+E. Ctrl/right-click, choose Convert to Smart Object. This will make the effect in the next step become an editable Smart Filter.

18 ADD A LITTLE WATER PAPER
Go to Filter>Sketch>Water Paper. Set Fiber Length to 25, Brightness 80, Contrast 70. Click OK. This helps smudge the detail. Apply a layer mask, fill it with black. Paint white with varying brush Opacities (40-70%) to add the effect to key areas.

19 COLOUR SOME HIGHLIGHTS
Click the Create new adjustment layer button in the Layers palette, choose Hue/Saturation. Pump up the Saturation to +75. Fill the mask with black, then paint white at 80% brush Opacity to the areas that you want to highlight.

20 DROP THE VIBRANCE
Click on the Create new adjustment layer button in the Layers palette, choose Vibrance. Drop Vibrance to -90 to tone down colours overall. With black, paint out areas you don't want to dull.

21 RESTORE YOUR DANCER
Some of the dancer may be texturally buried. Select the unaltered layer and Opt/Alt-Click+drag above the top layer. Apply a layer mask and fill with black. Paint white in some areas to restore the original dancer.

22 ENHANCE GRITTY DETAILS
Sharpening helps to bring out the gritty details. Merge the layers again as in Step 17. Go to Filter>Sharpen>Unsharp Mask. Set Amount to 95% and Radius to 1.5px. Click OK. Then, with black, paint out the areas that you don't want sharpened.

CHARACTER

LEARN HOW TO CREATE
CHARACTER CONCEPTS
AND THEN HOW TO
DEVELOP THEM IN TERMS
OF STYLE AND ATTITUDE

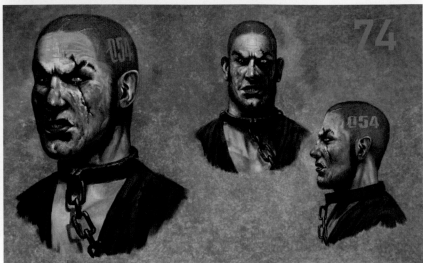

82

52

68

62

PHOTOSHOP

CREATE CHARACTER CONCEPTS

WORK WITH PERSPECTIVE, LIGHTING AND CONTRAST USING PAINTING TECHNIQUES

The process of creating a digital painting in Photoshop can be very complex, so in this tutorial you will learn how to control your workflow. We'll guide you from your initial thought process to any techniques you will have to bear in mind before diving deeper into the different aspects of creating a strong, readable digital painting. This includes, perspective, lighting and contrast.

The majority of your time here will be spent understanding the different steps, from the initial thumbnails to the final rendered painting. The tutorial is meant to be performed in Photoshop, for the sake of getting an efficient workflow by using some of its essential tools such as adjustments layers, blend modes and masks.

The inspiration and idea for this specific painting comes from a long-lasting fascination for dinosaurs, and is a comical new take on the discussed evolution theory about T-rex's way of hunting!

DEVELOPING YOUR CHARACTER CONCEPT
DON'T BE AFRAID TO EXPERIMENT FROM THE START

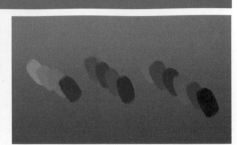

01 THUMBNAILS

The first step is to do some character exploration sketches, to get a better sense of the style and theme. In this case we want something stylised and cartoon-based with a comedy twist. As you do this, look up some references or write down some keywords to help you explore the direction to take. It is important to keep this step as simple as possible, so do yourself a favour and work at a small scale; create a new document and set the size to A4, then zoom out to 12.5%. Use a hard-edged brush.

02 SHAPE LANGUAGE

When we have finished sketching in some interesting thumbnail silhouettes that feel suitable for the style and theme, we can start exploring the shapes a bit further. Make the resolution higher on your chosen thumbnail design by going to Image> Image Size>Resolution and then begin exploring the personality, features and background of your character. Your thought process is the key at this point, so keep it loose and try to go with the flow of your character concepts.

03 THE GOOD IDEA!

Once you have fully explored the first two steps, you will hopefully find that you have some good ideas for what is to come next. Start by creating a new document and then set it to Width: 5000 pixels, Height: 2800 pixels and Resolution: 300 pixels/inch. The technical approach from here can vary a lot, but in this tutorial we want to go straight in with colour. Pick a colour palette that you like and start by creating a two-coloured gradient layer reflecting sky and ground.

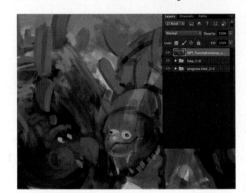

05 LIGHT

An important decision to make that will affect the rest of your painting is the light. In this case we work with three light sources: a direct light coming from the sun located to the right; an indirect light coming from the illuminating blue sky; and finally, the bounce light that is caused by both the direct and indirect light. The choice of light directions will affect your composition and the overall readability of your painting, so try to think about which elements are the most important to highlight.

04 SKETCH IT ALL OUT

When you start your painting you once again want to work on a small scale. Have a clear idea of what you want to achieve, and make sure that you paint with a large brush in the beginning so that you force yourself to work with the overall shapes first. Set your chosen brush to 100% Opacity and Flow, and colour pick from your palette and your gradient layer until you can see all the elements of importance in your painting. Don't be afraid of doing this roughly, as long as it follows your idea.

QUICK TIP
SAVE TIME WHEN ADJUSTING

To save time when you are adjusting your steps, use Hue/Saturation or Color Balance for any colour adjustments, and Levels or Curves for the contrast adjustments. Layering with different blend modes can also be useful, and using layer masks for controlling the affected area is very handy indeed.

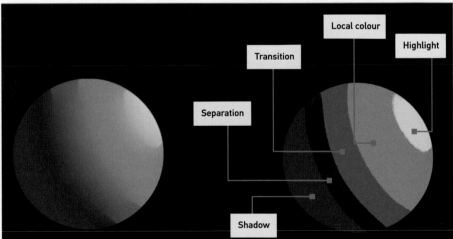

06 SHADOWS AND VOLUME

In order to define the individual shapes, it is crucial to understand the basic functions of light and shadow and the volume within. In this example we use shadows to create an interesting layer effect on the three dinosaurs in the foreground. The main function of this is to help us separate the characters from each other and also to clarify the volumes.

07 VALUE

Now it's time to work into the contrast values a bit further. To make the painting more readable, we turn it into black and white only for the sake of checking the values. Open the Adjustments palette. Click the Hue/Saturation icon and, in the dialog that appears, pull the Saturation bar back to -100. Now you can always check your values by switching the adjustment layer on and off. We want to have the highest contrast value in the foreground, and the further we travel into the image then the lower this contrast gets.

08 COLOURS IN LEVELS

To keep this painting colourful and playful, we want to have some more refined local colours. ('Local colour' means the colour of an element, such as a green leaf, that is not being affected by colour.) This is also a good way of clarifying the levels in the painting's foreground, midground and background. A basic rule of thumb when it comes to environmental colours is to have the warmest colours closest and the coldest colours furthest back. So in this painting we want to apply the warmest colours to the characters in the foreground.

09 SHAPES IN SPACE

Making the shapes clearly readable in a detailed painting like this is a challenge in itself. In this case we don't really have a clear dominant shape – it's more a matter of achieving a symmetry in the painting that makes the intruder, the T-rex, mix in with the two plant-eating dinosaurs on either side. This means that we end up having a round repetitive shape that creates the line of action that we want. We also want the surrounding space and the environment to support the characters' shape language in the best way possible.

10 SHORTCUT FOR ADJUSTING COLOURS

For a more efficient adjustment of your colour work there are some helpful tools you can use in Photoshop to achieve what you are looking for. Head to the Adjustments and select Hue/Saturation. This will bring up the options to adjust the Hue, Saturation and Lightness. In this case we want to increase the amount of red. Choose the drop-down menu named Master and select your Red channel for adjustment. This is personal preference at this stage so feel free to play until it is right.

11 SHORTCUT FOR ADJUSTING VALUES

For the same reason as when adjusting the colours, we want to have an easy way of adjusting the values of our painting. Go to the Adjustments window and select Levels. This will bring up the options of adjusting the image's levels. In this case we want to reduce the amount of whites. Choose the middle icon, then pull the midtones to the right to add more black. Again, wait until the picture is updated before saving and hit Cmd/Ctrl+Z to undo any changes if they do not look right.

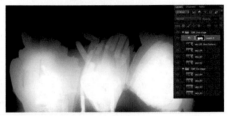

12 LAYERED MASKS

To control areas of affection for a certain layer, you can use layer masks. In this case we want to work with the previously added Levels layer, in order to decrease the amount of black furthest back in the painting. Select the Levels adjustment layer, then click on the layer's white icon. Now you can start masking out the blacks by painting with a soft-edged brush set to black. The advantage of a layered mask is that you can always change where it should affect and how much it should affect by painting in black for hiding and in white for revealing.

13 BLEND MODES

Try out different colour variations in your painting by using the blend modes. Be careful when using blend modes, as the result can become quite random if you don't know what you're looking for. In this case we want to use the blend mode called Overlay, in order to increase the saturation in different places. Create a new layer in your Layer stack, then click Overlay in the menu at the top. Now you can start colour picking from your painting and paint saturated colours into the different areas.

14 LIQUIFY

Sometimes, you just don't like a specific shape or area, or there's curvature that feels wrong. A helpful tool to warp these into place is Liquify. Go to Filter>Liquify and select the Forward Warp tool. As for all of the mentioned tools, use them carefully. What you don't want to end up having is stretched areas in your painting, so at this stage you should keep this to a minimum.

15 EVALUATION

When you have finished your painting, thoroughly evaluate what you have created. Rest your eyes, go back to it with fresh, critical eyes, and try to ask yourself the questions: 'How does it feel? Does it read as intended? Do the adjustment layers make the painting better?' and so forth. Making artwork is a matter of trying things out and exploring all the time. There is no recipe to a perfect painting – it's mostly hard work and a lot of small victories until you eventually master the piece. Good luck!

BRING CHARACTER CONCEPTS TO LIFE

DEVELOP A CHARACTER CONCEPT AND BRING IT TO LIFE USING PHOTOSHOP'S DIGITAL PAINT TOOLS AND TECHNIQUES

This tutorial will teach you how to create an illustration suitable for a children's storybook. You will be guided through the entire process, from the very first tiny thumbnail sketches, all the way to the final image. Learn how to handle composition, colour schemes, overall readability, effective shortcuts, and other tips and tricks. The main focus will lie in creating an illustration that tells a tale.

The painting was made for a spread based on a short story. It was commissioned by a Swedish youth magazine. This painting is a good example of story-driven art that's geared towards a younger audience, which can be great fun to work on. Being able to paint cute, expressive and appealing illustrations that really reach out to the viewer can be very rewarding.

If you have a Wacom tablet, it is worth using it from start to finish for more control. The image was also partly painted using some basic brushes, but a few custom brushes were used from a free brush set created by the talented artist Shaddy Safadi. You can download and use his brushes at www.shaddyconceptart.com/download.

SOURCE FILES ✓
WWW.SHADDYCONCEPTART.COM

PHOTOSHOP

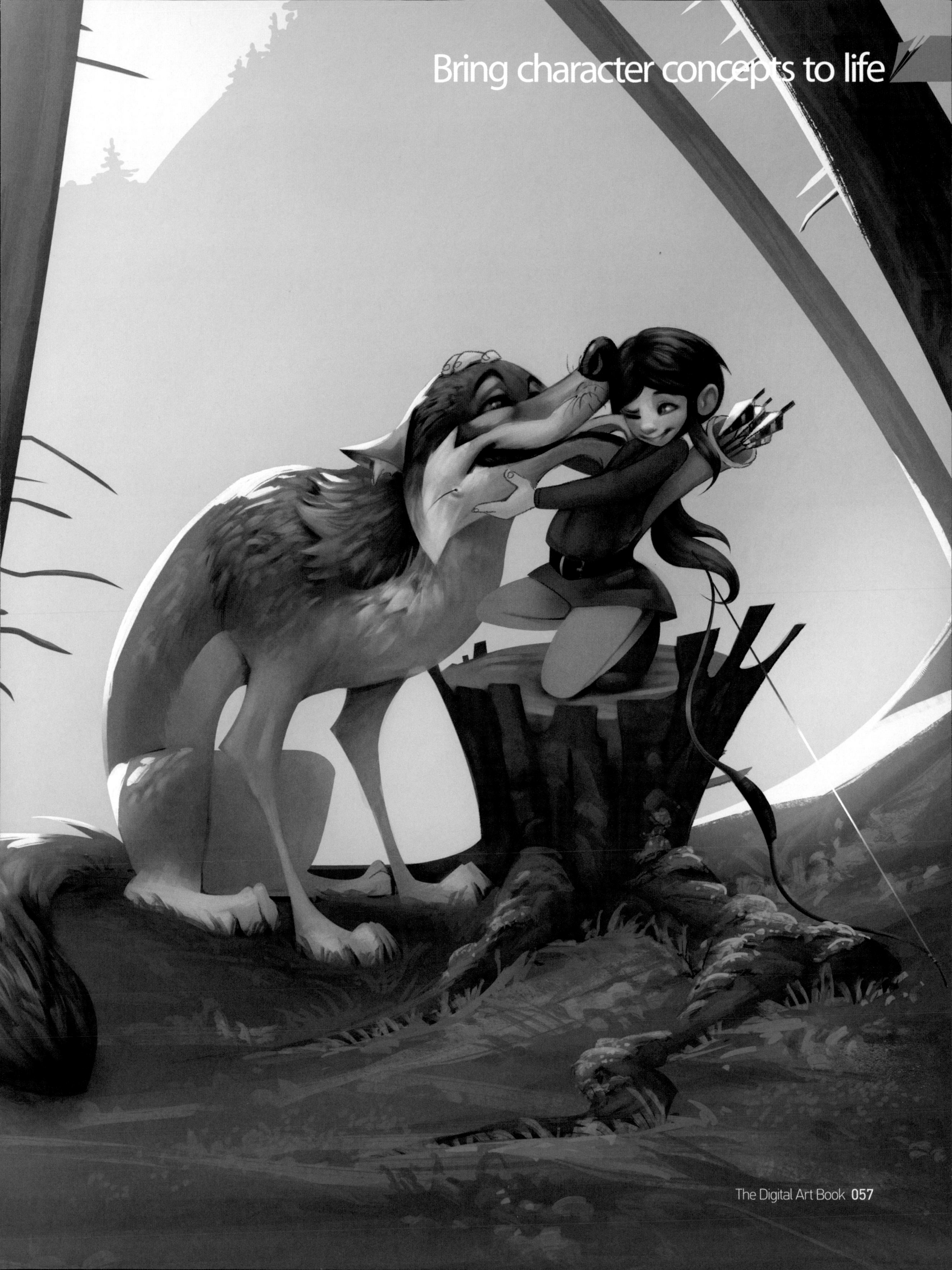

BREATHE LIFE INTO YOUR CHARACTERS
FROM SKETCHING TO PAINTING, DEVELOP YOUR CONCEPTS AND MAKE THEM REAL

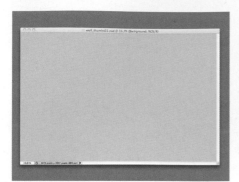

01 CREATE A NEW CANVAS
First, you'll need a brand new canvas. Start by creating a document by going to File>New and create a canvas that is 210mm x 148mm, and at 300dpi. It's better to keep the canvas rather small at this stage so that you can pay attention to the whole of the image. Fill the background layer with a light-grey tone. It's often better to work on a darker canvas, since it's more comfortable for your eyes. Then create a new empty layer on top – that's the layer you're going to sketch on next.

02 THE VERY FIRST THUMBNAILS
Start by quickly putting down a bunch of thumbnails. Keep them small and pick a medium-sized brush that you feel comfortable with. This is the 'sandbox' phase, and any idea is allowed at this stage. Focus on experimenting with pose, composition and proportions. The position of the little thumbnails is not that important, just make sure that you get every single idea out of your system. Stay very loose and feel free to play around a lot before settling entirely with your idea.

03 CREATE A ROUGH SKETCH
Pick the thumbnails that are closest to your idea and start arranging them on your canvas. Lower the opacity of that layer and create a new one on top of it. Keep sketching until the entire image works, and keep experimenting. It's great to constantly ask yourself questions such as: What's the purpose with the image? How does the story go? Which moment works best for this illustration? What style should it have? Who's the audience? Does the composition direct the viewer properly?

> **It's often better to work on a darker canvas, since it's more comfortable for your eyes**

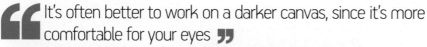

04 REFINE THE CHARACTERS
Now you will need to create another document to implement your final design. Feel free to make it even larger this time and fill the background with a light-grey tone. Select the character sketch with the Lasso tool from the rough sketch, copy the selection and paste it into your new document. After that, scale the characters so that they fill out the whole canvas and lower the opacity of the layer, then create another empty one and start refining the sketch further. To do this, use a brush with hard edges, and with the opacity settings activated.

05 LOWER THE OPACITY

When the characters are more refined and you feel happy with them, copy the layer and add it to the previous sketch document. Remove the rough version of the characters and merge the sketch layers together. The sketch should only work as a vague guideline for the painting itself, so lower the Opacity to about 30% and lock that layer. Most of the other layers (except some adjustment layers that affect the entire image) created for this painting will stay underneath the line drawing.

06 TRY IT OUT IN GREYSCALE

It's time to play around a bit with the values. Block everything in with flat tones just to find some suitable values that will work well with the composition and mood. Paint on a new empty layer that's created underneath the sketch layer. A nice rule to go by is that if things work well in greyscale, then it will definitely work out in colour as well later on. In general, it's also nice to have several possibilities to choose from before you start to colour a new piece.

07 COLOUR TEST

Before getting too serious with the illustration, it's a good idea to quickly flatten the greyscale sketch and create and save a new version that will serve as a colour palette later on. On the new document, create a new empty layer and set the layer blending mode to Color. Now you can start painting some colours in without affecting the tones. This one will work well with lots of greens as the dominating hue, with a slight touch of brown, yellow and red.

QUICK TIP
FLIP IT TO VIEW WITH FRESH EYES

This shortcut that can be created through Actions is very handy when painting digitally in Photoshop. Simply create an Action that flips your canvas horizontally when pressing a specific key, perhaps F2. Flipping your canvas often makes you look at the painting with fresh eyes, and you can immediately see and fix any proportions or compositions that may be a bit off.

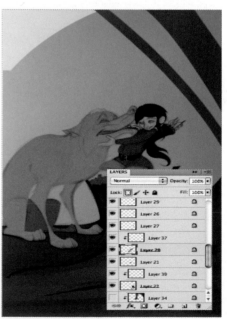

08 BLOCK IN THE BASE COLOURS

After settling on a nice colour scheme, it's time to block everything in. This will make things so much easier when starting to paint the illustration. The base layers can be created using the Pen tool. Start by drawing the main shape to create a new path, then make that path a selection and fill it with a basic colour. Proceed by creating basic shapes for the different background elements, the wolf and the girl. Lock the transparency of each layer when done.

09 CREATE CLIPPING MASKS

This stage really is a true time-saver, and it's one of my favourite Photoshop shortcuts. Start by creating new layers on top of each 'blocked' layer, then press Opt/Alt and hover the cursor in-between the two layers. The lower layer will become the parent of the upper one, and it will then stay within that shape, no matter how messy you paint. It also means that you only need to block in the main parts once. You can then focus on the fun part – the painting itself!

10 DOUBLE-CHECK IN GREYSCALE

When all the base colours are added to the painting and you're all set, it's helpful to create a Hue/Saturation adjustment layer. Keep it on top of the entire painting and adjust it so that the painting gets completely desaturated. You can then turn this layer on and off to keep checking the values when painting. Is the painting readable in greyscale at this stage? Good! Then it's ready to get painted for real.

11 TIME TO PAINT!

Keep blocking in base colours with a large brush. The basic brushes will work perfectly at this stage. Use big, bold strokes in the beginning and switch between hard-edge and soft-edge brushes, keeping the Opacity at 20-50%. Stay loose and always work on the entire painting. To get a better overview, open the document in two separate windows using Window>Arrange>New window.

12 FLIP YOUR CANVAS REGULARLY

Go to Image>Image Rotation>Flip Horizontally on a regular basis to check the proportions, balance and composition. When you flip the canvas, you'll see immediately if the nose looks off, or if the position of the eyes is awkward. It's a lot easier to spot mistakes. The great news is that you get to make the changes in time. If the image is working in both angles, then it's probably balanced.

Rough it up
If you increase the Scattering value from the Brush palette, you can rough up the edges of your brush and make it look more realistic. Uniform strokes are the hallmark of digital – real media is more random

Balance
Now that the image has been flipped, you can check that the composition is still well balanced

Character details
Take a step back and think about which parts of the characters need some extra work, like the fur and eyes

Rendering
Start with slightly rendering the form of the characters and tree trunk, keeping the direction of the light in mind

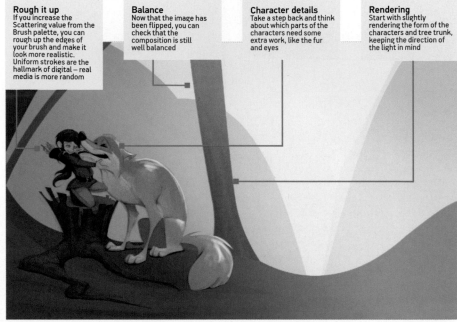

QUICK TIP
KEEP LIGHT SOURCES SEPARATE

It's always a good idea to keep your light sources on a separate layer to your base image. This way, you can turn those layers off when you need to, and you can then focus entirely on rendering form and putting down those basic values in your painting.

13 SECOND PAINTING PASS

Keep fleshing out the illustration, working on the entire painting and correcting smaller mistakes that you encountered when mirroring the image. Keep comparing the image in the smaller window as you proceed and make sure that it looks good and readable when it's smaller as well. Although it's tempting, don't dive into the smaller details just yet; just keep painting with a slightly lower opacity and render the forms.

14 ADD SOME LIGHT

It's a bit dark here, isn't it? To solve this, create new layers for the background and the characters, then connect them to the layers underneath as clipping masks. Set the layer mode to Color Dodge and pick an orange midtone to paint with. Use a hard brush without any opacity settings and paint in highlights, ensuring they are in keeping with the direction of the light source. Let those layers stay rough for now, as long as it looks good overall.

15 THIRD PAINTING PASS

The image is now ready for some slight detailing and early polishing. Play around with different textured brushes to get that traditional, painterly feel. Safadi's custom brushes will suit perfectly for this phase. Vary the opacity of the brushes to gain full control while you paint. Create new empty layers on top of the parenting layers if you feel unsure and want to redo, or remove unnecessary changes as you paint.

16 DOUBLE-CHECK IN GREYSCALE AGAIN

Turn on the Hue/Saturation adjustment layer that you placed at the very top and check the values. Is the illustration still readable? This part is really crucial, and as mentioned earlier – if it's working in greyscale, then it will most likely work in colour as well. So it's a very good habit to just double-check your illustration on a regular basis while working with colours. We can't encourage this part enough. Is it still working? If it still reads well, then it's fine.

17 REFINE THE FUR

You can see that the wolf's fur needs some more details. Keep painting with a medium-sized brush and render the forms a little bit more. After that, pick a brush that feels more like a traditional brush that slightly imitates hair or fur. Having photo references is always a huge benefit; so don't be afraid to search for some nice photos that clearly show what a wolf's fur really looks like. References will always be important, even if you paint in a rather cartoon-like style.

18 FURTHER DETAILING

Keep adding in smaller details where they are needed. Paint them all in while keeping a careful eye on the entire illustration. Remember: less is more. Another good thing to keep in mind is to spend some extra time on characters' eyes and faces in general. These features are one of the first things that the viewer looks at, so it's important that the eyes and expressions read well and show clear emotions. Getting this part right definitely helps to tell a story.

> "References will always be important, even if you paint in a rather cartoon-like style"

19 FINAL TOUCHES

Finally, you can add the smallest and finest details to the painting. These include the whiskers, hair and sparkles in the eyes. Evaluate the entire painting by flipping the canvas horizontally as in Step 12, turning the Hue/Saturation adjustment layer on to check values once again, and last but not least, make sure that it reveals your story. You can also flatten the entire painting at this stage, so you don't have to handle all the different layers anymore.

20 PREPARE FOR DELIVERY

Since this was made for a magazine, it's especially important to make sure that all of the settings and modes are correct. To start with, check that the image is scaled or cropped properly. Most publishers handle their images in CMYK, so make sure that it is converted. You can also sharpen the image a little bit. Go to Filter>Sharpen>Unsharp Mask. Play around with the settings and make sure that the image looks nice and crisp, and then you are done!

Concept: The little girl is so happy that a bee decided to taste her lollipop. The bee doesn't look as happy. This sketch will be our guide through the tutorial.

PHOTOSHOP

3DS MAX

V-RAY

ZBRUSH

CREATE STYLISED CHARACTERS

CREATE A 3D ILLUSTRATION WITH SHORTCUTS

Both illustration and film use 3D but, even though the techniques are similar, the approach for each can be quite different. An illustration gives the artist a lot more freedom and skips a few technical steps that would be essential when preparing for animation.

Creating a 3D illustration can be a lot faster if you plan ahead, so you know what to skip and where to invest the details. Here we will be

preparing a 3D illustration following a concept to optimise the production process. ZBrush and 3ds Max will be used together for modelling and posing. We will also be making extensive use of the new V-Ray 2.2 for the rendering and materials, especially its new Hair Material that enables hair to cast reflections, receive Global Illumination and V-Ray lights. We will learn all the necessary tricks to achieve a good result with this most recent feature.

> Creating a 3D illustration can be faster if you plan ahead, so you know what to skip and where to invest the details. Here we will be preparing a 3D illustration following a concept to optimise the production process

BEGIN WITH BASIC SHAPES
WORK FROM THE CONCEPT SKETCH TO BEGIN THE MODEL

01 BEGIN COMPOSITION IN 3DS MAX

In 3ds Max, set units to Meters. The correct scale is very important for accurate light and hair rendering. Set the render size to 767 x 1,000px and enable Safe Frames (Shift+F) on the viewport to match the concept's proportions. Set the concept image (free with this issue) to be the viewport background (Opt/Alt+B and Load Image).

Build a ground plane and a rough version of the girl 1.5m high using primitives. Make sure that the centre of the girl's body is at the co-ordinates 0,0,0. Create a camera with a 33mm lens and place it so that the perspective matches the concept on the background. For the lollipop make a 0.25m radius Cylinder with 18 sides and six different Cap segments.

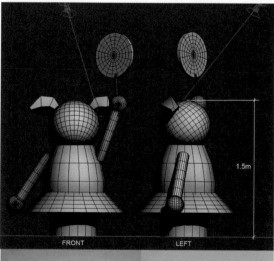

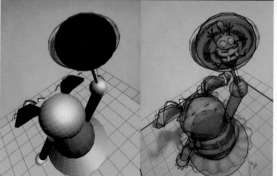

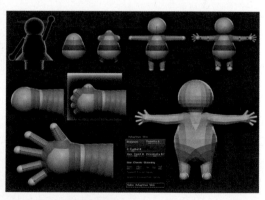

02 ZSPHERES BASE

Select all objects and pick the GoZBrush from the GoZ menu, ZBrush will then open. Drag the document and hit T to edit the model. This rough model will be used as a reference for proportions.

Press Append (Subtool menu) and pick ZSphere. Enable Transparency (Trans button) and scale the ZSphere to be the girl's belly size. Activate Symmetry (X) and create a new ZSphere to make the trunk. Extend the head, arms and legs. Add ZSpheres at the wrists and knees, then extend the feet. From the hand extend the fingers and press Make Adaptive Skin. ZBrush creates a new Skin_ZSphere tool. Press Append and select to add it to your tool.

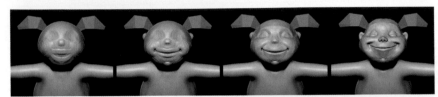

MODELS AND MAPS
PREPARE TOPOLOGY AND UVS FOR THE NEXT STAGE

03 SCULPT THE BODY

Subdivide the body three times, slide the DynaMesh Resolution to 8 and press DynaMesh (choose No when prompted for Freeze Subdivision). When working in this mode every time you hit Cmd/Ctrl and drag on the background, the model will be remeshed and generate new geometry as you need it. Enable Symmetry and, using the Clay Buildup brush, start marking the main facial features. Detail the features just enough to use them as a guide as they will be retopologised. On the body refine the hands' volume and mark the main body masses. Remesh every time the surface starts to become stretched and you need more detail.

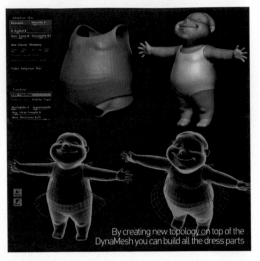

By creating new topology on top of the DynaMesh you can build all the dress parts

04 RETOPOLOGY – BODY

We will retopologise the DynaMesh to create a lighter model and enable cleaner UVs. Append a new ZSphere and under Topology choose Edit Topology. As you click the surface you create vertexes that close as polygons, creating new geometry. Enable Symmetry and, following the facial features, create polygons looping around the mouth and eyes. Create a nose and ears connecting the surfaces. Extend the surface to cover the back of the head and neck. Create polygons looping around the fingers, extending along the hands and arms until they connect with the neck. Create polygons along the legs and close feet. Under Adaptive Skin set Density to 5 and click Make Adaptive Skin. Append the new model to your tool.

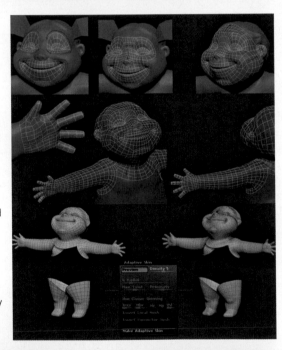

05 RETOPOLOGY – DRESS

Append a new ZSphere and start topology for the dress. Create a bathing suit shape with openings for arms, legs and head. Under Topology set Skin Thickness to 0.25, click Make Adaptive Skin and Append. Create new topology with a loop of polygons around the waist and shoulders. Add a thinner loop that will represent the elastic that holds the cloth. Activate Transparency and Ghost mode to move vertexes freely, creating the edge of skirt and sleeves. Include several new edge loops. Under Topology set Skin Thickness to 0.25 and lower the Density to 1. Click Make Adaptive Skin and Append. Set Crease Tolerance to 25 and press Crease to prevent the edge that defines the elastic from smoothing. Finally, subdivide the parts.

QUICK TIP
A WORD ON TOPOLOGY

Topology is very important. Creating geometric edges that follow the surface landmarks results in models that are lighter, easier to apply UVs to, more suited for animation or posing and better for sculpting. However trying to create the perfect topology for a model whose form we are still busy defining is difficult. Try dividing the model creation into two stages: one that is 100 per cent artistic and another that is 100 per cent technical.

The first phase must be flexible and careless regarding polygon count and edge flow. Use DynaMesh and its capacity to generate new geometry as you extend your model to visualise and test your ideas. Don't detail too much at this stage.

The second phase is retopology. Having established your idea, create geometry on top of your 3D sketch with the best edge flow. You can detail it comfortably as the direction of surface geometry matches the direction of the details. This strategy gives you the best of both worlds: unrestricted creativity and accurate topology.

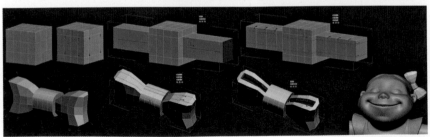

06 RIBBONS AND PIGTAILS

In 3ds Max, create a 0.06m cube with 4 x 3 x 3 edges. Apply Edit Poly and Symmetry modifiers. In Edit Poly, move the edges and extrude the central side faces. Add two horizontal loops and three loops along the extrusion. Move vertexes to shape the ribbon to a butterfly shape. Add two extra loops and extrude the central top faces on the bow inwards. Press GoZBrush in the GoZ menu.

In ZBrush, append the ribbon to the girl tool. Position the ribbon on the head and shape it with the Move brush. Append the ZSphere and create a chain with a pigtail shape. Click Make Adaptive Skin and shape it with the Move brush. Using the Subtool Master (ZPlugin menu) mirror the ribbons and pigtails.

COMBINE ASSETS
UNWRAP YOUR UVS AND MAKE A POSE

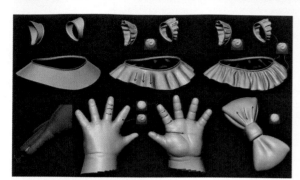

07 MAKE FINE DETAILS

Using the Standard brush, stroke from the inside to the outside to create folds. Subdivide and sculpt detail on the folds. With the Dam Standard brush create a rim at the edge of the sleeves and skirt. Subdivide the dress, mark the edge around the openings then sculpt folds at the waist and chest. Subdivide the body. Using the Clay Buildup brush, detail the face. Mark the mouth and eyeline with the Dam Standard brush. Unmask one fingernail at a time and rotate from a side view to create the nails. Use the brush to mark the wrinkles and sculpt hair ribbons with the Clay Buildup brush.

08 CHARACTER UVS

Select each subtool and press GoZ to export to 3ds Max. Apply the UnwrapUVW modifier, select edges where UVs will be cut and set Convert Edge Selection to the seams. Choose Open UV Editor, click the Peel mode button and disable it. Choose Tools>Pack UVs to separate the UVs and enable Peel mode again. To shape the UVs select vertexes that you want to be fixed and choose Pin Selected. Move other vertexes to reshape the UVs and get a good layout. Click GoZ>GoZBrush to update the ZBrush subtool with these UVs. On the body, keep seams behind the head and follow the hair line. Create seams to separate the ears and arms, leaving easily identifiable UV islands that will make the texture painting task easier.

An illustration consists of a very specific point of view of a certain moment in time. As a result there are many occluded parts. You should take advantage of that to make your work quicker and more enjoyable. Here are a few shortcuts.

The back of the girl hasn't been detailed as it can't be seen. The legs have only been modelled roughly as their only purpose is to create shadow. The UV seams have been placed on the back of the girl and the belly of the bee to hide texture-continuity problems. Posing was made with Transpose Master instead of rigging the character as we won't be using it for animation or different poses. The lollipop was only detailed on the visible side.

In the next chapter this logic persists, keeping the scenario only as big as the field of view of the camera, ensuring the objects that are out of focus are very simple. Minimum effort and maximum impact is the idea here.

09 ADD CLOTHING FEATURES

On the dress, make seams at the openings and a vertical one at the back. In Peel mode, select the vertical edge loops on the sides and align their vertexes using Align Vertical (under Quick Transform) this will enable an undistorted layout, easing the task of pattern creation later on. For the skirt, shape the UVs into a rectangle and align the vertical and horizontal edges to allow for a pattern. On the ribbons, use seams to separate the central knot from the bows. Regarding the lollipop, create a seam at the back edge of the cylinder.

10 POSE THE CHARACTER

Delete the subtools, except the final parts and lollipop. Under ZPlugin>Transpose Master choose TposeMesh. Unmask the trunk and rotate it to the character's right. Unmask the right arm and rotate it up to reach for the lollipop stick. Adjust rotation of the right hand. Unmask and rotate the left arm down and rotate the left hand up. Under ZPlugin>Transpose Master pick Tpose>SubT. The pose will transfer to the original subtools. Using the Move brush, correct any deformations caused from posing. Select the body subtool and by unmasking each of the fingers and using Rotate mode, pose each finger to make the hand grip the lollipop.

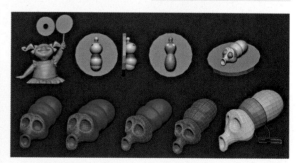

11 SHAPE THE BODY

Duplicate the lollipop subtool; move it to the centre for ref. Using ZSpheres create the body, head and nose of the bee against the lollipop. Click Make Adaptive Skin, append a primitive sphere and place as an eye. Using the Transpose Master, mirror it and mark an iris on the eye for ref. Subdivide the body and sculpt it with the Clay Buildup brush, marking the eyebrows and mouth. Sculpt the body sections of the bee. Create new topology, starting with edge loops around the eyes. Extend to the nose and create a loop around the mouth. Extend polygons along the body sections, give a different polygroup to each body section, isolate them and press Crease to keep a hard edge between sections while subdividing.

MODELS AND MAPS
TIME TO CONSTRUCT THE BEE CHARACTER

12 BUILD BEE SECTIONS
Create a new topology on top of the bee's mid-section with the shape of a wing. Under Topology set Skin Thickness to 0.03. Click Make Adaptive Skin and position the wing on the bee's back. Delete the lower subdivision level and using GoZ export the body and wing to 3ds Max. Apply the UnwrapUVW modifier and mark seams as in the image using Peel mode. Adjust UVs and use GoZ to update them on ZBrush. Using ZSpheres, create one arm, a leg and an antenna. Subdivide and detail with the Clay Buildup brush then duplicate the extra arm from the existing one and position it. Mirror all these parts using Subtool Master.

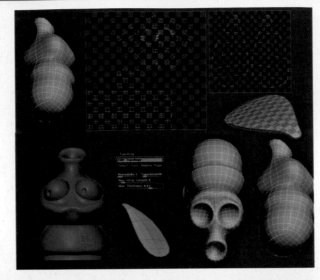

> Mask the lollipop and place the bee on it. The bee's tongue will be glued to the lollipop, so pose the body as if the bee is trying to release itself by pulling its head up

13 POSE THE CHARACTER
You can delete the lollipop duplicate. Select all the bee parts and the original lollipop. Under Transpose Master choose TposeMesh. Mask the lollipop and place the bee on it. The bee's tongue will be glued to the lollipop, so pose the body as if the bee is trying to release itself by pulling its head up. Unmask the upper body and rotate up, then the head and rotate it right. Unmask the mouth and rotate it left as if it's being pulled. Rotate the arms and legs to counter balance the pulling action. Under Transpose Master choose Tpose>SubT to transfer the changes to the final model.

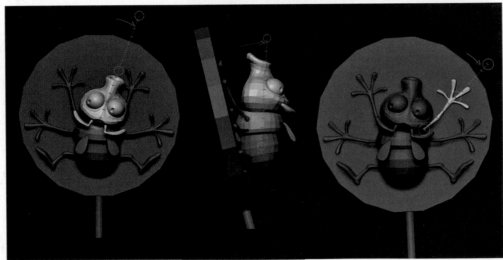

QUICK TIP
GOZ BACK AND FORTH

GoZ creates a bridge between ZBrush and 3ds Max. Polygon selection tools are superior in 3ds Max, use them to assign Material IDs that will be interpreted as polygroups in ZBrush.
On the other hand, ZBrush is better at reshaping organic forms. Export geometry, reshape and send it back to 3ds Max. Take advantage of the best in each software.

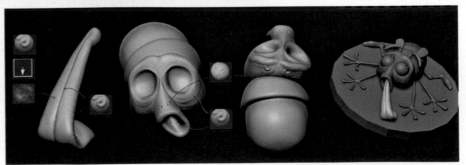

14 FOCUS ON THE BEE'S FEATURES
Create a ZSphere at the mouth and extend to create the tongue base. Click Make Adaptive Skin, subdivide and shape with the Move brush. Sculpt the tongue with the Clay Buildup brush. To create UVs, start by deleting lower-level subdivision and press GoZ. In 3ds Max, apply UnwrapUVW, select edges indicated on the image as seams and use Peel mode to unfold UVs. Press GoZ to update ZBrush model UVs. Create a surface texture using the Standard brush in Drag Rect mode using the LeatherySkin15 Alpha (in Lightbox) and dragging onto the surface. Use the Dam Standard brush for wrinkles on the tongue and face (around eyes and lips). Mark nostrils and connection with antenna with the Clay Buildup brush.

FINAL DETAILS
FINALISE AND EXPORT FOR THE NEXT PHASE

15 ADJUST THE LOLLIPOP

Select the lollipop cylinder, set Ctolerance (Crease Tolerance) to 41 and press Crease. This will prevent the cylinder's edges from smoothing. Subdivide twice then Press Shift and Uncrease All. Subdivide three more times and, using the Clay Buildup brush, mark the lollipop spirals by stroking lightly to produce an irregular surface. With the Dam Standard brush mark the frontier between the two spiral colours.

With the Clay Buildup brush, sculpt around the tongue as if the surface had been licked. Also add volume around all body parts that touch the lollipop surface.

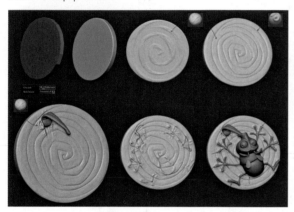

16 EXPORT TO 3DS MAX

The model has ten million polygons. To export a lighter model to 3ds Max, choose the adequate subdivision level for each subtool as indicated in the image. Set this subdivision level and press DelLower to delete lower subdivisions. We have to do this because ZBrush will always export to 3ds Max with the lowest subdivision level through GoZ.

Most subtools will be exported at subdivision level 3. However, here we are exporting the lollipop at its maximum level to keep all the contact details with the bee. Near GoZ button press All to export all subtools to 3ds Max. The exported model has about 475 thousand polygons.

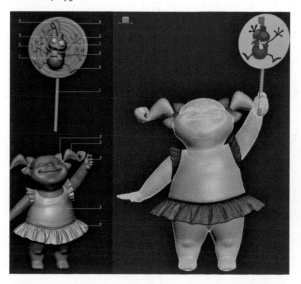

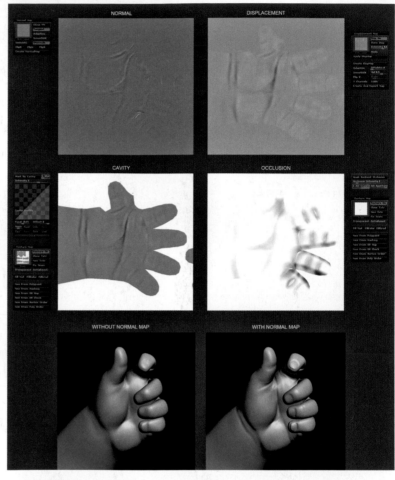

17 EXPORT THE MAPS

We will export normal maps for all subtools that have UVs to use later in materials. Also export cavity, occlusion and displacement maps in order to help in the creation of textures in the next chapter.

To export normal map, go to lowest subdivision. Under NormalMap disable SmoothUV, press Create NormalMap. Press CloneNM and under the Texture menu choose map and press Export to save it. To export displacement map at the lowest subdivision, under Displacement Map press Create DispMap. Press CloneDisp, go to the Alpha menu, select Map and Export. For cavity and occlusion, set the highest subdivision and under Masking press Mask Ambient Occlusion or Mask by Cavity. For cavity set Focal Shift to 0 and Intensity to 1. For occlusion, set AO ScanDist to 1. Under Texture Map, choose New from Masking. Clone Txtr and export it (Texture menu). Everything is set to start next phase.

QUICK TIP
EXTRA MAPS FOR MORE QUALITY

Occlusion, cavity and displacement maps can be easily extracted in ZBrush. These maps work very well as a base to create other maps (like specular, glossiness or bump) and are also useful for adding extra information to colour maps. Use the occlusion map on top of your colour map using a Multiply or Linear Burn blending mode for a dirt effect. Cavity and displacement maps also work really well using the Overlay blending mode to provide extra visual detail and reinforce the normal map's effect.

IMPROVE YOUR CHARACTERS

ACHIEVE SIMPLE, STRIKING AND STYLISED CHARACTER DESIGNS USING MODO AND PHOTOSHOP

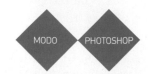
SOURCE FILES ✓
AVAILABLE ON THE FREE DISC

MODO   PHOTOSHOP

In this tutorial we're going to cover the steps towards achieving a stylised portrait that can be used to present, for example, a character concept. The main consideration for an image like this is first and foremost design. The piece needs to convey the personality and appeal of the character, so anything else should be secondary. This means that lighting, environment and staging should all serve the purpose of conveying and enhancing the character. As such these aspects should all be kept simple so as to avoid distracting the viewer from the subject itself.

Approaching this project from a design point of view simplifies the whole approach to the image-creation process. It also means that a few changes could well be needed as the project matures and the final result takes shape.

Only the areas of the model that are absolutely essential to the design need to be created. In terms of topology it really is vital that the face is modelled to a high enough standard to show off the expression, however, in other areas, it is okay for the modelling to be far less rigorous.

Concept image

START WITH THE HEAD
SCULPT AND ADD TOPOLOGY

01 DEFINE THE FORM OF THE HEAD
Working with your initial sketch as a reference, add a sphere and set it to Multiresolution mode with six subdivisions to create a very high-resolution mesh. We'll use the Sculpt tools to shape the head, but at this stage things can be kept very loose, so just think of this as a 3D sketch that's more convenient to work from than a 2D image. Once the rough form is finished, we can sculpt the nose and lips.

02 BEGIN RETOPOLOGISING
With the main form of the head fleshed out, it can now be retopologised. Because this element will need to show a facial expression, it's important to get the topology around the mouth and the eyes right. The main loops that surround the eyes and the mouth are tackled first and then the rest of the topology is built around them. The mouth is very important because it requires a wide range of movement, so it needs some wide loops around it to enable smooth deformations.

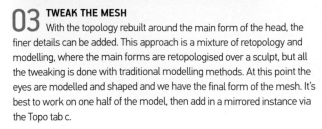

03 TWEAK THE MESH
With the topology rebuilt around the main form of the head, the finer details can be added. This approach is a mixture of retopology and modelling, where the main forms are retopologised over a sculpt, but all the tweaking is done with traditional modelling methods. At this point the eyes are modelled and shaped and we have the final form of the mesh. It's best to work on one half of the model, then add in a mirrored instance via the Topo tab c.

QUICK TIP
RETOPOLOGY

Many artists are uncomfortable with the idea of retopologising a model, fearing that this means doing a job twice. However, this is a short-sighted view, especially when modelling your own designs.

Retopologising over a sculpt ends up saving a huge amount of time. This is because this workflow enables you to break down the process into two logical steps: the sculpting stage is solely for creating form and the topology stage can be used for edge flow. Trying to do both together is far more difficult. The other big benefit is that it frees you from requiring any 2D reference in the viewport. Also, retopologising in 3D is much faster than working from viewport-based 2D references.

FINALISE THE BASIC FIGURE
ADD DETAILS AND INSERT MORE ELEMENTS INTO THE SCENE

04 SHAPE THE EXPRESSION

Once the model is complete, the instanced side can be deleted and the final geometry mirrored over. Apply a new Morph map from the Vertex Map List to be used to shape the character's facial expression. The lopsided smile is made with the Soft Select Move tool and moving vertices with the Transform tool creates the wink. You can speed up the modelling process by having Select Through active, which will let you quickly move one vertex and then another without dropping your tools.

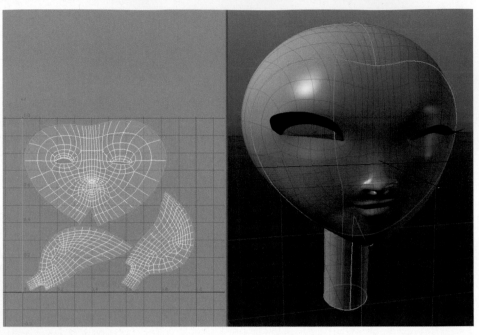

05 ADD THE UV MAPS

Prior to any texture painting, the UVs need to be created. In modo this process is relatively straightforward: simply select the edges that will define the borders of the UV map and run the Unwrap tool in the UV viewport. It's usually worth experimenting with the different settings in the Unwrap tool to get the best possible projection. Unwrapping heads is generally best done with Spherical mode, but in some cases Cylindrical might work better. Testing each axis is worthwhile in order to get the best possible projection. Running the Relax tool after unwrapping is usually a good idea.

> **With a female face concentrate details in certain areas such as the lips, eyes and nose, leaving the rest of the face smooth**

06 SCULPT WITH MULTIRESOLUTION

In order to add details with Multiresolution sculpting, the mesh must be in Catmull-Clark Subdivision mode (hit Shift+Tab to do this). For the head, set the highest subdivision level to 6, which creates a total of just under seven-million polygons. This amount enables very fine details to be sculpted onto the model. With a female face it's best to concentrate details only in certain areas such as the lips, eyes and nose, leaving the rest of the face smooth.

07 TEXTURE PAINT THE FACE

With the details sculpted, texture maps can then be painted with modo's Paint tools. In this case we'll use the Airbrush to paint some colour onto the nose and cheeks and a harder brush to paint the lips. Also paint a black-and-white mask to define the glossy parts of the lips, then apply this as a group mask in the Shader Tree to add a glossy material to the lips. Finally some translucency was added to the materials, using the colour maps painted for the skin and lips.

QUICK TIP
CHARACTER DESIGN

Producing interesting characters requires some individuality on the part of the artist. In order to make something original, you need to work on developing a personal style, so that your characters become distinct and therefore have a chance of standing out from the crowd.

Your sketchbook, whether physical or digital, is the best way of getting noticed. If you regularly try out new ideas in your sketchbooks and try to push your designs, you will soon find plenty of original material for later development. The crazier you can be in your sketchbook the better – even if you need to tone some of the ideas down later.

08 START TO BUILD THE JACKET

By roughly extruding and shaping a cube we can shape the basic form of the jacket, then retopologise it for better edge flow. The folds can be added using Multiresolution sculpting and the jacket is UV-ed and textured with Image maps. To evoke the feel of fabric, a Bump map along with Anisotropic Reflections can be applied. Controlling these is dependent on a good UV map, so the care we took over the topology will pay off at this stage.

09 MODEL THE EYES

When shaping the head mesh, some placeholder spheres are positioned to guide the contouring of the eyelids. To create convincing eyes you will need to model a cornea and an iris as well as the eyeball. You can start with a standard sphere, then rotate it by 90 degrees and delete the triangles at the pole. Inside the hole, use a disc for the iris and model a hemisphere around that for the cornea. Inserting these details will enable the proper reflections and refractions to occur, resulting in very lifelike and appealing eyes.

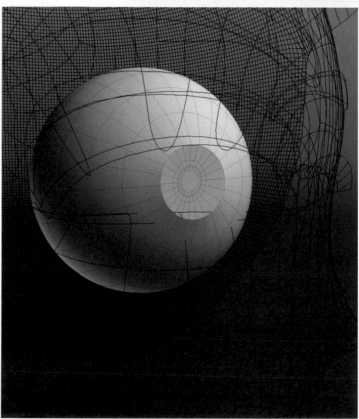

10 TEXTURE THE IRIS

The best way to create the iris texture is to paint one in Photoshop. You can start by filling in a dark brown and then paint streaks of a lighter shade in a radial pattern coming from the middle. Break these streaks up and vary the patterns you paint. Add some lines in a more saturated shade at the halfway point to simulate the patterns commonly found on the iris. Also use this map in the Subsurface slot for translucency .

APPLY HAIR AND BACKGROUND ELEMENTS
COMPLEMENT YOUR FIGURE WITH EXTRA FEATURES

11 CONSTRUCT THE HAIR
A simple hairstyle, such as the one used here, can be created relatively easily. Keeping elements such as the hair as simple as possible helps to speed the whole process up. Copy and paste the polygons that the hair should grow from into a new layer, then apply a black material to them. Add a fur layer and adjust a few settings; for instance increase the number of segments to 20 to ensure there is enough curvature. The Density and Length should also be increased, but reduce all the Jitter settings to ensure more even growth. To finish this element, increase the Flex and Root Bend settings to give the hair some weight, then set Specularity to 100% to create a bright highlight.

12 SHAPE THE PARASOL
You can shape the character's parasol with a hemisphere and then arrange the ribs around a radial array. The Work Plane in modo can be activated in order for you to comfortably work at the angle that the umbrella will be occupying in the 3D space. Paint some folds on a Square map with a radial pattern in Photoshop and apply these as a Bump map to add to the fabric material. To finish, add various maps to define the diffuse and translucent tones.

QUICK TIP
HAIR ADVICE FOR MODO

If you have created hair guides or custom curves to act as guides, there are a couple of very important settings that are needed to ensure the hair follows the guides correctly. In the Fur Material tab make sure the guides are set to Range and that the Guide Range Distance is set to a high value, otherwise the guides will have no effect. Finally, be sure to create enough segments for your hair to follow the guides accurately. To soften the look of the rendered hair you might need to render multiple frame passes.

13 MODEL THE TREES
 The tree elements are a breeze to create in modo: simply start with a flat polygon at ground level and use the Sketch Extrude tool to create an organic trunk. Branches can be pulled out from polygon selections using the same tool. With Select Through activated, you are able to pull new branches out without dropping the tool. The entire process can be completed in just a couple of minutes. Use the Scale and Spin settings on the Sketch Extrude tool to add variety to the branches.

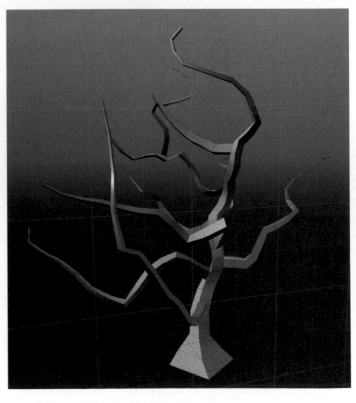

MAKE THE FINAL TOUCHES
WITH THE CHARACTER COMPLETE IT'S TIME TO BRING EVERYTHING TOGETHER

14 BUILD THE LEAVES
The easiest way to create a canopy of leaves is to use particle clouds distributed among the branches of the trees. Once these are placed, you can model a few leaves and make a group out of the leaf meshes. Next, add some Replicator items that will use the leaf groups to duplicate the leaves into the particle clouds. You can add some colour variation very easily by using a gradient set to Particle ID to give each leaf a slightly different colour from the others.

15 APPLY THE BLOSSOM
The blossom can be created in a similar way to the leaves, with the main difference being that the shape of the flowers can be driven by Stencil maps. In Photoshop the blossom shape is painted on a transparent background, which can be used as a Diffuse map. The transparency can also be used to drive a Stencil map, which will define the shape of the petals. The flower can be spread with particle clouds and Replicator items.

16 LIGHTING AND RENDERING
With all of the modelling and texturing complete, the scene is ready for final lighting and rendering. The main light is a simple Directional Light with a faint yellow tone to simulate sunlight. An Area Light is placed to the right to create some reflections in the clothing and eyes. The parasol is backlit with a Spot Light to enhance the translucency. In terms of rendering, the scene is straightforward since it's set outdoors and lit mainly with direct light. The global illumination will render cleanly on default setting.

QUICK TIP
USING THE SHADER TREE

In modo's Shader Tree there are several ways to apply materials to a mesh, either with Polygon Tags, Item Masks or even Selection Sets. If you want a simplified workflow you should exclusively use Polygon Tags to apply materials. This feature has the benefit that materials can be reapplied throughout the scene and objects can be duplicated without losing their materials. Item Masks and Selection Sets can then be used without any materials for things such as item level Alpha channels, and without affecting the predefined materials.

17 RETOUCH IN PHOTOSHOP
With the high-resolution render complete, some final touches can be added in Photoshop. With the default brush tool, apply some retouching around important areas, such as the eyes and lips, to enhance the rendered details. You can retouch the skin using an airbrush to even out any CG harshness. Add some glowing layers (use a solid black layer and set its blending mode to Linear Dodge) and paint subtle airbrush highlights in them over the hair and clothes. Finally, use some basic Color Balance adjustment layers to warm the image and control the contrast.

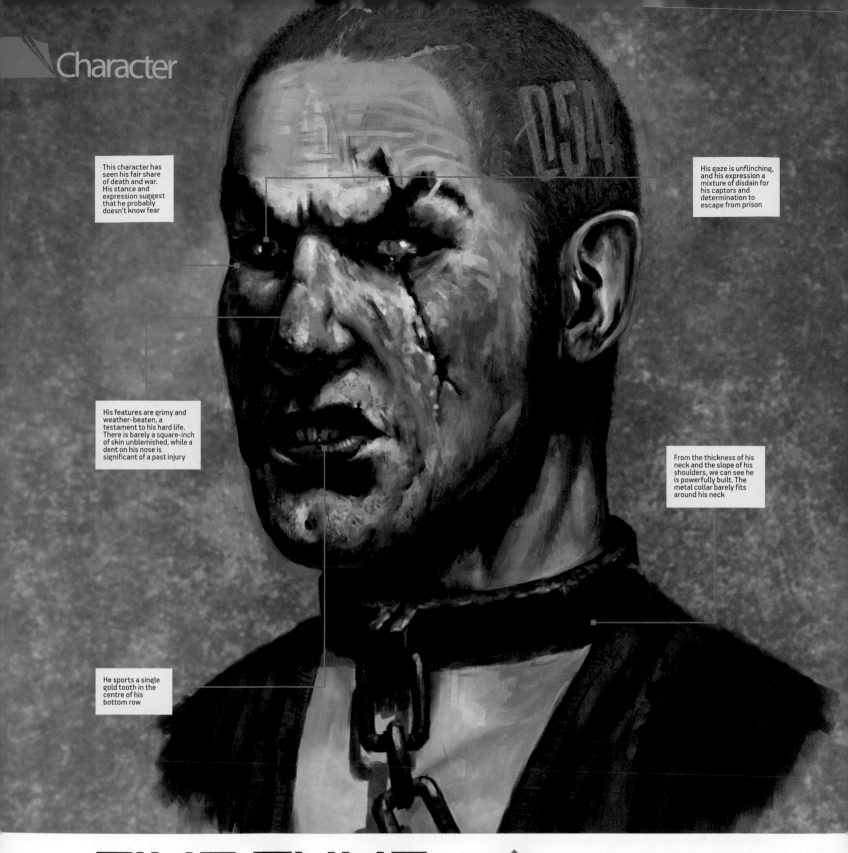

This character has seen his fair share of death and war. His stance and expression suggest that he probably doesn't know fear

His gaze is unflinching, and his expression a mixture of disdain for his captors and determination to escape from prison

His features are grimy and weather-beaten, a testament to his hard life. There is barely a square-inch of skin unblemished, while a dent on his nose is significant of a past injury

From the thickness of his neck and the slope of his shoulders, we can see he is powerfully built. The metal collar barely fits around his neck

He sports a single gold tooth in the centre of his bottom row

FINE-TUNE PORTRAITS

PAINTER

ZBRUSH

FOLLOW THIS ZBRUSH WORKFLOW TO CREATE A 3D INTERPRETATION OF A STYLISED CHARACTER CONCEPT

SOURCE FILES ✓
AVAILABLE ON THE FREE DISC

A deep scar runs from his forehead down to his left cheek. The injury has left him blind in one eye and this contrasts strongly with his undamaged right eye, which is a striking blue. The scar isn't recent and has clearly occurred in battle

His jaw is powerful and his jutting chin emphasises the strength of his will

As an extra feature, his prisoner number has been cut into his shaven head. Once safely in his cell he is not expected to leave, though he may have other ideas

A rusting metal collar is secured around his neck with a thick chain. The simplicity of the collar signifies that he is being kept in Spartan conditions

The goal here was to produce concept art for a 3D artist to replicate into a convincing character bust. When creating concept work for 3D artists you need to ensure there is enough information captured in the design to help them interpret materials, textures, expression and so on.

To present a challenging project for the 3D artist, we have included some scarring, facial hair, shaved details in the hairline and lots of aging. The expression is of paramount importance here, because it makes the character engaging for the audience.

The final result shown on these pages is a rugged male character portrait – a strong and charismatic fellow that has been through the wars. To get to the final design, thumbnails were very helpful to explore different ideas. Reference images from the likes of Dreamstime.com also helped to achieve realism in the expression and skin imperfections.

The concept sheet supplied to the 3D artist provided him with a front-on, side and three-quarter view to give him as much 3D information as possible to tackle the project. You can see the results and follow along on the next pages.

ESTABLISH INITIAL FORM
BLOCK IN THE BASIC SHAPES OF THE CHARACTER

Taking the concept of this menacing convict, we'll go through the workflow for creating a character bust, from sculpting the main forms to refining the model with pore and wrinkle details. We'll be using DynaMesh to create the clothing and the chain, FiberMesh to add facial hair and we'll also go over some Polypainting techniques to bring the character to life.

ZBrush is the tool of choice for this process because it gives us the freedom to create without the need to jump between multiple software packages or worry about technical limitations. Once our character has been sculpted and Polypainted, we'll pose him and render multiple passes to be composited in Photoshop.

01 BUILD THE BASE MESH

With the DynaMesh tools in ZBrush it doesn't really matter if you're starting with a sphere or a pre-existing base mesh. The main thing is to keep the subdivision low at this point. Try to keep the brush size large and avoid zooming in on the character early on. This way you're only concentrating on the overall silhouette of the character. To start, we'll concentrate on getting the main shapes and proportions of the head, neck and shoulders. Hitting Y will toggle between the default white and black of the SubTool, enabling you to check the silhouette easier.

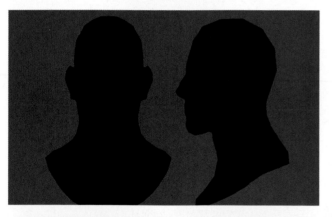

02 WORK OUT THE MAJOR FORMS

Try to exclusively use the Move brush early on to manipulate the major shapes into place. Looking at the concept we'll try to establish where the eyes, nose and mouth sit in relation to one another. At this point we can begin to subdivide and, using the ClayTubes brush, block in the major forms and structure. Using the DamStandard brush we can also cut in some guidelines for skin folds and concave shapes, such as the nasolabial fold, philtrum, eyelids, brow and lips.

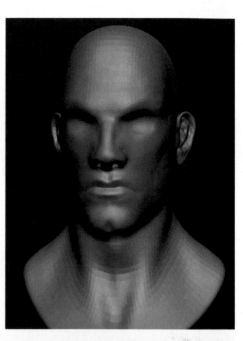

QUICK TIP
CONTROL SUBDIVISION

When starting a sculpt it's important to keep the subdivision level low, especially when blocking in proportions and main shapes. You can then slowly subdivide (Cmd/Ctrl+D) to add polygon density as needed. Doing this helps prevent your sculpts from looking bloated and gives you more control over your mesh. If you are working on a higher subdivision level and need to make large changes to the mesh, drop down to a lower subdivision level (Shift+D) to enable smoother transitions and easier control.

03 ADD EYES AND TEETH

For the eyes, click on Append in the SubTool palette and choose Sphere3D. Using Deformation>Size, scale down the eye to fit the character's head. Then, using Transpose Move, we can position the eye in place. To create the other eye, simply use ZPlugin>SubTool Master>Mirror and choose Merge Into One SubTool. Once the eyes are in place, make adjustments to the eyelids to fit the curve of the eye. For the teeth we can append a Cube3D and resize it using the Transpose tools. Under Geometry>DynaMesh, set the Resolution to a low amount (such as 128) and create a U shape for the gums and teeth. Turn off DynaMesh, increase the subdivision, then block in the teeth and gums using the Clay brush. Slowly refine the teeth with the DamStandard and Standard brush while increasing the subdivision level.

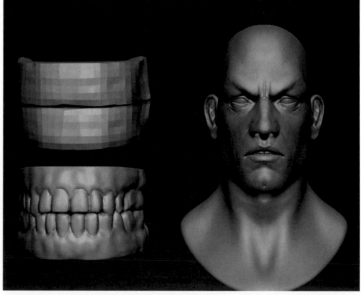

ESTABLISH INITIAL FORM
BLOCK IN THE BASIC SHAPES OF THE CHARACTER

04 SCULPT THE SCARS
In the concept this guy has some pretty gruesome scars. The one over his left eye and upper lip are indented, so we'll start by using the DamStandard brush to create the initial line and flow of the scar. Next we'll go back over the line and include some irregularities, then by using small strokes and the ClayTubes brush we can build up the scar tissue around the edges. The ClayTubes brush is great for these kinds of details and we'll use it again for the small raised scars on his head, by blocking in the rough flow and shape of the scar. To add some more irregularities we'll set the Intensity a little lower. Using short strokes that alternate between Zadd and Zsub (holding Opt/Alt) we can build up the grisly scar texture.

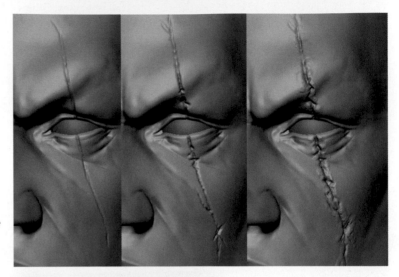

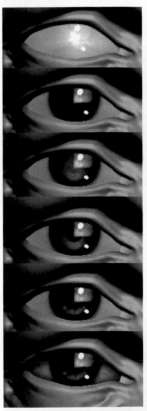

05 IT'S ALL IN THE EYES
Apply some Polypaint to the eyes before you finish the sculpting phase, to bring some life into the character as you're working on it. The MatCap to use is the zbro_EyeReflection and can be downloaded from http://luckilytip.blogspot.com.au. Select a base off-white tone and, with MRGB turned on, go to Color>Fill Object. Next, choose the Standard brush, turn off Zadd and only have RGB turned on. We'll select a brush size that fits the size of the iris and paint the darkest outer-edge of the eye. Next we'll choose a lighter saturated tone and paint in the iris, giving a slight taper to the lower half. This enhances a concave effect around the iris. Add some lighter flecks to the iris, then include a black pupil as well as some subtle veins and colour variation to the sclera. To finish this element, we'll paint in some fake occlusion to give the eyes some grounding in their sockets.

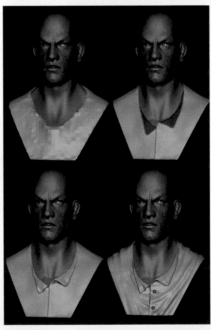

06 CREATE THE SHIRT
To clothe our character we'll begin by appending a sphere and resizing it to roughly fit. With the DynaMesh resolution low, we can use the Move brush to block in the basic shape of the shirt. We can then begin to subdivide the mesh and build up details. For the collar area of the shirt, we can mask the areas where we want to create the appearance of an overlap and use the Move brush to pull these areas up and over. Use the DamStandard and Standard brushes to refine the details.

07 BUILD THE CHAIN COLLAR
To shape the chain collar we're going to use DynaMesh to subtract and merge different meshes. Subtract one cylinder from another to create the neck opening, then merge a cube and subtract another cube to produce the area where the chain links in. To subtract one mesh from another in ZBrush, go to the SubTool palette, move to DynaMesh (A) above the SubTool (B) you are going to use to subtract. The lower SubTool (B) needs to have the Difference SubTool icon selected, which is the second icon. Select the top SubTool (A) and go to SubTool>Merge>MergeDown to combine both SubTools. To create the subtraction, hold down Cmd/Ctrl, then click and drag on the canvas to re-DynaMesh.

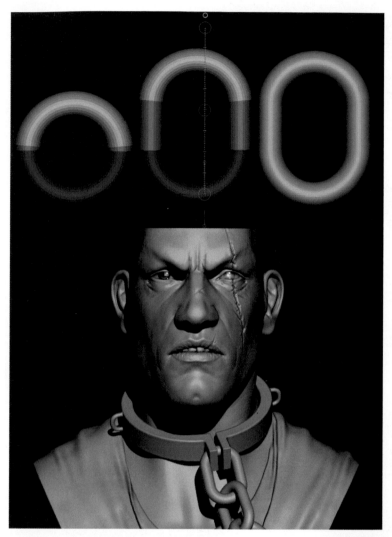

08 ADD THE CHAIN LINKS

For the chains we'll need to append a Ring3D. Go to Deformation>Inflat to add some thickness. By masking half of the ring we can use the Transpose Move tool to drag half of the ring upwards to extend the middle area. Next we'll use DynaMesh to reconstruct the topology. With the first link created we can now duplicate and position a few more links using the Transpose tools. This enables us to add a sense of movement to the character.

QUICK TIP
MORPH TARGETS AND LAYERS

The use of Morph Targets and layers can be extremely beneficial to non-destructively add detail. For example, you can store a Morph Target then start to sculpt scars and if you aren't happy with a particular area, use the Morph brush to paint back to the stored version of the sculpt. Layers can be helpful for controlling tiny details like pores. By placing the pore details on their own layer, you can increase or decrease the amount that they're visible, giving you greater control over them.

---

09 DETAIL THE ACCESSORIES

We can now do a cleanup pass over our accessories and apply some more detail. For instance, we'll want to add some wear and tear to the chain links. To do this we can use the Mallet Fast brush which can be found in Lightbox>Brush>Mallet>MalletFast.ZBP. Just use small strokes to add some dents and scratches to the collar and chains. We can add some seams to the shirt using masking with the Move and DamStandard brushes, then also add some more folds to the shirt using the Standard brush.

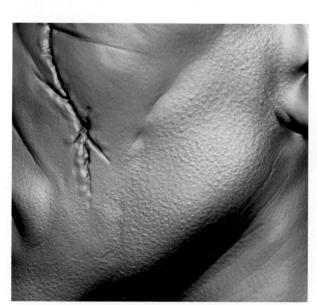

10 FOCUS ON THE FACE

With the sculpting phase almost complete, it's now time to add some finer features. DamStandard should be the main brush used for applying wrinkles and the smaller details. For the pores and stubble texture, use the Standard brush with a pore Alpha and the Stroke set to Spray with a low Intensity. Try to keep in mind places like the nose, which tend to have larger and more visible pores. You can also use a mask for areas like the lips, where you don't want any pore detail.

FIBERMESH AND POLYPAINTING
APPLY THE TEXTURE AND BUILD THE HAIR

11 APPLY AND ADJUST THE HAIR
FiberMesh works by applying hair strands to any masked area of a SubTool. To create the head stubble, we'll first need to create a 054 black-and-white image in Photoshop to be used as a mask. We can then mask the area of the head we want to add hair to and subtract the 054 shape using the created Alpha. Click the Preview button under the FiberMesh palette. Under Modifiers, change Length to 10 and Coverage to roughly 70. Change the Width Profile to create thinner strands and the Base and Tip colours should be a dark brown. Use the BPR Render (Shift+R) to test what this looks like. Once you're happy with the results, go to FiberMesh>Accept.

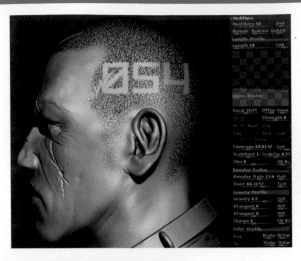

QUICK TIP
MASKING TIPS

There are some masking tools in ZBrush that can be used to help speed up the workflow and create some interesting effects. Masking>Mask PeaksAndValleys can be used to quickly create versatile patterns for texturing. In this case it was used for Polypainting the chain. Masking>Mask By Smoothness is also very useful for quickly painting edges and dents, especially when working on hard surfaces. Play around with the sliders to see what you can come up with.

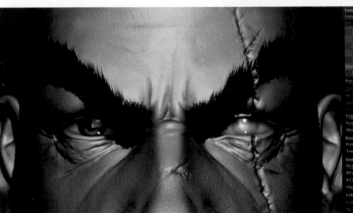

12 SHAPE SIDEBURNS AND EYEBROWS
Mask the sideburns area and select Lightbox>Fibers under the FiberMesh menu. This will provide some presets to choose from and edit. For the sideburns we can use the Fibers196 preset. Set Length to 14, Coverage to 10 and adjust the Width Profile. Turn the texture off and set the Base and Tip Color to brown again. Click Accept and then mask the area for the eyebrows. This time we'll use the Fiber160 preset and change Length to 110, Coverage to 2.25 and Gravity to -0.5. We'll also need to adjust the Width Profile, and change the Twist and Revolve to approximately 135. Select dark brown for the colours and render to test the hair. When happy with the results click Accept. Now we can use the Groom brushes to style the eyebrows a bit more and really get them looking rugged.

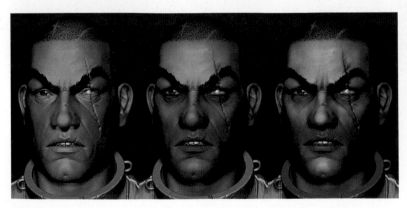

13 BEGIN POLYPAINTING
For the skin, use the zbro_Viewport_Skin2 MatCap, which can be downloaded from http://luckilytip.blogspot.com.au. To begin painting the skin, fill the SubTool with a neutral skin tone as the base colour. Using a Standard brush, with just RGB on and a blue selected, block in the beard area and around the eyes. Add some red around the nose, lips and cheeks, then a yellow tone on the forehead and slightly on the cheeks. Using these more saturated colours will give us some nice variation and a good foundation to work from. We can then begin to build up on the darker and lighter skin tones and use a pore Alpha with the Stroke set to Spray in order to add some more texture to the skin. Now we can slowly build up and refine the textures and values.

FINALISE THE SCULPT
ADD THE LAST TOUCHES TO BRING OUT REAL PERSONALITY

14 FINAL POSING
To finish we will need to add asymmetry and pose the character. This can be done with ZPlugin>Transpose Master> TPoseMesh. Then, using masking and the Transpose tools, we can position the character into an interesting position. In this case we are trying to achieve a pose that would fit the concept artist's description of this character. When this is done, go to Transpose Master>TPose-SubT to transfer the pose back to the SubTools. We can now tweak the mean expression.

15 SET UP THE RENDER
When the sculpt is finished and ready to be rendered, we'll need to find a nice camera angle and store its position in Document>ZAppLink Properties>Cust1. For the lighting setup, use one main light from the front and two rim lights from behind. We'll render these out separately to be composited together in Photoshop. To create a rim light, simply click on the dot in the Light Placement Preview window in the Light palette. This will send the light source behind the character. When rendering the rim lights, turn off Polypaint for each SubTool and use the Basic material. Also set the colour to black.

QUICK TIP
EXPERIMENT WITH MATCAPS

Don't be afraid to experiment with layering different MatCaps in your render passes. You can also edit existing MatCaps to suit the material you're trying to render. Trying out different MatCaps and blend modes can lead to some interesting effects and an overall more engaging render.

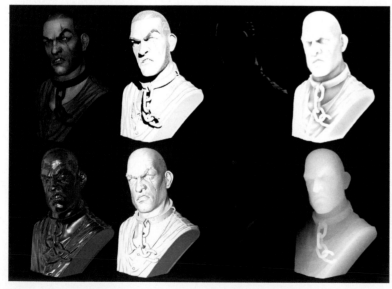

16 MAKE RENDER PASSES
Once the lighting is set up, you are then able to begin to render out the different passes. The starting render passes to use are the main BPR Render, Shadow, the Rim Lighting passes, Ambient Occlusion and Depth. The next passes to render are the Cavity, using the SketchShade2 MatCap; a Specular pass, using the Basic material and the Color set to black; then finally a Reflection pass for the chains, using a combination of the Reflected Map and Chrome materials.

17 UNIFY THE BUST
Once we've rendered out our passes it's time to put everything together. Experiment with the different layer blending modes in Photoshop to see which effects you can find. In this case, Ambient Occlusion, Cavity and Shadow passes are all set to Multiply with the layer opacity lowered. For the Rim Lighting, Reflection and Specular passes we will use a combination of Color Dodge and Screen. Once you are totally happy with how the image is looking, you can make a final Levels and colour correction to really make the image pop.

MARMOSET
TOOLBAG

MUDBOX

NDO2

LIGHTWAVE

PHOTOSHOP

ADD TEXTURE AND DETAILS

ACHIEVE A CHARACTER READY FOR A CLOSE-UP, COMPLETE WITH FINELY SCULPTED DETAILS AND TEXTURES

This tutorial will guide you through the entire process of modelling, sculpting, texturing and rendering a chameleon character with a high level of detail. First you'll work out what the building blocks for the base mesh of the model will be. Second, you'll be guided through the creation of custom organic stencils, which will enable you to sculpt rich and varied details for the skin. You will learn which tools can easily be used to refine your sculpt and blend in the different details. You'll see how you can use Mudbox to easily pose your model for different shots. Next up, check out the process of unwrapping UV layouts and extracting Normal, Displacement and Occlusion maps from your model. Learn how to convert a Normal map into a Cavity map with the help of the nDo2 plug-in for Photoshop. Finally, you'll get to know Marmoset Toolbag's real-time rendering engine and learn how to set up a basic scene and define useful material and lighting properties.

START WITH THE BASICS
DEFINE YOUR MODEL IN LIGHTWAVE

02 BORN FROM A BOX

Darwin's *On the Origin of Species* will tell you that a chameleon should come from an egg. Well, Trippy, our chameleon friend, comes from a box in LightWave. Evolving from this basic object enables us to quickly form the rough volumes that comprise the character. We'll employ basic and well-known tools such as Extrude, Extend, Spinquad and Mirror, while not being too concerned with exact proportions at this stage. However, do prepare a few appropriate loops for the limb articulations, the eyes and the mouth limits, which should be refined in a later step. After a few fixes regarding topology, you should have a base mesh that serves its purpose and keeps the potential to be aesthetically pleasing when refined.

01 DO YOUR HOMEWORK

As with all artwork, research plays an important role in defining your goals and identifying your challenges. Given the specificities of the subject, you should carefully pick your references in order to get a good feeling of form, weight, common qualities and intricate features. For a start, any search engine will provide you with plentiful photo references of chameleons. You'll want to roam free with your creativity, but picking a particular gender and subspecies will provide your creation with consistency for those who know this creature well. However, the balance you strike between realism and artistic license is of course completely up to you.

QUICK TIP
MODEL WHAT WILL BE SEEN

As soon as you lay your eyes on Trippy, the thought of a really long, slimy tongue probably crosses your mind and you may wonder what the inside of his mouth looks like. Here's a hint: nothing! Whenever you're assigned a project where your characters will be presented in a 3D-illustration format, or in a very limited animated piece, settle your scope of work beforehand and agree on which parts will never be seen or used in animation. This will keep your model as light as possible and will enable you to allocate your attention to what really matters.

03 FROM BASE MESH TO SCULP

After settling for a base mesh, import it into Mudbox and start sculpting the general forms that perfect the rough model. You may feel drawn to sculpting the chin's skin intricacies early on, so to achieve these features only use the Wax brush with the bw_strip stamp. You can experiment with the default brush without the stamp to realise the difference in results. To better control the affected areas, try locking all the objects or sections that you don't want to accidentally sculpt. Go to the Object list and click on the lock near each of the objects you wish to protect.

 BUILD UP THE DETAILS IN MUDBOX
CREATE CUSTOM ORGANIC STENCILS AND APPLY INTRICATE FEATURES

04 LEARN YOUR SCULPTING TOOLS

The Knife tool and Wax brush are used frequently throughout the sculpting phase. The sharpness of the Knife tool satisfies tasks such as the tooth-like patterns surrounding the mouth. Features such as the eyebrow patterns and the details near the eyes are the result of alternating between the Wax brush and the Knife tool.

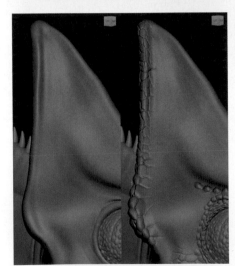

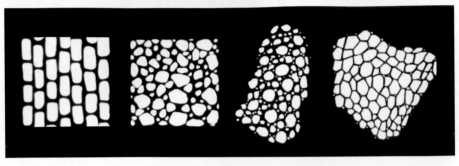

05 CUSTOMISE ORGANIC STENCILS

The most eye-catching skin details are achieved through custom-made stencils, which can be prepared manually in Photoshop (the ones used here are supplied with this tutorial). To create your own, find a few photo close-ups of chameleon scales to work from. For each reference, create a new file with a transparent background, a layer for the reference and a top layer to paint over. Paint the emphasised forms in white and save as a PNG without the reference layer, as shown. While in Mudbox, find the Stencil tray, click the right arrow on top, choose Add Stencil and load your stencil images.

06 GO WITH THE FLOW AND BLEND IN

You should scale and rotate your stencil according to the natural flow of the skin intricacies. An automatic repetition (pattern) will not produce realistic results and so will appear much less organic. Pay close attention to the types of scales that are adequate for each area. To achieve a nice blend between different styles, you can choose to leave some blank areas between them and fill them in with custom-sculpted details. You will achieve different results according to the tool you have selected in the Sculpt Tools tray, but Sculpt was used for Trippy (the first icon on the tray). After applying the stencil, use the Wax tool to make a few sporadic spots stand out. As you can probably tell, this stage will very much depend on the result you're trying to achieve, so it's best to find your own preference when applying these details.

07 KEEP REFINING AND BUILDING DETAIL

The Knife tool provides a means of sharpening the stencil's results. A few well-positioned strokes can deepen the skin wrinkles and define prominent details. The head and casque are also sculpted with the Wax and Knife tools to achieve a well-defined silhouette for the model. Start with a higher intensity and soften the application towards the top. A stencil can also be applied.

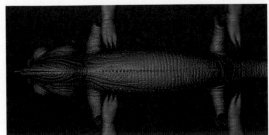

08 FINISH THE DETAILS

These methods are sufficient to achieve the sculpted details for the body and limbs. Keep a natural flow for the skin while minding articulations, creases and volume oscillations. Use the brick-wall-like stencil to sculpt the tail with a gradual blend towards the body's scales. The corn-like stencil is used to sculpt the feet soles.

09 MAINTAIN THE BALANCE

We'll now model and sculpt a simple branch for the chameleon to stand on. This is built using the bw_skin02 stencil and some custom details. Feel free to be more creative regarding small protruding leaves or even add little critters to enrich your piece.

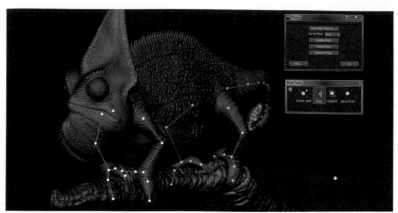

10 STRIKE A POSE

You can use Mudbox's Pose tools for a minimalist approach to posing. Let's be clear on the fact that this is not the equivalent of rigging, but it will provide you with the basic means to deform the model and achieve a simple pose variation, which suits our goals for this particular work. The skeleton of the pose will be automatically placed on a homonymous layer as soon as you create your first joint. Before actually creating any joints, make sure you deselect the One Joint at a Time property so that each new joint connects to the previous one. Upon selecting a joint, the Weights tool enables you to customise the way pose transformations affect the object. Our chameleon has one joint on the neck with weights extended all the way to the head. To make sure these weights affect the eyes and spikes, select them immediately after creating the joint. Select the Weights tool, apply 100% Strength in the Properties tray and click the Flood button on the bottom. You should be able to move the whole head without leaving the eyes or the spikes behind. You may choose to create their joints with the Mirror property set to X. The tail holds many joints to achieve its curvature. Once you're happy with a pose, you can save it for reference (Windows>Poses).

UNWRAP AND EXTRACT
UNPACK YOUR UVS AND REMOVE MAPS WITH YOUR SCULPTED DETAILS

11 APPLY LIGHTWAVE UV LAYOUTS

PLG_Make_UV_Edit is a free plug-in (www.cglounge.com/plugins/plg-make-uv-edit) that enables you to easily unwrap your UVs in LightWave Modeler. Select a surface to unwrap and press the Q key to trigger the Change Surface window. Specify each surface properly, then open the plug-in's interface. Click Make Atlas From Surface, which will show you the edges of each surface, then click Make UV. Use the Move and Rotate tools to compose a neatly organised map. The spikes that compose the crests are unwrapped differently. Use the plug-in to select each spike's centre edge and then click on Advance Edge. After doing this for all spikes, just select all of the edges and Make UV to attain their shells. This piece comprises a total of five UV layouts.

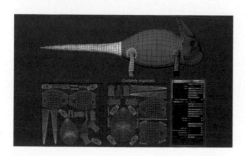

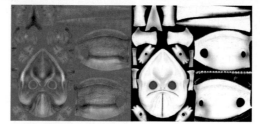

12 MUDBOX MAPS

Choose File>Import UV, making sure your object is set to the base subdivision level (Level 0, by pressing the Page Down key). If you haven't edited the object in a way that might have changed the number of vertices, select the Match by: Vertex ID import option. After doing this for each object (each UV layout), extract your maps for each object with its own UV layout. Use the Select/Move tools to make sure your desired object is fully selected (marked in yellow). Select Maps>Extract Texture maps>Normal map. For the Extraction Options, click the Add Selected button near the Target Model and Source Model boxes. Refer to the supplied screenshot named 'maps_extraction_config.jpg' for the remaining extraction configurations. Follow the same procedure to extract the Displacement and Occlusion maps (Mudbox recalls previous configurations). The Occlusion map requires a specific Advanced>Filter property configuration: set it to 0.001000 l.

13 PHOTOSHOP AND NDO2

Cavity maps nDo2 is a Photoshop plug-in created by Quixel (http://quixel.se), which enables you to enhance Normal maps. Use it to convert a Normal map into a Cavity map. Open the plug-in's interface and then your Normal map files in Photoshop. Click the small Convert... link in nDo2, define Normal as your Origin, Cavity as your Target, then click Active Doc. The plug-in does a great job of picking up on slight sculpting nuances, which are a perfect base for Specular and Diffuse maps. After a few tweaks to the exposure, the Cavity map is ready. Get better acquainted with nDo2's potential with the free trial supplied, or visit http://quixel.se/ndo m.

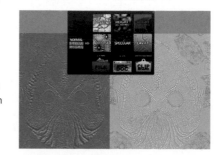

CREATE DETAILED TEXT
USE PAINT TOOLS AND YOUR EXTRACTED MAPS TO ACHIEVE THE FINAL TEXTURES

14 PAINT LAYERS AND CHANNEL TIPS
Mudbox enables us to work with separate paint layers. Always keep your colour scheme flexible by painting each colour onto a distinct layer. This means you can adjust each colour area's hue, saturation and brightness at any stage without affecting the remaining areas. Here we've adorned Trippy with turquoise, purple and orange tones as the main colour scheme. The painting process itself is straightforward: use the Paintbrush tool for colouring and the Paint Erase brush for corrections. To achieve the glossy irises, paint one layer with jet black, then duplicate it (Ctrl/right-click then pick Duplicate Selected). On the Layers panel, create a New Layer with Channel as Specular. Repeat the process for the Gloss channel and drag your duplicated layer to the top of the newly shown Specular channel. Ctrl/right-click this layer, then choose Adjust Color>Select a Preset>Inverse. This results in an intense and unique shine. Now duplicate this specular layer and drag the result to the top of the Gloss channel.

15 APPLY MAPS TO TEXTURES
The Paint Tools tray enables you to import a layer from an image. Import the Cavity map as a layer for the Diffuse channel and place it on top of all other paint layers. This is the main channel for all the coloured paint layers. Ctrl/right-click the Cavity map layer and choose Adjust Color>Select a Preset>Inverse. Now that your cavities are white, apply the Overlay Blend Mode with 35% Opacity and you'll achieve a reptilian look for the skin's intricacies. Import your Occlusion map into another layer and set it to Multiply Blend Mode to achieve soft volumetric shadows, including the contact shadows between the feet and the branch. Any layers that you create within the Specular channel will affect the shininess of the underlying objects. Bright paint will result in a shiny area, whereas black will result in a matte area. Here we duplicate various layers from the Diffuse channel: drag the duplicates to the Specular channel, convert them to greyscale and then slightly adjust their contrast values. As a finishing touch, create a noise-like stencil and paint it onto the Specular channel.

RENDER IN MARMOSET
CAPTURE ASTONISHING DETAIL WITH AN AFFORDABLE GAME ENGINE

16 RENDER IN REAL-TIME WITH MARMOSET

Marmoset Toolbag is a software developed and maintained by Marmoset that empowers artists to render low-poly models in real-time with very high quality (www.marmoset.co). Real-time artists who wish to portray their work on a showcase will benefit from this tool's qualities. A recent software update enables the use of Displacement maps with DirectX11 tessellation. The first step is to export your model from Mudbox at subdivision Level 2 in OBJ format. A final round-trip to LightWave Modeler is required to name the final exported object layers: eyes, body, branch, chin crest and body crest. Import your OBJ to Marmoset and notice the Chunks and Material trays. Import your Displacement map (extracted in Step 12) into the Material tab, under Displacement Input. Notice that you have many properties to experiment with, such as Translucency. To soften the edges of your rendered model, scroll to the bottom of the tab and adjust the Tessellation value to 1,000 (this will require a graphics card that supports DirectX11). Incredibly easy to work with, Marmoset comes packed with various lighting presets that are swappable in one click. Select the Light tab and pick your favourite Sky Lighting preset. Given this character's natural habitat, we'll choose Pine Forest. You can adjust the Focus and Depth of Field amounts in the Render tab and tweak the Chromatic Aberration to simulate lens-like effects p.

17 POST-PRODUCTION IN PHOTOSHOP

Marmoset Toolbag enables us to save screenshots with High Dynamic Range, giving us further control over the colours in Photoshop. You will also be able to export an Alpha channel in order to separate the model from the background. When you open your file in Photoshop you'll realise it's a 32-bit image, which provides you with the means to make colour corrections without losing any of the model's gradients. In this case, Marmoset's output was very satisfying, so there was very little post-processing to be done. If you'd like to indulge in colour-correction adjustments, you can add goal-specific adjustment layers (Layer>New Adjustment Layer) and tweak their values without affecting your image irreversibly. Afterwards, flatten the image to 8-bit and add a Translucent Noise layer (Filter>Noise>Add Noise) q.

TYPOGRAPHY

ACHIEVE CREATIVE, EYE-CATCHING TYPOGRAPHY USING FONTS, GRAPHICS AND IMAGES THAT WILL GRAB ATTENTION

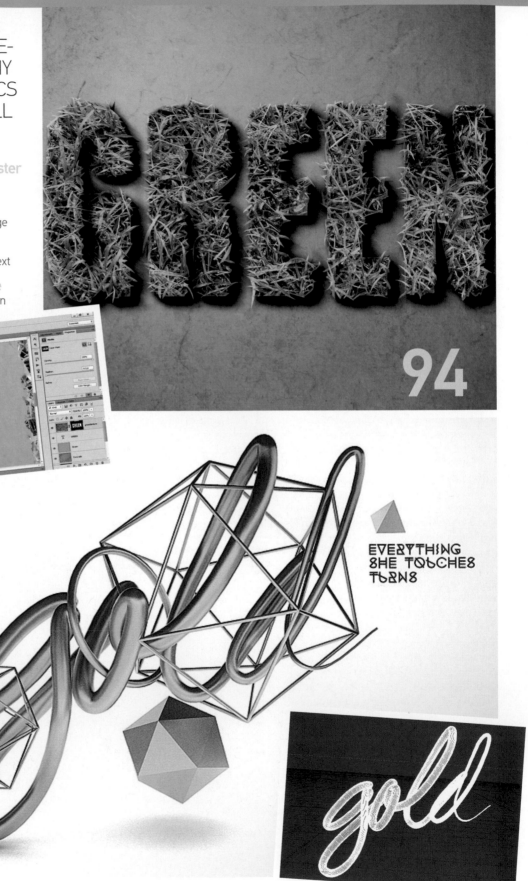

90

102

TWO POSSIBILITES EXIST: EITHER WE ARE ALONE in the universe, or we are NOT. BOTH ARE EQUALLY TERRIFYING

- ARTHUR C. CLARKE

DESIGN A GRAPHIC PRINT POSTER

PHOTOSHOP

LEARN TO PLAY WITH FONTS TO MAKE YOUR OWN INSPIRATIONAL POSTER FROM YOUR FAVOURITE QUOTE OR SAYING

Graphic print posters are great to adorn your walls at home or at work – and if you're making your own, you can get the exact quote or saying that you want. The great thing about them is that you don't even need to be able to create labour-intensive detailed artwork to make them look good. Some simple typography and icons work just fine.

It's impossible to talk about bold, printed, type-orientated posters without acknowledging the primary influence – Modernism. This movement really kick-started the big, bold, brash design aesthetic, with propaganda posters and advertisers using graphic designs based around one simple concept or message. Straight lines, limited colour palettes and bold type helped make the messages stand out for both political and commercial agendas. In particular, it's hard to see a screen-printed black-and-red poster and not think about the posters from the Soviet Union.

PERFECT POSTERS
BRING QUOTES TO LIFE BY ILLUSTRATING THEM IN PHOTOSHOP

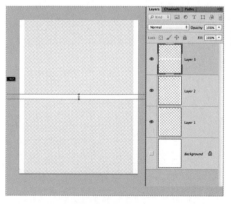

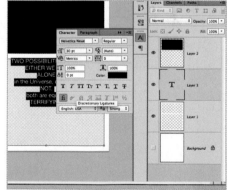

01 SKETCH AN IDEA
Pick an idea that you really like and come up with a rough idea of the way you want to make the poster. It's ideal to use a sketched-out rough idea so that you'll have something to refer to.

02 ESTABLISH MARGINS
Make margins around the page, so you have something to snap to. Draw one margin with the Marquee tool (M), fill with white, then copy and paste it, transforming for the top and bottom.

03 USE RAW TYPE
Now make a text box using the margins and put in your type with the line breaks in the right place according to your mock-up. Place a black rectangle to get a feel for the layout.

> " The great thing about graphic print posters is that you don't even need to be able to create labour-intensive detailed artwork to make them look good. Some simple typography and icons work just fine "

04 EDIT YOUR TYPE
Using the Character window, you can change the Font, Leading, Tracking, Width and Height to get the desired look. You can use pre-installed fonts or free ones from **www.dafont.com**. Spend some time on this step to get things right.

05 REALIGN YOUR MARGINS
After working on the fonts to get everything to fit together, you may want to alter the margins. Make sure your image box lines up with your text to keep everything clean and bold.

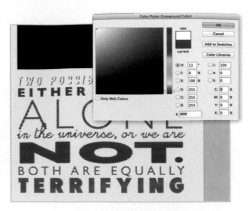

06 BRING IN COLOUR AND TEXTURE
Remember, this is a screen-print imitation! Bold, primary colours and a papery texture layer (set them to Multiply) are essential. Try out different combinations to find the right blend of tones that perfectly suits your piece.

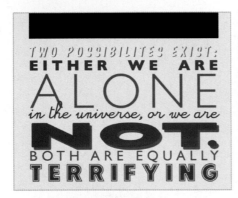

07 CUSTOMISE THE FONTS
You can make your fonts different with some customisation. Here, on the word Terrifying, we have selected the pixels of the text (Ctrl/right-click and choose Select Pixels) and contracted the selection, filling it in white in a new layer.

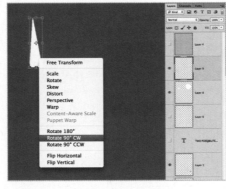

08 DRAW THE IMAGE
The image used here is also quite bold and simple. You can add this element with the Marquee and Lasso (L) tools, filling in a layer with white. Get creative with the Transform tool (Cmd/Ctrl+T) to make shapes relevant to your theme.

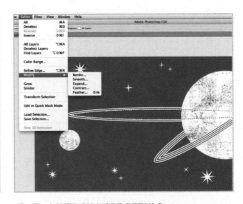

09 LAYER ON MORE DETAILS
Use the Elliptical Marquee tool (M) to make the planet's rings (and the spaceship's trail) by contracting the selection (Select>Modify>Contract) by 10px each time and alternating between filling and deleting the white.

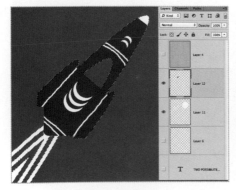

10 FOCUS ON THE EFFECTS
Use the Pencil tool (B) to add some details to the spaceship (in a new layer for red). Use a Non-Contiguous selection from a papery texture to delete part of the white layer. Head to **http://blog. photoshopcreative.co.uk/tutorial-files** to download the one we used now.

11 SEPARATE THE COLOURS
Once you're happy, Rasterize the text (duplicate first if you want to change it). Use the Magic Wand to select one colour at a time, filling in a layer for each colour. Now set all these to Multiply and offset them.

12 MESS THINGS UP A LITTLE
Finally, add some Noise (Filter>Noise> Add Noise) to make the colour look like ink on paper. You can also add another paper texture on a layer set to the Multiply blend mode to make it look like an old poster.

ALTERNATIVE POSTER DESIGNS
EXPERIMENT WITH DIFFERENT FONTS FOR AN ARRAY OF DIFFERENT STYLES

Depending on what you want to go on the poster, you need to change the colour palette and the design the poster to fit it. There's so much room to play around with simple bold ideas, it's no wonder that there are hundreds of re-imagined film posters out there. It's best to take inspiration directly from the idea, rather than trying to imitate the exact look of another poster that you like. This way, you'll come up with something new, using a style and method that's very much in vogue.

LIGHT A CANDLE

This fairly basic stock photo makes a visually strong poster, as there is a central object to work around. We drew the candle by hand, with a black Pen (P), and used the shape created to make selections to work with in a block of colour on the poster. Again, we offset the colours to give it that print look, and used textures to get the image a vintage poster feel.

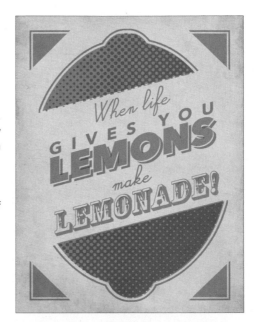

LEMONS

This is an old quote that has a strong central image. The large graphic shape of a lemon with text running through is visually striking. Using the right colours and bold visual imagery means that even with a glance at this poster you know what the text says without fully reading it. This is the main aim of a bold graphics poster, because it's the original intent for the design.

UNION FLAGS

Here, a half-tone screen shades parts of the artwork. Create a grey or gradient fill in the shape that you want the half-tone to be in. Copy it into a new file and make this file into a Bitmap image (Resolution of 300 and a Frequency of around 20). Now copy this into your original file and use a selection of the black to create a Multiply layer of any colour you see fit.

RUN

Simple, bold, large and to the point. This is probably the most to-the-point inspirational poster. We modified the type using a pen-like shape drawn for the tails of the letters. You can do this by copying and pasting the shape on the back-ends of the letters.

We used the shapes to make print-style colour blocks, using the methods from the rest of this tutorial.

> It's best to take inspiration directly from the idea, rather than trying to imitate the exact look of another poster that you like. This way, you'll come up with something new, using a style and method that's very much in vogue

USE CREATIVE TEXT EFFECTS

PHOTOSHOP

GET GREEN FINGERS AND LEARN TO GROW YOUR OWN TEXT USING A SINGLE IMAGE AND SOME CAREFUL TRIMMING!

There's nothing more eye-catching than a funky text effect. As fancy as it appears, the steps are pretty simple. Beginning by using your own base layer, or the grass stock in the supplied resources, you'll quickly produce an impressive piece of photo-manipulation that is also functional. Use this effect to create any word you want which you can then use in flyers, posters, invitations or anything else that you can think of. The essence of this manipulation is

attention to detail: being able to single out and define individual strands of grass to create a realistic feel – think organic! Letters will lose their perfectly straight edges and gain a new rugged quality with a cool natural look. The background is made up of a few different textures to help add to the rustic theme, blended with custom colours and gradients to give it a vibrant feel. For those not so confident with the Pen tool, the Brush tool or even the Polygonal Lasso tool can be used instead.

FROM GRADIENTS TO TEXTURES
FIND A STYLE THAT SUITS YOUR MESSAGE

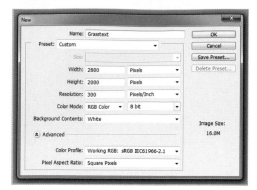

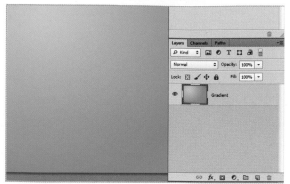

When cutting out images, the Pen tool is a good way of getting smooth straight or curved edges accurately. It works using Bézier curves, controlled by a start point, end point and two adjustment points for each. When you've drawn a point, hold Cmd/Ctrl as you drag it to move it, and Opt/Alt+drag to move the adjustment points. If you want to symmetrically adjust the curve, Ctrl+drag on the adjustment points! Try it out for yourself!

01 CREATE A NEW DOCUMENT
Open Photoshop and create a new document. Enter the size you'd like the overall canvas – your text can take up as much or as little space as you'd like. 300 Pixels/Inch will give you a high resolution.

02 ADD A GRADIENT
Select the Gradient tool (G). Set your foreground colour to a yellow-green and your background colour to a darker green. In the gradient tool bar, select Radial Gradient and draw a line across from the top left of your canvas to near the centre.

03 ADD SOME TEXTURE
Add 'Paper.jpg' to your image. Set the blend mode to Multiply at 50% Opacity. Next, add 'Chalkboard.jpg', blend mode set to Overlay at 70% Opacity. Finally, add 'Concrete.jpg', blend mode set to Overlay at 50% Opacity.

04 INCREASE VIBRANCY
The background is looking pretty grungy and vintage now. To make it a bit more vibrant, create a new layer with Cmd/Ctrl+Shift+N and Fill (G) with a yellow-green. Set the blend mode to Soft Light at 70% Opacity.

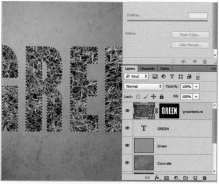

05 ADD YOUR TEXT
Insert the text you want using the Text tool (T) in a different colour to the background in your desired font/size etc. Here we have used the font Impact with some adjustments to make the text slightly thinner and slightly more spaced out.

06 INSERT THE GRASS
Add 'grasstexture.jpg' to your image. Cmd/Ctrl+Click on your text layer to create an outline of your word. Select the grass layer and add a layer mask using Layer>Layer Mask>Reveal Selection.

07 OUTLINE BLADES OF GRASS
With the line still there, click on the grass layer (not the layer mask). Go to Select>Refine Edge (Alt+Cmd/Ctrl+R). Set the Radius to 20px and Contrast to 50%. This will detect changes in colour and contrast and outline blades of grass.

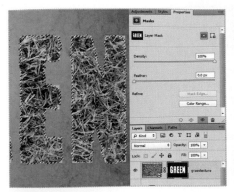

08 REFINE EDGES

Select the grass layer. Have your background White, then hit Cmd/Ctrl+ Backspace in order to add detail. Press Cmd/Ctrl+ Shift+I to invert. Set background to Black. Tap Cmd/Ctrl+Back to hide surrounds.

QUICK TIP
GET THE BEST FROM BLEND MODES

To create a grungy background you don't necessarily need a load of grungy images to get a good effect. By utilising blend modes you can use the same photo to create an entirely new image. Here the concrete photo from the tutorial, has been duplicated eight times, each time selecting a different blend mode and a different opacity. You can also use Transform (Cmd/Ctrl+T) to give it more interest, or add a fill or gradient layer with different blending modes to create a new Hue. Experiment and play around – there's no wrong way to create a background.

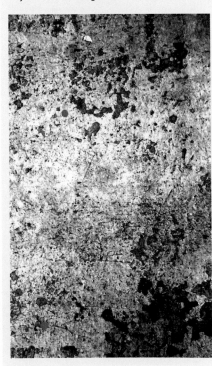

09 NEATEN IT UP

This may have caused some letters to merge. Using the Pen tool (or a black Brush), draw in your own gaps, right-click Make Selection, Feather at 0px. Select the layer mask and fill in black.

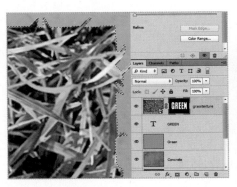

11 DO IT IN SECTIONS

If using the Pen tool it's rather nice to do it in sections. Right-click>Make Selection>Feather 0px. On the layer mask, Fill your selection in with White. Invert with Cmd/Ctrl+Shift+I and then use the Brush tool in order to paint in black the edges outside of your selection.

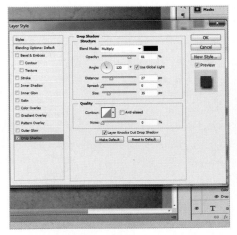

13 ADD LAYER STYLES

Now you've cut out all the letters, hide the text layer. Next, double-click on the layer and select Drop Shadow, set to Multiply, 81%, Distance 27px and Size 35px to give an immediate 3D effect.

10 CUT THE GRASS

Using whichever method you prefer, continue to neaten up the letters by drawing around the edges of blades of grass as well some straight lines of the letters. Use the text layer and grass layer as a guide.

12 KEEP GOING!

Continue to cut out all the letters. This will take a while and will be the longest part of the tutorial! Use a creative eye, switching between using Black and White to show and hide new areas of both stuck out blades and straight edges.

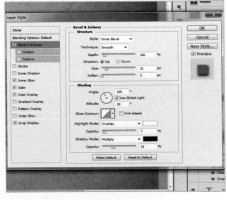

14 MORE LAYER STYLES

Add a Bevel & Emboss style, Depth 100%, Size 21 px, Soften 0px. Highlights set to Overlay, 7% Opacity and Shadows set to Multiply, 33% Opacity. Add a green Inner Glow, 65% Opacity and size 20px. Add a dark green Satin, at an Overlay of around 19% Opacity.

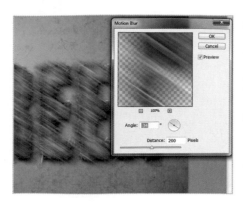

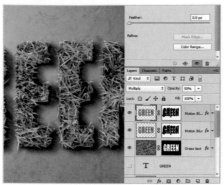

15 REALISTIC SHADOWS
For a better shadow, duplicate the layer, right click on the mask and select Apply Layer Mask. Double-click and remove all layer styles except Drop Shadow. Go to Filters>Blur>Motion Blur and set it to -34 degrees at 200 px. Hit Ok.

16 DARKER SHADOWS
Set the blend mode to Multiply. Cmd/Ctrl+Click on the original grass text layer mask. Go to Layer>Layer Mask>Hide Selection. Paint in black on the mask on the left of the letters, as if the sun is on the left. Duplicate for a darker shadow.

17 ADD A 3D EFFECT
Go back to your original grass layer and duplicate (Cmd/Ctrl+J). Select the bottom copy and move it down and right so that it is offset. Double click and remove the Inner Glow layer style. You can edit the layer mask slightly using a black brush.

18 MAKE THE LAYER DARKER
To keep the image as realistic as possible, the sides of the text should be darker. So, add a Hue/Saturation adjustment layer above the offset layer. Set the Hue to -28 to give it a redder tinge, Saturation -19 and Lightness -44. Right-click on the adjustment layer and select Create Clipping Mask.

> To create a grungy background you don't need a load of grungy images to get a good effect. By utilising blend modes you can use the same photo to create an entirely new image. Experiment — there's no wrong way to create a background

19 CREATE A NEW LAYER
Create a new layer underneath the text, but above the background. Call it 'Shine'. Set your foreground colour to white, select the Gradient tool (G) and set the Gradient settings to Foreground to Transparent. Hit OK.

20 ADD SOME SUNSHINE
Drag the Gradient across from top left down to near the middle to create a bright spot. Set the blend mode to Soft Light to help it blend into the background, and then you are done.

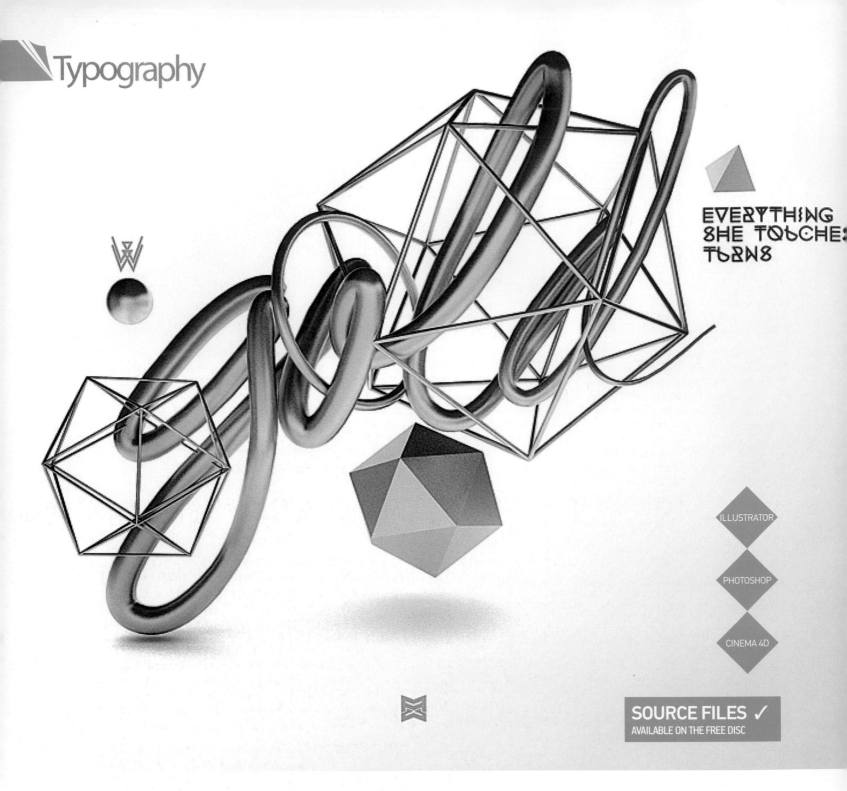

EVERYTHING
SHE TOUCHES
TURNS

ILLUSTRATOR

PHOTOSHOP

CINEMA 4D

SOURCE FILES ✓
AVAILABLE ON THE FREE DISC

DESIGN 3D TYPE

COMBINE CINEMA 4D, PHOTOSHOP AND ILLUSTRATOR TO CREATE 3D GOLD TYPOGRAPHY

I n Greek mythology there's a king called Midas who, as the story goes, had the power to turn anything that he touched into pure gold. Inspired by that tale, we will turn a simple vector line into a 3D, minimalistic gold typography using Illustrator, CINEMA 4D (C4D) and Photoshop. You'll learn how different tools and software can come together to produce a richly designed artwork with killer execution. The project will take, at most, four or five hours to create, including render time. You will be spending that time perfecting the curves in Illustrator, as well as getting the perfect lighting and shaders in CINEMA 4D.

To complete the tutorial you will need to use the V-Ray plug-in and the GreyScaleGorilla HDRI Light Kit in CINEMA 4D, which can be found at **http://tinyurl.com/GorillaPlug**. These are not strictly necessary, but are recommended for getting the best results. Once we have rendered the objects in C4D, we will move to Photoshop for post work. You will learn how to adjust lights and shadows by applying different adjustment layers and filters. After completing this tutorial you will then have all of the skills for creating 3D typography using your own handwriting.

BEGIN WITH ILLUSTRATOR
PREPARE VECTORS BEFORE TURNING THEM INTO GOLD

01 SET UP YOUR DOCUMENT
Create a new document in Illustrator at the size of 7 x 7 inches. Select the Pencil tool (N) and make sure that the Stroke Size is 1pt. It's very important to write in cursive, because when we have to transfer the vector into C4D, we will use the overlapping of the strokes to create more depth.

02 ADD YOUR WRITING
Don't fill up the canvas, just keep writing in order to actually see how the letters flow to form into cursive. It's also important to remember to keep the lines connected as one stroke, because if there is more than one path, the stroke won't be connected and it won't be smooth in C4D.

03 SMOOTH LINES
After writing 'gold' many times in cursive, pick the smoothest one and delete the rest. Now switch to the Smooth tool (Opt/Alt) and stroke around the writing to make it perfectly clean. Smooth performs similarly to Smudge or the Liquify tool, but in Illustrator it's used to change the curves of a path.

04 FINISH IN ILLUSTRATOR
It's almost impossible to get the smoothest curve with one stroke of the Smooth tool, so keep brushing along the path to get the best you can. Once you're satisfied with the writing, you'll have to export the path to C4D. Exporting the file in Illustrator is quite an important step because if you save the Illustrator file in the wrong format, you won't be able to import the strokes into C4D. Name the file 'Gold.ai' and save it in the Illustrator 3 format.

05 STEP INTO CINEMA 4D
Open your Gold.ai file in C4D and see if the lines need smoothing. If so, you can modify them in C4D using Point Mode. Select the point that needs fixing and use it like the Anchor tool in Illustrator and Photoshop. Fix the curve by moving the two sides of the point and ensure that your path doesn't include any small dots. If you see any dots lying around the path, delete them. After cleaning up the path, you can move to turning the path into 3D.

06 WORK IN POINT MODE
Remember that when you're in C4D you're working in three dimensions, which means that there's an extra variable to consider. You will see in the following screenshots that the stroke isn't flat, but more like a piece of string, because it has depth. This can be achieved by using Point Mode to move the points on the Z-axis in order to create another dimension for the word. We'll explain this further in the later steps.

07 2D WRITING INTO 3D
As we have discussed before, we have to move the path along the Z-axis too. Think of your handwriting as a pipeline. It has a start point, where water flows from, then curves and loops a bit like a rollercoaster and then, finally, there is an end point where the pipeline thins out. So, if you take a look at your own handwriting from the Perspective view, it should have smooth loops and curves just like an everyday rollercoaster has.

08 INSERT NURBS AND A CIRCLE
Before moving to the next stage, take a look at your writing and check to make sure that you now have the smoothest path possible. If you're happy, create a new Sweep NURBS and drop the path onto that NURBS. You won't notice any change because at this point the NURBS doesn't have an object that it can rely on to make it into a pipe. In this case it's a circle, so get the circle and drop it onto the NURBS again.

DEVELOP YOUR 3D
APPLY MATERIALS TO TAKE YOUR CREATION TO THE NEXT DIMENSION

09 GET THE SMOOTHEST GOLD
Working in 3D is just like using your hands to sculpt. You have to consider the material, the lighting on the model and most importantly the additional Z-axis. You'll also have to look at the writing as a pipe that has a defined beginning and end.

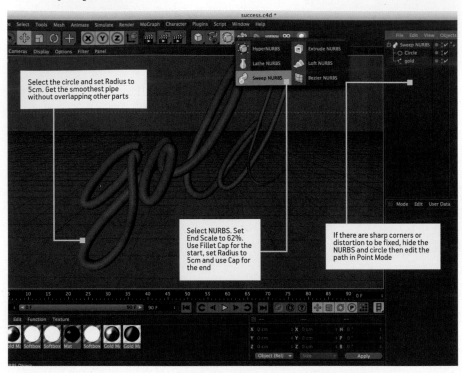

Select the circle and set Radius to 5cm. Get the smoothest pipe without overlapping other parts

Select NURBS. Set End Scale to 62%. Use Fillet Cap for the start, set Radius to 5cm and use Cap for the end

If there are sharp corners or distortion to be fixed, hide the NURBS and circle then edit the path in Point Mode

10 V-RAY SHADER
We'll now enter different values to produce the material, so create a new Advanced V-Ray Material. Make sure you check the boxes for Luminosity and Specular Layer 1 and 2. We'll be using these three layers in the shader to get the gold material. The eponymous Luminosity layer is used to add the brightness of the material. Set the Color to white with an Amount of 5%. For the Transparency, set the Color to white and the Amount to 100%.

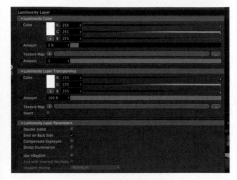

> " Working in 3D is just like using your hands to sculpt. You have to consider the material, the lighting on the model and most importantly the additional Z-axis "

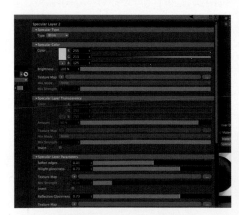

11 SET UP SPECULAR LAYERS
The next layers to edit are the Specular layers 1&2. Select Specular Layer 1 and set its Color to a light yellow at: R:255, G:228 and B:172. Set the Brightness to 100% and the Texture Mode to Fresnel, with the Gradient Shader of R:214, G:219 and B:179 to R:216, G:179, B:136. Set Reflection Glossiness to 0.5, Anisotropy to -0.5, Glossiness Subdivision to 18 and Trace Depth to 10. For Specular 2 guidance please see the screenshot above.

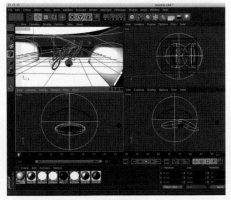

12 ADJUST THE LIGHTING
Here we'll be using GreyScaleGorilla HDRI Light Kit. Use the overhead soft box, but instead of just placing the light over the word, place one light on top and two on the sides. Set the top and left soft boxes to have higher brightness settings. This will make the light source enter from the left when rendered. You can also add a floor with a generic light-grey material. Select the NURBS and move the text just above the floor to produce shadow.

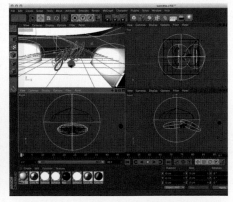

13 BEGIN RENDERING
Ensure you drop the material shader onto the Sweep NURBS. We're going to render using VRayBridge with Global Illumination. No settings are changed in GI, but the result should be your writing in 3D with the gold material and a little noise texture. You can add more objects to make the piece more interesting, but remember to drop the shader on top of the objects to keep the artwork uniform. When happy, render at 2,560 x 1,600px in TIFF format.

POST-PRODUCTION
POLISH UP YOUR RESULTS AND PERFECT YOUR RENDER

14 MOVE TO PHOTOSHOP
Now it's time to boot up Photoshop. Create a new document at a size of 3,500 x 2,800px, fill the Background with a light grey and File>Place your rendered image into your canvas. Create a Quick Mask, then cut out the letter and its shadow. Make a new layer underneath the text and paint with a large white soft brush in at the side of the light source in order to create gradient behind the text.

15 ADJUST THE EXPOSURE
Currently the lighting on the word is dull, so you can improve this by painting in light using blend modes. Grab a soft brush set to a light grey and paint over the word, using Overlay as the blend mode. Also reduce the Opacity of the brush to 50% and create a clipping mask over the word's layer. This is a quick way to brighten certain areas of an artwork without using any adjustment layers. The word has now been brightened up, but we'll also need to make the shadows darker.

16 TWEAK THE SHADOWS
This method is different from using just one adjustment layer to edit and we'll specifically select dark areas of the word and enhance them. Use the Eyedropper to select the darkest area in the 3D type, go to Select>Color Range, then select all the shadows of the type. Ensure you have selected the 3D type layer and then hit Cmd/Ctrl+J to create a new layer from the selection. Use Levels to lower the brightness and tweak the opacity to get the best transition between the midtones and shadows.

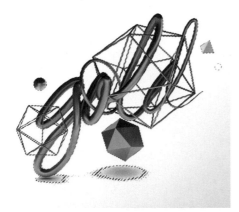
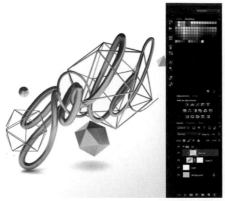
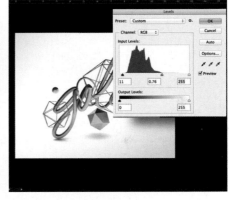

17 ADJUSTMENT LAYERS
We'll now use adjustment layers to enhance the colour and contrast of the image as a whole. Add a new Vibrance adjustment layer, then set the Vibrance value to 97 and Saturation to -6. There are many different shades of gold, but we'll lean more towards a white than a regular gold. Feel free to increase the saturation to get a more yellow finish and add a Levels layer to modify the light and shadows.

18 FINAL EDITS
Create a new layer at the top, select Image> Apply Image, then select OK to flatten the image into one layer. Another way to do this is to create a new layer and hit Cmd/Ctrl+Opt/Alt+Shift+E. Select the merged layer and apply Filter>Sharpen>Smart-sharpen, setting the value to 190%. If you want a more pronounced effect, create another merged layer and apply the Oil Paint filter with Shine at 0% and Smart Sharpen on. Add some text and symbols for the finishing touch and you've turned a vector line into golden 3D handwriting!

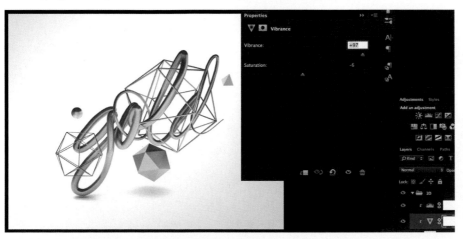
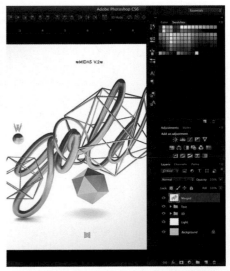

QUICK TIP
SHADOWS AND HIGHLIGHTS

When retouching a photo or an object, pay more attention to the shadows and highlights. By simply adjusting the light and shadows of an object, you can make it more dynamic. Also use adjustment layers to quickly edit the artwork's brightness, saturation and colours.

BLEND GRAPHICS AND TYPE

PHOTOSHOP

LEARN HOW TO MAKE A TYPOGRAPHIC ILLUSTRATION WITH IMPACT USING THE POWER OF PHOTOSHOP

They say a picture says a thousand words, so imagine the possibilities in conveying a message if you were to combine the two? In this tutorial, you will learn how to blend elements and shapes to create an energetic and dynamic typographic illustration. During the implementation process, you will use many different techniques in Photoshop to balance elements and vary their proportions and shadows, and learn how to give volume to the shapes you draw with the Pen tool.

Using a digital tablet can be useful, as the opportunity to play with the pressure of the pen works wonders when building quality into your final image. You'll see the composition and balance of illustration is not only about knowing which elements to include, but also knowing when to remove them. Finally, you'll learn that colours play a vital role in obtaining a composition with a consistent atmosphere. This tutorial requires a sense of subtlety, but you're free to create anything.

SETTING THE TONE
CHOOSE A FONT AND COLOUR PALETTE THAT WILL HELP CONVEY YOUR MESSAGE

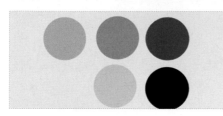

01 PICK A COLOUR PALETTE
Launch Photoshop and create a new document, then select the colour palette that you will use. Be creative with a limited number. The colour palette helps you to visualise your project as a whole, so choosing it beforehand saves you time later on. The colours used in this example are #0b58a8, #001451, #de9e22 and #f0d2a0.

02 CHOOSE THE FONT AND TEXT
Add a new text layer (T) and choose a font in a large size. 'Impact' was chosen in this case, but you are free choose your own. Type 'Be Creative' and align your text in the centre of the image. This is the main element and the focal point of your illustration.

03 ADD A GRADIENT
Duplicate your text and go to Layer>Pixelate>Text. Double-click it and choose Overlay gradient. Add a Radial gradient from colour #c16205 to colour #d89543. You are free to choose other colours – the purpose of the exercise is to be creative, so if you prefer the look of others, go ahead and indulge yourself!

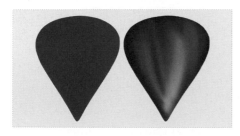

04 CREATE A PETAL
Import the 'Petal' file into the document. Using the eyedropper tool (I), select colour #0157ac, hit Cmd/Ctrl+U, click Reset and push the Saturation to 45. Add a new layer, change it to Multiply mode, and with a soft edged brush and Opacity set to 35%, paint the shadows of your form. Repeat the process on another layer set to Overlay mode and paint the highlights to give volume to the petal.

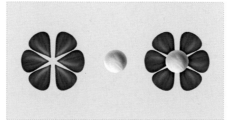

05 MAKE A FLORAL SHAPE
Using the petal you made in the previous step, you can now create a floral shape. Duplicate the layer five times and position them so that it forms a rosette. Create a circle with the Elliptical Marquee tool, fill it with a grey Radial gradient and place it at the centre of your petals. The use of horizontal and vertical symmetry will help to balance your image. Go to Edit>Transform>Vertical Symmetry Axis.

06 ADD A FLOWER
Open the 'Flower' file provided on the source disc and copy and paste the image into your scene. Apply an Invert adjustment (Cmd/Ctrl+I) to create a negative version of it. Put it to the side, as you will use it later in the process. For a more personal look, this flower was created from a photograph, with shadows and light painted on with a digital tablet. Feel free to do the same.

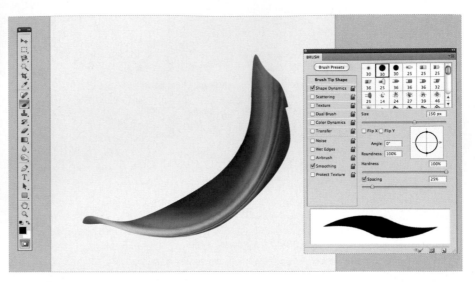

07 DRAW A CIRCLE AND DETAILS
With the Pen tool (P), create a circle. Double-click on your layer and add an Inner Shadow to give volume to it. Now draw a pattern. Be creative and take inspiration from tribal art or other designs. Ctrl/right-click on the background of the plot and add a focused shadow (Layer>Layer Style>Drop Shadow). Set the Opacity to 40%, Distance to 0px, Weight to 10px and Height to 80px.

08 CREATE AN ABSTRACT FORM
You will now create the last main form of your illustration. Add a new layer (Layer>New>Layer) and name it 'Abstract form'. Take the Pen tool and draw a shape similar to the one you see in the example above. Repeat the process that was outlined Step 4 to give volume to the shape. A Wacom tablet is often useful for doing this.

Duplication
Feel free to duplicate each form as much as you want and play with their size and rotation in order to make your artwork dynamic

Colours
Your colour palette is one of the most important factors when creating an illustration, so make sure you plan this in advance

Balancing the scene
Balance your scene up. Simplicity is your best friend most of the time. Take a step back to assess the usefulness of a form

10 ADD CURVED SHAPES
Give a little bit of dynamic movement to the artwork. To do this, add some elements that I particularly like: curves. Draw them with the Pen tool. If you want to be really accurate then this is the time to use a digital tablet, as it will allow you to play with the pen pressure. Fill them with a grey colour. Build flowing shapes that appear to be suspended in air and give them volume for realism – see Step 4 for an example. Arrange the shapes so that they intertwine with the text.

11 INSERT PATTERNS
Add a new layer and with the Pen tool create a rectangle. Double-click the layer or click fx in the Layers panel and select Pattern Overlay. Select an existing pattern or one from your library. While adding organic geometric elements to an illustration can be good in terms of balance, keep in mind your main objective, which is to make the text the focal point of your composition. Place large elements in the background and smaller ones in the foreground.

09 BUILD THE COMPOSITION
The next step is to import the file named 'Sphere grid' into your document. Now that the main elements are at your disposal, you can begin the most exciting part of the tutorial: the composition. Take the time to find the right balance.

12 PAINT IN SHADOWS

Now that you have your shape elements, it's time to add a little more realism. When you overlay forms, the credibility of these is achieved through shadows. Use them to create a 3D effect of depth. Paint them using a soft brush set to 40% Opacity with your layers in Product mode. Obviously there are other means to add shadows, like using drop shadows, but I prefer not to use this method. Painting your own offers a more personal touch.

13 PASTE IN THE BIRDS

Bring some life into your composition by adding an extra element. Download a bird image from **morguefile.com/archive/display/843318** and import it into your document. Duplicate the image once or twice, and place your birds in dynamic ways by varying their size (Edition>Free transform or Cmd/Ctrl+T). Playing with the variation in size allows you to provide a depth of field, to create the illusion of a foreground, midground and background.

FINAL ADJUSTMENTS
USE LAYER MASKS, ADJUSTMENT LAYERS AND FILTERS TO COMPLETE YOUR ILLUSTRATION

14 CREATE DECORATIVE CHIPS

To bring even more energy and vitality to your illustration, add a few chips with features brushes. To do this, draw random shapes and turn them into brushes (Edit>Define Custom Shape). Hit F5 to open the Form panel and play with the settings of the dynamic forms, and those of Diffuse. Don't go too far, even if this effect is fun. It can give a rough look to your composition if you add too much. Be subtle.

15 ADD A LAYER MASK

There are always points that can be improved during the creation, like masking imperfections or removing elements you don't want to see, as you think they are useless. Layer masks are ideal for this as they allow changes to be non-permanent. Add one and remove unwanted areas. Layer masks have an important role in the integration and credibility of an illustration, so spend time applying them.

16 MORE DEPTH

Duplicate the flower in Step 6 and choose a neutral colour like grey to increase depth between the foreground, second plane and background. Using a bright colour will draw attention to the element, which you don't want. Go to Layer>Smart Objects> Convert to Smart Object. Increase size (Cmd/Ctrl+T) and set the layer to Overlay mode. Duplicate this layer, arrange it differently and play with the opacity.

17 APPLY ADJUSTMENT LAYERS

Now you need to give the composition a balanced chromatic scale. Add a layer of brightness and contrast adjustment to bring out some elements (Layer>New Adjustment Layer>Brightness/ Contrast) and a Curves adjustment layer (Layer>New Adjustment Layer>Curves). This is almost essential for me, as it offers so much more flexibility in colour correction and also contrast. Experiment with the settings until you are happy with them.

18 STRENGTHEN THE COMPOSITION

To finish, select all your layers, duplicate them and then merge them . Apply a High Pass filter (Filter>Other>High Pass) with a radius of 1.2px. Set the layer mode to Overlay. Attenuate the effect of the background using a layer mask. Perform these final touches, zooming to 100%. Your picture is now complete, but of course you are free to go even further and add more forms and elements if you feel it is necessary.

MIXED MEDIA

COMBINE TRADITIONAL
ARTISTIC METHODS WITH
DIGITAL TECHNIQUES AND
PRODUCE MIXED-MEDIA
MASTERPIECES

112

134

116

130

108

138

124

COMBINE SKETCHES WITH DIGITAL TECHNIQUES

PHOTOSHOP

MIXING MEDIA CAN PRODUCE SOME WONDERFULLY CREATIVE RESULTS

The long-boarding scene is getting quite big these days, so to stay competitive companies always need to remain innovative with their boards. They also need to stick out in a more obvious way; graphics. Of course, there's absolutely no necessity for a great long-boarding deck to have any graphic at all – it would still work. But people will always prefer to

have something good-looking that stands out from the rest, rather than having an ugly board under their feet. Graphics help to create images for a brand, which is why customers like designs that have some personality within them – so they prefer artists who have their own style. A lot of these designs are now a mixture of traditional and digital art. Our example here is the design for the Landyachtz Chinook 2012.

Here we'll combine traditional hand-drawn sketches with the possibilities of Photoshop. Starting with a simple pencil sketch, we'll create a rough mockup, which will lead us to a symmetrical layout made with fine-liners and markers. After scanning, we will use some cutting and colouring techniques to create a graphic that combines the aesthetics of street art with an almost Indian style.

FROM PAPER TO COMPUTER
BE CREATIVE MORE THAN REALISTIC

01 PRODUCE AN INITIAL SKETCH
Start with a simple pencil sketch as a rough layout. Always use reference photos, but for a piece like this you can also work freehand. We're not planning to create something realistic here, so try whatever you want and just create a broad impression of a lion. Always attempt to keep your work symmetrical at this stage.

02 LAY OUT ONE HALF OF THE PIECE
Now scan in the sketch and open it in Photoshop. Since the design is based on symmetry, we'll only need to create one half of the detailed drawing. The challenge is to correctly set it up. Erase one half, copy the other one, mirror it and put them together. Correct every part that doesn't look good, then erase one half again until the result works.

03 DIVIDE THE SKETCH
Print your (half) layout at an A4 size and trace it on a new piece of paper using a pencil. This next part all comes down to style. You can split the piece in a way that looks pleasing, there are no real rules here. Keep in mind that some parts are more important than others – like eyes and mouth – these should be accentuated.

04 REFINE THE FINAL LAYOUT
Using the sketch, you can now start to prepare the detailed sections. Retrace all the single pencil lines with a black fine-liner (0.3mm), while trying to stay as clean as possible. Don't rush this, as sometimes fine-liners tend to take a few moments to dry. Every mistake made will have to be corrected later in Photoshop, so it's advisable to be patient at this point. After you've traced your sketch, erase the overlapping pencil lines.

QUICK TIP
EXPERIMENT

Check out various kinds of markers and pens, as each brand can work in unique ways. Some are better to work clean, others can turn out looking traditional. Also try different kinds of paper, depending on how much you want line bleeds.

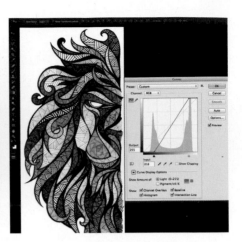

05 FILL THE FRAGMENTS

Working with fine-liners sized at 0.03 – 1mm, you can start to fill all the single fragments. Again, this is a matter of taste. Here we're using different kinds of hatching everywhere, but the same thing would work using dots, circles, waves or whatever you prefer. What's vital is that you create different shades of grey, because that's what gives depth to the drawing. Try not to use the same pattern on two parts that are next to each other.

06 FINALISE OUTLINES

To finish, you need to emphasise the outlines of every single fragment, as well as the lion itself. This should help accentuate the skull against the mane. You can also correct little mistakes made while hatching by covering them up in black. While a fat outline may help to keep the whole drawing together, it often also adds a street art look. Changing the thickness of the outlines in some places will also make the drawing more dynamic.

07 TURN YOUR DRAWING DIGITAL

After finishing your drawing, scan it at 800dpi. Always keep in mind that it may be necessary to resize the image later, so it's best to work with larger files now rather than needing a better resolution afterwards. Since no colour information is needed here, greyscales are enough. Now open your file in Photoshop and adjust its contrast by applying a Curves adjustment (Cmd/Ctrl+M). This way you should get the paper almost plain white, while the drawing should be black.

08 PREPARE TO MIRROR

Now you can remove any dirt that appears on the scanned images. Here it's useful to invert the drawing (Cmd/Ctrl+I), as this will help you spot stains (white on black is easier to see than black on white, at least on screens). You can now use the simple Brush tool to remove some flaws. After this, use the Burn/ Dodge tool (O) in case there are some shades of grey. Finally, change the canvas size so that there's enough space for the whole graphic.

QUICK TIP
FINDING YOUR OWN STYLE

People often wonder how they can create their own style. The artist here has always used crosshatching in drawings and, after a while, began exaggerating it a bit. Try analysing the work of other artists you like and adopt some of the ideas and techniques found there to incorporate them into your own work. It's all a never-ending process and there's never something like a final style. It's truly important to get inspired; look for other artists and what they do, but don't just copy! If you mix your own ideas with inspiring things from the outside, there's a good chance something new will emerge.

09 FINALISE THE DRAWING

Now remove the overlapping parts at your central line. Copy your layer, mirror it and change the blending mode to Multiply. You may need to redo this a few times if the original drawing is not at a perfect 180-degree angle. When done, put both layers together exactly pixel to pixel and reduce them to one layer.

Centred axis
The final layout is strongly based on a centred axis. No line is crossing another one in the middle!

Cut out
Now we have to cut out the final drawing from the white background in order to move on with our graphic

Black and white
There should be almost no shades of grey left, so what we see is nearly completely black and white

10 CUT OUT THE DRAWING

This is a process used a lot in these projects. Select everything by hitting Cmd/Ctrl+A, copy this, add a mask to your layer and click on it while holding Opt/Alt. This way you'll remain inside your mask, where you'll paste your drawing. Invert the whole thing and you should see a white drawing on a black background. Leave the mask and return to your layer. Fill the canvas with black, hit Cmd/Ctrl+G, then Cmd/Ctrl+E and your drawing should be cut out.

11 ADD THE MAIN COLOUR

While the final graphic should have strong colours, here we'll keep it down to just two main tones; turquoise/green and yellow. Use different grades of green to fill the lion's head by selecting the space surrounding the drawing. Invert this selection (Cmd/Ctrl+Shift+I) and go to Select>Modify>Contract. Depending of the size of your drawing about 5 pixels should be enough. Create a new layer below the drawing and fill the selection with a selected tone.

12 USE DIFFERENT GRADES

Now lock the opacity of your layer in the Layers palette. This way it's easier to work without watching for the exact outlines of the graphic all the time. Now fill all the fragments using different tones of green, maybe almost some shades of grey to the different parts of your drawing. Think about where you could include darker colours and where injecting some lights might help achieve depth. You can use the simple Brush tool with a graphics tablet for this.

13 ACCENT THE DETAILS

Now the second colour comes in. Here we've used a very warm, almost orange, yellow. It's complementary to the green tone, which helps the eyes stick out a lot. This should be used very subtly, without overdoing the effect. Of course, it's still best to use different grades and even add a bit of red surrounding the eyes. This is something you have to practise a bit to really get a feeling for what works and looks good in the end.

14 LAYER ON THE SHADING

To give the design a little bit more depth, it's a good idea to add some shadows. Create another layer on top of the colours, but beneath the drawing. Now apply the Brush tool again, setting its Opacity to 30%. You can either use just plain black, or different shades of dark green. As ever, this is just a matter of taste, so there are no limitations at this stage. In this piece, we worked especially around the skull to accent it further against the mane.

Original

COMBINE ARTISTIC PROGRAMS

PHOTOSHOP

ILLUSTRATOR

CREATE THIS COLOURFUL AND DYNAMIC PORTRAIT BY TEAMING UP PHOTOSHOP WITH ILLUSTRATOR

SOURCE FILES ✓
AVAILABLE ON THE FREE DISC

Working cross-platform can create interesting and unique results. Combining programs means you can get the best from each of them, mixing and matching tools and techniques to create some really unusual mixed-media styles. We will show you how to create a bright and colourful

portrait image, working from a photo to create a sketch in Illustrator, then moving onto Photoshop to add splashes of colour.

Before you start, have fun sketching lots of different portraits on paper. It's important to understand shading and colour, and which details have the biggest impact on your portrait. As you

progress, you will see that the eyes are often the trickiest part to get right, yet they are also the most important aspect of a portrait. Study plenty of photo stock to ensure that you master their shape and shading, for a more engaging and convincing design. Don't be put out if this takes you some time, though, as you'll learn from each mistake.

ILLUSTRATE THE PORTRAIT
SKETCH THE PORTRAIT SHADE BY SHADE

01 CREATE A NEW DOCUMENT
Start up Illustrator and create a new A3 document with Color Mode set to CMYK. If you prefer using different settings or sizes, feel free to do so. Here you will need a portrait orientation. Make sure that you do not change the raster effects and keep it at 300dpi.

02 FIND YOUR PHOTOGRAPH
Use a photo as a base for your illustration. To spot a good picture from the rest, you need to check a few important details. First, you must make sure that the size is okay; the bigger, the better. It's also important that there is enough contrast, as this helps a lot when you are sketching the image.

03 LAYER ORGANISATION
If there is something that will always help you in the future working as a designer, it's a nice and clean layer organisation habit. Start your document by naming your layers. In this tutorial you will only need a few, depending on how many colours you wish to use.

04 START WITH BLACK
To create this portrait, always start with the darkest colour to draw the most important elements of your portrait (these are the eyes, nose, hair etc). It's important to use your fresh energy in the beginning to make sure that these features are just perfect! Use your Wacom or mouse with the Pencil tool if you have some experience of drawing in Illustrator, or use the Pen tool and create your paths point-by-point if you are a beginner.

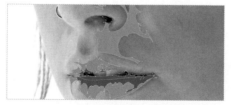

05 DRAW WITH WAVES
After you have finished the most important details in black, continue drawing with a dark grey. Select 'Only web colors' in your Fill(x) menu to work with the six shades of grey. Now you can draw in the darker areas and build your portrait. To create paths, draw with a 'wave' technique, and try to draw in waves and curves. This way you can create some experimental colour paths – perfect for lips and shadow from the hair and chin.

06 CONTINUE THE PROCESS
When you are shading your portrait, you will see how important it is to start with the darkest colours first and then the lighter colours in the layers below. Make sure you look at the whole image, to keep your focus and not get lost in one single detail. After a few hours of drawing portraits, you will pick up your own ways to recognise and handle different shapes on a face; for example, how you like to draw a mouth or an eyebrow.

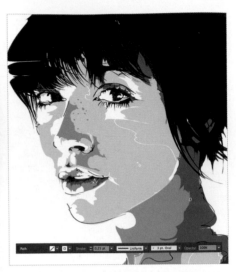

07 MAKE IT DIRTY

You should now be almost finished with your black and white illustration. The next step is to add a dirty paint effect to your portrait. Create a new layer on top and call it 'Dirt'. Then imagine you have a dirty, rough brush in your hands and wipe black and white paint over the portrait, in particular coming from the highlights. Take the Pencil tool and draw your dirty paint strokes and place them around so they still fit and add value to your portrait.

08 ADD SOME LINEWORK

Before you are completely finished in Illustrator, create a new layer group called 'Linework' and take the Paintbrush tool (B) with Stroke on. Set the Stroke up with a Size of 0.25pt (depending on your image size), a Brush Definition of 3pt Oval and a Uniform variable brush width profile with Opacity of 100%. Now draw lines to emphasise the curves of your portrait and add flow to your model's face. It's also a perfect tool to add details and outlines.

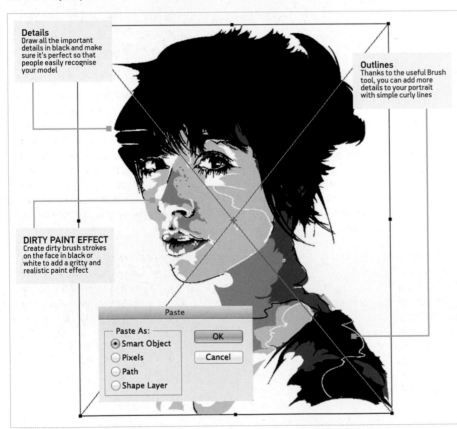

Details
Draw all the important details in black and make sure it's perfect so that people easily recognise your model

Outlines
Thanks to the useful Brush tool, you can add more details to your portrait with simple curly lines

DIRTY PAINT EFFECT
Create dirty brush strokes on the face in black or white to add a gritty and realistic paint effect

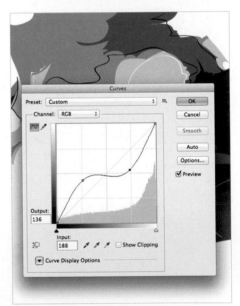

09 OPEN PHOTOSHOP

Time to start working in Photoshop. Copy all the paths from your Illustrator document by pressing Cmd/Ctrl+C. Open a new A3-sized document in Photoshop and place your illustration. Photoshop will then ask you how you want to paste it. Pick Smart Object to allow easy updates to your drawing later.

10 ADD HAZE

For the next step, you need to search for high-resolution images of dark clouds with lots of details in them. Once you have found some, paste them into your Photoshop document, desaturate your layer (Cmd/Ctrl+U) and adjust the brightness using Curves (Image>Adjustments>Curves or Cmd/Ctrl+M) until you have a high-contrast black and white image. Now change the layer's blend mode to Multiply and place it over the shoulders and hair to add a foggy feeling to your portrait.

11 CREATE YOUR OWN GRADIENT BRUSH
You will now create different coloured gradient brushes. Use a soft round brush with Opacity of 70% and Flow of 100% and start by brushing one circle of 2500px in a pinky-red colour. Then create another at 2000px with dark orange, 1500px with orange and 1000px with yellow. Then transform your brushes with the Warp tool (Edit> Transform>Warp tool and pull around) and set the blending mode to Screen to place it over the portrait.

12 WARP YOUR BRUSHES
You can warp the gradient brushes around specific parts of your portrait; for example, around the shape of your model's hairline or neckline. Play around and see what looks best. Make sure you try and adjust the colours as well with the Hue/ Saturation option (Image>Adjustments>Hue/ Saturation) after you have brushed your own gradients. This way you can come up with unique colourways you would never have imagined before.

13 CONTINUE TO ADD ENERGY
By placing the correct warped brushes, you will experience a special effect where it feels as though your portrait has gained some energy. This result can come from the movement your brushes suggest and the colour. In this tutorial, you should try and stick with warm colours and pull your round soft brushes to one specific side with the Warp tool. This will give the impression that your model has stopped in time, but her surroundings are still moving.

FINAL ADJUSTMENTS
USE LAYER MASKS, ADJUSTMENT LAYERS AND FILTERS TO COMPLETE YOUR ILLUSTRATION

14 IT'S IN THE DETAILS
Your image is almost complete, but before you finish, search for images that will create textures to add to your portrait. For example, in this tutorial we have used a waving American flag with the red stripes and white stars to add details that matter to the model, in order to create a story behind the artwork. Then blend the texture with the illustration by changing the contrast (Image>Adjustments> Curves) and change the blending mode to Screen again to place it in the darker areas.

15 CHANGE THE OVERALL COLOUR
Create a new layer on top of your whole document and fill the layer with color #2a59ef, for example, then change the blending mode to Difference and the Opacity to 10-15%. You will find that you discover a fantastic colouring effect with this single step. You can also duplicate this layer and change the colour for another effect. When you do this, place white lines on top of this layer to emphasise specific details in your portrait – for example, below the eyes.

16 ADD A GRAIN
You may have noticed that recently a lot of digital art has a cool grainy effect in the colour shading. Ever wondered how this is done? Well, it's easy. Search for 'grain texture' in Google with the search option on large images and you will find a high-resolution grain texture image (grey and white dots like on an old TV). Paste this image on top of your work and change the blending mode to Overlay and the Opacity to 30-50%. This works just fine with the dirt brushes you created earlier.

17 MOVING IN TIME
Earlier in this tutorial we looked at how to add energy and movement to the portrait, to give the impression that the model is in a dynamic environment. To add a very obvious feeling of movement, you can add an extra group of layers with white lines on top of all your layers in a specific direction to create this really awesome movement effect. It's an easy step that has a very big impact on your portrait.

18 FINISHING AND SAVING
Since you are working on a high DPI with the purpose to print this artwork, it's important to change some things before you share your work on the internet. First you have to change the image size (Image>Image Size). Change the Resolution from 300dpi to 72di and resample the image to Bicubic Smoother (best for reduction). Normal quality will be just fine since you worked on a high-resolution image. Now you can sit back and enjoy your portrait.

MERGE COMPARATIVE STYLES

FIND OUT HOW TO TAKE YOUR TRADITIONAL IMAGE INTO DIGITAL SOFTWARE TO CREATE THIS VIBRANT STYLE

SOURCE FILES ✓
AVAILABLE ON THE FREE DISC

PHOTOSHOP

Collaboration is defined as a process where two or more people work together to realise shared goals – in this case, a super-vibrant piece of artwork. Two of the globe's most talented mixed-media artists, from totally different ends of the creative spectrum, have merged their comparative styles into one super style. Mixed media has never felt so energised.

Traditional artist Simón Prades (**www.simonprades.com**) puts pencil to paper in a productive way, showing you how to master physical application for an authentic result. Brush marks, paper types and post-production tools are all discussed in Phase 1. Andy Potts (**www.andy-potts.com**)

then picks up the baton, running with it headfirst into Photoshop. Phase 2 of this tutorial explores ways to digitise your image using photo stock, textures and more. These are combined with Prades' impressive scanned illustration to produce this vibrant masterpiece.

Photoshop makes this all possible, of course, and you will quickly discover how you can apply layer masks; crop, cut and paste texture and image stock in new ways; and boost colour by using adjustment layers combined with blending modes. By the end, you will have mastered this fresh mixed-media style, which is applicable to any of your future projects.

PHASE 1: TRADITIONAL MEDIA
SIMÓN PRADES SHOWS YOU HOW TO MASTER YOUR MARK-MAKING WITH HIS EXPERT DRAWING TECHNIQUES

01 PENCIL ON PAPER
Using the model in 'DSC_5534.psd' as a guide, sketch a face in pencil. Try to identify the significant parts, for example the nose, eyes and mouth. As all pencil lines will be erased later in the creative process, you don't have to be overly careful; just go with the flow instead. This lets you add interesting lines to work with when inking later on.

02 SIMPLE SHADING
Try not to go into too much into detail while shading with your pencil marks, as you'll want to save most of your efforts for when you're detailing in ink. All you need to do is present the areas of the face that create shadow and contour, like the brow and the nose.

03 FIND YOUR WAY
Also make sure you don't spend too much time obsessing over one area of the face – move around as much as possible. This way, you won't lose the view of the whole image. You can learn a lot by educating yourself on the hatching techniques of the masters like Rembrandt and Ingres, but you'll find your own way the more you work with pencil and paper.

05 DARK TO LIGHT

Remember: there is no going back when working with this medium. Every line you draw is permanent and you will have to live with it. A simple way to tackle mark-making with ink is to approach your drawing as you did with your pencil. Start working in the darker areas of the image, then move onto the lighter ones. Draw without fear and you'll make your inking look interesting in the end.

QUICK TIP
BEGIN IN ANALOGUE

A lot of people may ask themselves what the point of drawing on paper with ink is, when Photoshop, Illustrator and drawing tablets are available. The main reason is that your way of creating is always more unique when working in analog. This shows much more about you and your rhythm than if you were to start directly in digital media.

04 WORK WITH INK

Once you feel as though there is enough information in the pencil marks, move onto working with ink; in this case made by Rohrer & Klingner. You only need to use a normal nib and brushes. There are lots of different materials available for you to try and buy, but in the end what you feel comfortable using depends on your practice. This is more important than spending too much time looking for material in art shops. Sometimes it's a case of the simpler the better.

06 FIND YOUR RHYTHM

Try to switch between pen and brush often, so you achieve rhythm in your drawings. Rhythm is actually something that is very important, as the more you keep your hands moving, the more interesting marks you'll make. In parts like the hair, it doesn't make sense to show each and every strand. So again, look out for lighter and darker areas and use the brush, especially when there is not a lot of ink left on it, to create good textures.

07 EMBRACE THE MEDIUM

Little side effects of your ink drawing always add personality. These include strokes or points and circles you'll leave on the paper, and are things you can't experience when working digitally with a tablet. It's good just to let these happen, as you can still erase parts later. Also, keep sheets of paper at hand for cleaning the brushes or noting ideas. This is always a good source for textures you might want to use later when colouring digitally.

08 TIME TO STOP

One of the biggest problems when drawing freehand is knowing when to stop and say 'enough is enough' before moving on into the digital canvas. It's natural to spend too much time on something rather than quitting too early, but sometimes you overdraw the picture and regret doing it, by which time it's too late. A good drawing lives from the contrast between the light, sketchy parts and the areas where you really went into detail.

09 SCAN YOUR IMAGE

After the work is dry, move onto digital application by simply scanning the picture in. This is better than taking a photo. If you're working with an A4-size scanner, you'll often have to merge parts in Photoshop. Always aim to scan in around 200 per cent larger than the intended final size, as this gives you the possibility to crop the picture or rearrange the composition and still have a high resolution at the end.

10 SEPARATE THE BLACKS

The good thing about working with ink is that you don't have to worry too much about the tonal correction once you've scanned to Photoshop. You would if you had scanned your pencil drawing. Just try to filter out all good black marks and lose the paper colour, using Select>Color Range. Choose Select: Shadows, then duplicate to a new layer. Erase the original backdrop, create a new layer beneath your ink layer and add a new colour (#b0c6c2).

11 COLOUR YOUR BLACK MARKS

Your black marks may now seem too harsh when offset against your coloured background. You can add a new colouring to your black marks by again selecting Color Range to target your black marks (Select>Color Range>Select: Shadows), then fill the selection with a new colour. You might have to try a few times to get the right one, but to help why not try starting with a dark blue hue (#17293f) like the one used in the example, so contrast isn't lost?

12 INTERESTING AREFACTS

As mentioned before, there are little side effects that might appear in your image. Embrace the strokes and splodges caused by drawing in ink, as they add personality and individuality to an image, even if not every art director will let you get away with keeping them in. If you want to highlight certain elements in a graphical way, just paint beneath your line work on a new layer using a bright colour. Working with a drawing tablet helps a lot here, letting you paint precisely and keep inside the lines.

13 ADD MORE BRUSH MARKS

When you have areas that feel a bit too empty or perhaps just a little boring, you can always work with some of the brush strokes you created while drawing but didn't use. Recycle these by scanning them in, colouring them using the techniques in Step 11 and overlaying them on top of your background, beneath your line work. Edit these marks by lowering the layer opacity and working to layer masks. These always look more authentic than digital brushes. However, there are some very nice expert brushes on the web, such as those by Kyle Webster (**www.kyletwebster.tumblr.com**).

> Embrace the strokes and splodges caused by drawing in ink, as they add personality and individuality to an image

ANDY POTTS + SIMON PRADES

Keep it real
Switch between pen and brush often, so you achieve rhythm in your drawings. This is very important, as the more you keep your hands moving, the more interesting marks you'll makemore realistic. Uniform strokes are the hallmark of digital – real media is more random

Colour
Choose Select>Color Range and separate your marks from the original background by duplicating them into a new layer. This lets you re-colour these using a simple selection and the Fill command. Apply a colour that achieves contrast with a new background

Mixed-media effect
Recycle your leftover brush marks by scanning, copying and pasting these into your artwork. Position them between your line and background layers, then re-colour and edit with layer opacity and layer masks to create a mixed-media effect

New layer
With your ink marks on a separate layer and the old background deleted, you can now add a new one. Simply create a new layer at the bottom of your layer stack and fill this with a colour that again contrasts with your newly coloured ink marks

PHASE 2: GOING DIGITAL
ANDY POTTS NOW USES PHOTOSHOP TO DIGITISE THE IMAGE

14 INCREASE CANVAS SIZE
To add a little breathing space around the traditional illustration, extend the canvas at the top and sides. This provides more space at the top in particular. The decision to boost colours was made, implemented by adding a new blue base colour (#02498b) on a new layer. Add a vector mask to this. Apply a black to white Radial Gradient tool to the mask to make this colour layer faint around the edges and set the layer blending mode to Overlay. Duplicate this layer and remove the mask to strengthen the overall blue, but retain a more intense central area.

15 CUT OUT THE MODEL
Next, you'll add flesh tones to the illustration using the original photo. Open the 'DSC_5534.psd' file supplied, then choose Select>Color Range. Use the Color Picker to choose the white space around the model and set Fuzziness to 160, picking out fiddly hair edges. Inverse the new image selection choosing Select>Inverse. With the selection, activate the Lasso tool, hold Shift and quickly draw around the face and hands area to complete a whole model selection. Press Cmd/Ctrl+J to copy and paste your selection to a new layer.

16 PLACE THE FACE
Drag and paste the model cutout into your working PSD. Set the Opacity of the illustrated model layer to 50% to help position the photograph with the drawing accurately. Use Transform (T) to adjust the photographic face to fit the lines. Create a new path layer and use the Pen tool to trace around the model's face only. Select the Path (Cmd/Ctrl+Return). Press Cmd/Ctrl+J to copy and paste to a new layer and place this above the blue colour tints created in Step 15.

17 BLUE IN THE FACE
Hide the photo layer and reduce the opacity of the brush marks. Select the cutout layer, press Cmd/Ctrl+U and set Saturation to -100. Hold Cmd/Ctrl+L and set Levels to create a higher contrast. Duplicate this and place the new layer beneath the original version. Set the foreground to dark blue and the background to light blue, then apply a Gradient Map. Set the blending mode to Soft Light at 50% Opacity. Apply a layer mask to both layers and add gradients as shown to blend elements.

18 STYLE THE HAIR
Use Gradient Map to apply colour to the hair in the model photo layer beneath your face layer group. Choose a bright magenta foreground and a royal blue background in the palette, then apply a Gradient Map to the model photo, as shown in this example. This will pick out magenta hair texture in the drawing. Use a mask and gradient to fade out the body, leaving only the left side of the face affected. Use the Lasso tool to create two simple selections at the front of the hair, painting in a magenta tint.

19 EYES AND LIPS

Use your Lasso tool to create simple eye shape selection on a new layer under the drawing layer. Fill these with an off-white colour. Select the black-and-white face layer and create a selection around the lips using the Lasso tool. Copy and paste to a new layer, place above the illustrated model layer and set blending mode to Hard Light and Opacity at 50%. With the lip selection still active, create and fill a new layer above this one with a magenta colour. Set its blending mode to Color.

20 DETAIL FEATURES

Now that the colour, flesh tones and hair have been worked out, it's time to add a few simple finishing touches to the face to bring it to life. This is before working on the rest of the illustration. We'll do this by detailing certain key facial elements, like the eyes, lips and hair.

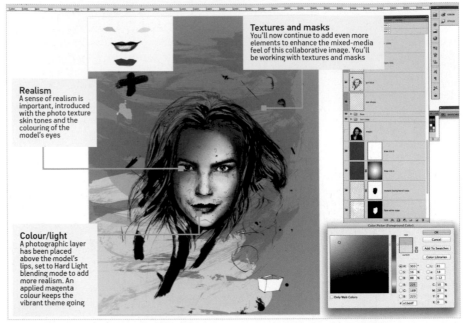

Realism
A sense of realism is important, introduced with the photo texture skin tones and the colouring of the model's eyes

Textures and masks
You'll now continue to add even more elements to enhance the mixed-media feel of this collaborative image. You'll be working with textures and masks

Colour/light
A photographic layer has been placed above the model's lips, set to Hard Light blending mode to add more realism. An applied magenta colour keeps the vibrant theme going

> " Adding digital textures to the illustration will help to blend the photographic elements "

21 ADD HINTS OF YELLOW

Now the face is in place, start to develop the illustration and composition around it. Open 'yellow_dots.psd' and drag it into your image, placing it beneath the illustrated model and eye shape layers created earlier. Apply a Hard Light layer blend mode to this new layer and do the same with 'yellow_shape.psd'. The yellow adds another colour dynamic to the illustration and highlights the model's eyes and hair in unusual yet interesting ways.

22 ZEBRA TEXTURE

At this stage, you'll want to add more visual interest to the image. This will be in the form of zebra marking in the brush marks in your backdrop. Open 'zebra_mask.psd' supplied on the disc and drag the layer into your image. Add a layer mask to the brush mark layers applied in Step 13. Select the zebra shape by hovering the cursor over the layer thumbnail and click while pressing Cmd/Ctrl. Activate the brush mark layer mask and fill the zebra selection with black to create the new mask shape in that texture.

23 EDIT SHAPES WITH MASKS

Open 'magenta_splat.psd' and copy it. Back in your image, activate the illustrated model layer and select Edit>Paste Special>Paste Into. Position the magenta shape in the lower-left area of the hair. Cmd/Ctrl-click the thumbnail yellow shape layer, create a new layer and fill your selection with magenta. Open and drag the circular 'mask.psd' into your image. Select it, activate the previous magenta shape layer and click Add Vector Mask. Move your mask over the magenta shape to create the desired effect. Place behind the model's hair.

24 ADD STRUCTURE TO YOUR DESIGN

Open 'bridge.psd' and paste it into the top-right of your image, under the blue tint layer. Open 'building.psd' and repeat, positioning it to the left of the model. Set both layers' blending modes to Overlay and Opacity to 70%. Add a layer mask and gradient to fade away the bottom edges. Cut out the lamppost from 'building.psd' using the Marquee tool. Apply Levels, add a Multiply blending mode, then place it at the bottom. Place the final 'building_2.psd' under the bridge, set to Overlay and at 70% Opacity.

25 TEXTURE IMAGE AREAS

Open 'texture_1.psd' and place it in the bottom-left below the blue tint layer. Add a layer mask and use a gradient to fade the right side. To get a smooth fade on the top edge, simply Cmd/Ctrl+J the texture, delete the existing mask, add a new one and edit again. Add another gradient mask to fade the remaining top edge and apply an Overlay blending mode. Add the 'texture_1.psd' again, place this above the bridge layer and set Saturation to -100. Mask out edges with the Gradient tool.

26 TEXTURE THE WHOLE IMAGE

Adding texture to the illustration will help to blend the photographic elements. Open 'texture_2. psd' and place it beneath the blue tint layers, filling the whole canvas. Add a Soft Light blending mode and set Opacity to 30%. Paste the same texture into the black-and-white face layer, using the Edit>Paste Special>Paste Into technique in Step 24 and setting the same Soft Light blending mode and 30% Opacity. This lets you move it to an optimum position and work with the facial features through the mask.

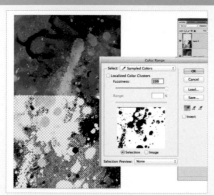

Being able to edit a photograph and cleanly take the texture you need is important when working in digital mixed media. Use Hue/Saturation to create a black-and-white image, then apply Color Range to cleanly select either black or white areas, adjusting Fuzziness to accurately decide selection amounts. To ensure you get the most from your selection, choose the opposite colour you need, then inverse your selection before cutting out. This picks up more pixels in tricky edges. You can then lift your texture and use this to mask detail from the original photo, or even fill it with colour for a pop art effect.

27 MORE GRADIENT MAPS

Open 'palm_tree.psd' and paste it into the bottom-left, above all the layers. Open 'texture_2.psd' and apply a magenta to blue Gradient Map. This creates colourful texturing. Edit>Paste Special>Paste Into a selection of the palm tree layer, then scale and position accordingly. Place the final 'yellow_shape_2. psd' over the main palm tree and set this layer's blending mode to Hard Light for a little final flourish.

28 ADD LEVELS

The image tones are quite subtle and could do with being a lot more vibrant. You can resolve this issue by merging your image, then selecting Layer>New Adjustment Layer>Levels. Set Shadows to 15, Midtones to 0.90 and Highlights to 245 to boost the contrast. This will result in an exciting, digitally fleshed-out ink drawing of a beautiful woman in a tropical urban environment.

CREATE VIVID PORTRAITS

PHOTOSHOP

EXPERIMENT WITH DIGITAL AND TRADITIONAL MEDIUMS TO CREATE VIVID PORTRAIT ILLUSTRATIONS

Being able to create art digitally has sped up our workflows and allowed us to apply effects that would previously have been impossible. However, digital art can be quite generic and artists often miss the unique yet random styles that can only be achieved with traditional media. However, with Photoshop, digital artists can integrate traditional art into modern methods, allowing them to push boundaries and create new art forms. This tutorial will show you how to do just that with this eye-catching mixed media portrait.

When creating a portrait, there are many ways of approaching the concept and executing it. The processes shown here are carried out using basic Photoshop brushes and tools that are applied in more unusual ways. Following the tutorial step by step will lead to an understanding of the process, but by experimenting and using your own techniques you will be able to create fascinating new forms that will be unique and special. Experiment with colours or even monochrome, because this can really change the mood and density of the artwork.

LAYING THE FOUNDATIONS
CREATE A PAINT-EFFECT BACKGROUND AND SKETCH THE PORTRAIT

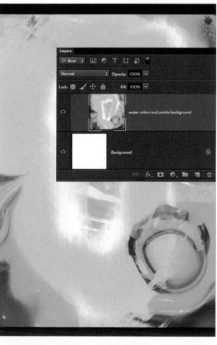

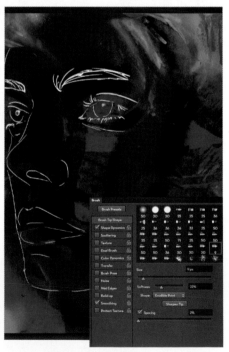

01 THE BACKGROUND
Use traditional media to create a paint-effect background. One way to do this is to take three different coloured paints and mix them in a bit of water, swirl them around and take a picture with a high-definition camera. Another method is to create an abstract mix of colours on a canvas or piece of paper and then scan it into the computer, which is what has been done in this example.

02 IMPORT THE BACKGROUND
Once the paint image has been scanned or imported into the computer, create a new document (Cmd/Ctrl+N) and a new layer. Drag the painted base into the new layer and use a soft brush to create a soft circular surface over the paint-effect background. This is important, as the portrait will be painted over this area.

03 SKETCH THE OUTLINE
Invert the layer to change the blue tones to red. The next step is to sketch the portrait. With a small fine brush tip, draw the silhouette and features of the face, making sure the composition is central and just above the soft brush area you created in Step 2. Select the default pencil brush in Photoshop and activate Smoothing and Shape Dynamics.

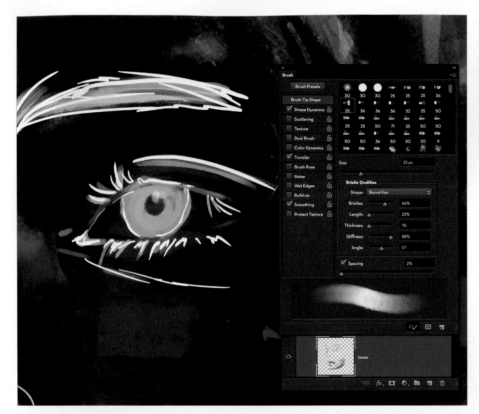

04 PAINT THE EYES

You can now start painting your portrait, beginning with the eyes. The aim is to paint using colours that contrast with the red tones but that also give a mysterious and dramatic effect to the image. Using shades of aqua blue and light lime green, take a soft round brush and paint the eyeballs and eyebrows very softly in a circular motion. The eyelashes are created using fine strokes drawn from the eyelid outwards. You can refer to the screenshot above to see exactly how the eyes were painted in this example.

05 ADD HIGHLIGHTS AND SHADOWS

Shadows and highlights are what give depth to an otherwise flat-looking portrait. It's a good idea to create these in the initial stages of the design to make it easier when applying the colours. First, create a new layer and call it 'Tones', then using a soft round brush at 70% Opacity and a white colour, create highlight strokes as shown in the image. After that, select a dark shade such as black or dark grey and apply darker strokes in areas like the back and sides of the face and below the lips and neck. Creating shadows and lights can often be tricky. Look at different photographs of faces to study the light and shadow in them.

QUICK TIP
USE THE LASSO TOOLS

Apart from using just the brush engine in Photoshop, a nice idea is to play around with Lasso tools. It is such a flexible yet simple tool to create interesting new effects and shapes.

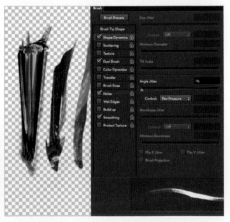

06 PAINT SKIN WITH COLOUR

Next, create a new layer below the Tones layer and name it 'Coloured paints'. Select two colour tones of blue and lime green. While painting, keep switching between different shades of each, for example, different shades of blue, green and yellow. Take a distorted brush and use it to create strokes in random directions with each colour for an unusual colour palette. After the blue and yellow-green colour range, do the same with orange, red and magenta tones.

07 CREATE ABSTRACT SHAPES

You can use Photoshop's Lasso tool (L) to create some really unusual effects and shapes that will add interest to your portrait. To apply them, you will first need to create a new layer called 'Lasso shapes'. Select the Lasso tool and create a branch-like, slightly abstract geometric shape like the one in the screenshot. Use any Brush tool with slight texture and a darker mix of colour tones to randomly paint inside the lasso selection to create interesting effects.

08 PAINT COLOURFUL STROKES

Open a new document (1000 x 1000px) and create a new layer. Remove the background layer. Select any hard-edged brush and draw strokes while holding down Shift. Try and make each stroke a different colour so you get a beautiful range of colour tones. The colour palette used here consists of reds, oranges, lime green and yellows. The idea is to create strokes in one straight direction so that they blend in nicely. Try and do this several times so that there is a nice range of colours and depth.

ADDING IN DETAILS
MIMIC TRADITIONAL EFFECTS TO ADD EXTRA INTEREST

09 FUSE THE STROKES INTO THE PORTRAIT

Copy the layer of shapes you created in Step 8 into your main artwork file. Place the shapes below the lips, jawbone and over the eyebrows, as seen in the screenshot. You need to tweak the shapes so that they fit in nicely with the composition, and you can play around with the colours as well.

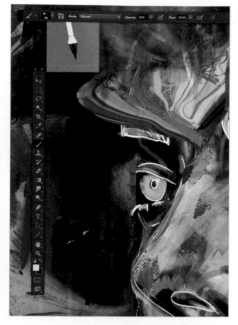

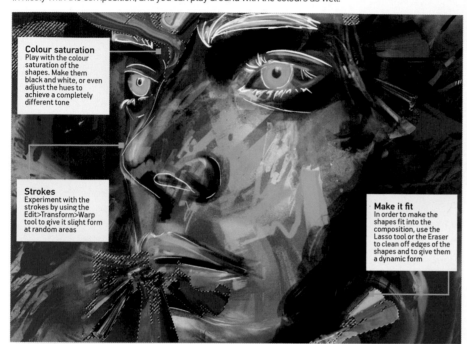

Colour saturation
Play with the colour saturation of the shapes. Make them black and white, or even adjust the hues to achieve a completely different tone

Strokes
Experiment with the strokes by using the Edit>Transform>Warp tool to give it slight form at random areas

Make it fit
In order to make the shapes fit into the composition, use the Lasso tool or the Eraser to clean off edges of the shapes and to give them a dynamic form

10 MORE BRUSH STROKES

You can add extra depth by creating even more interesting, colourful strokes. Use a hard brush and zoom into the portrait. Reduce the brush Opacity to about 55% and play with the opacity of different strokes. Apply brush strokes on areas that you could highlight, as shown in the image. You could even use a hard Eraser with a very small size setting to create uneven edges.

11 CREATE PATTERNS

One way to add an additional element to the portrait is to create fan-like patterns from multiple duplicated shapes. To do this, use the Pen tool (P). Create a new layer and label it 'Shape repeat 1', then draw out an organic point shape as shown in the screenshot. Make sure that the starting point of the Pen tool meets the end point so that it forms a closed shape. Ctrl/right-click and choose Make Selection.

12 FILL THE SHAPES

Take two tones of grey and use the Gradient tool (G) to fill the selection you have created with a gradient. Take a soft round brush and brush the edges of the shape while the selection is still on. This will add depth to the shape. It will also help when you repeat the shapes to create a shadow. After that, use the Lasso tool (L) or the Pen tool (P) to create an almond-like outline in the centre of the shape. Make a selection and fill it with a dark grey colour. You are now ready to form the pattern.

13 FORM THE PATTERN

Now you can create a fan from the shapes. Press Opt/Alt on your keyboard and drag the Shape repeat 1 layer to duplicate it, or Ctrl/right-click on the layer to do so. Rotate the new duplicate shape by 30 degrees and place it over the pattern layer. Repeat the steps again until a chain of shapes is created. Each shape needs to be rotated and aligned over the previous one to create a beautiful, seamless pattern.

14 LINE ART DETAILING

You can create extra interest by adding a line art drawing into the visual. Select the white colour and use a thin pencil tool to draw some flowing organic shapes near the eyelids and the back of the portrait. Experiment and play with other areas too. This effect needs to be very minimal and should be added as a touch of detailing.

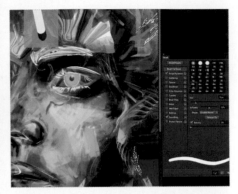

QUICK TIP
KEEP BRIGHTNESS THE SAME

Keeping 'Preserve Luminosity' checked prevents the image from changing brightness as you adjust the colour balance.

15 FINAL IMAGE ADJUSTMENTS

For the final step, create a new Color Balance adjustment layer. Select Midtones from the Tone tab and drag the Cyan-Red slider to +7, the Magenta-Green to + 3 and the Yellow-Blue to -7. Set the layer's blending mode to Color. This is a nice way to give a lovely tone to the artwork, especially when working with many colours at once.

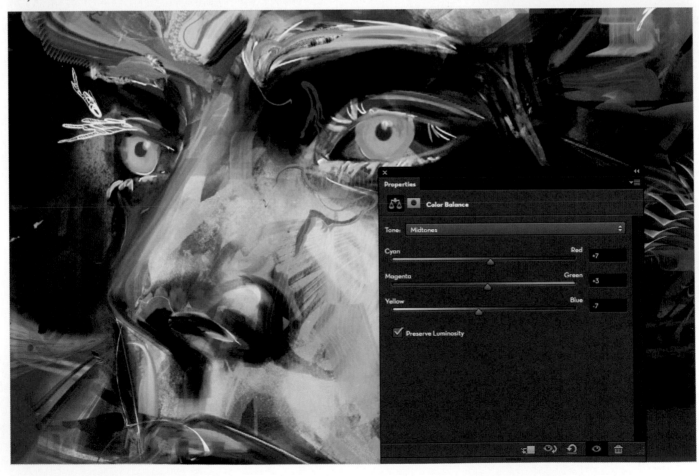

PAINTING AND PREPARING THE BACKGROUND
CREATE A BASE WITH TRADITIONAL MEDIA

One of the most fascinating aspects of digital art is the ability to fuse different mediums. It really pushes experimentation to another level. Initially, when conceptualising the artwork, it was going to be completely digital, but the idea to create the background paint texture manually using acrylic paints sounded fun. The aim when creating the background is to just go wild with the paint and have fun, and then later on fuse it with the digital painting in Photoshop. The results can be quite interesting, as every brush stroke is random and very spontaneous, and can lead to something new and vivid.

01 MONOCHROME BASE
First, take a white A3-sized sheet of paper or card. Prepare a medium-grey shade by mixing black and white together. Then take a large sized brush and create paint strokes in an elliptical direction around the edges of the paper. Try and leave the middle portion white for now. Apply some water to ensure a nice consistency and add layers to the stroke.

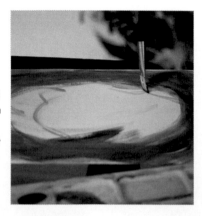

02 ADD COLOUR
Next, you will need to add some colour to your base design. Mix different shades of green, yellow, blue and white until you get a slight aqua tone to the mix, then paint this all over the grey background. Have fun and experiment with creating interesting strokes on the sheet. What you are wanting to achieve is something relatively solid but completely abstract.

03 PERFECT THE BACKGROUND
Play with water to blur out certain areas, or even mix some dark tones again. You want to create a beautiful fusion of both grey and blue tones, which you can import into Photoshop to start creating the artwork from.

MERGE PHOTOS WITH ILLUSTRATIONS

LEARN HOW TO COMPOSITE A MIXTURE OF TEXTURES AND STYLES TO CREATE EYE-CATCHING PIECES OF DIGITAL ARTWORK

This illustration is a fun mix of media. We'll be working with hand-drawn illustrations, photography and block colours in Photoshop. Be prepared to spend a bit of time tracing and selecting elements, all great skills worth mastering!

We will go through experimenting with different layer styles and building colours to create a bold and original piece of artwork. This kind of style is very easy on the eye and is really great to use for your own posters, greetings cards, wall prints and much more!

Here we've used a selection of photographs – you can download them from the supplied resources. Or why not put your own spin on things and incorporate loved ones into the composition? Scan in your family photos and get editing!

Original

> We will be working with hand-drawn illustrations, photography and block colours in Photoshop

PIECE IT ALL TOGETHER
STITCH UP A COMPOSITE USING PHOTOS, BLOCK COLOUR AND DRAWINGS

 01 PREPARE YOUR FILES
Kick off by cutting out the elements that you need from your photographs then start compositing them together. Let's start from the back and work forwards, so we'll begin with a lovely paper-texture background.

02 ADD SKY
Open your sky background, select all (Cmd/Ctrl+A), copy (Cmd/Ctrl+C) and paste (Cmd/Ctrl+V) your sky photo on top of your paper layer. Position this in the top third of the composition, then click on your layer and set layer style to Hard Light.

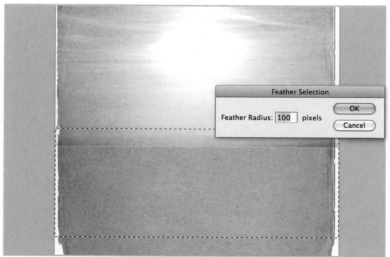

Mixed media

03 ADD MOUNTAIN PHOTOGRAPHY

Cut out the mountain photographs and also add a scan of some ripped-up sandpaper just to mix things up a little. Now you can have a play here – move the photographs about until you're happy with the layout.

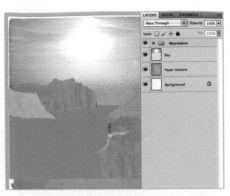

04 BASE COLOURS

Cmd/Ctrl-click on a mountain's layer icon, highlighting its area. Add a new layer underneath it and Edit>Fill (or Shift+F5) with your chosen base colour. Click back on the mountain layer, change to Multiply blend mode and lower Opacity to 60%. Repeat for the other elements.

05 BLOCK OUT THE COLOUR

As well as these slightly textured mountains, you can also add in a few mountains that are simply block colour. Draw a mountain shape using the Lasso tool (L) and then fill in the whole area with your selected colour.

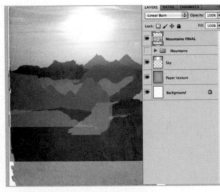

06 COMPLETE YOUR ENTIRE MOUNTAIN RANGE

Duplicate the Mountains folder and hide the original. Click once on the new folder and hit Cmd/Ctrl+E to flatten it into one layer. Change this element's blend mode to Linear Burn.

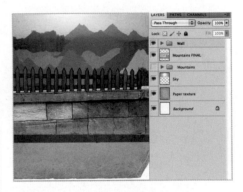

07 WALL PHOTO AND ILLUSTRATION

Open 'Wall original.jpg' and use the Magnetic Lasso (L) to cut around the fence and wall (hold Alt to get rid of the fence post gaps). Paste the selection onto your main project. Now place 'Illustration 2 original.jpg' on a new layer set to Multiply. Rotate clockwise using Edit>Transform.

08 CREATE A BASE TONE FOR THE WALL

Hold Cmd/Ctrl and click the Wall layer icon. Create a new layer underneath and Edit>Fill (Shift+F5) with your desired colour (for instance #bb998b). Now go back to your Wall layer and change its style to Overlay at 50% Opacity.

09 MAIN FIGURES

Now for the main figures. Use the same technique you used for the wall with the supplied figures. Trace over them using a black Pen tool (P). Draw some extra lines to join the characters together and give them something to sit on.

10 DELETE THE OBJECTS

Scan and clean the illustration and add it on top of the photographed figures. Delete the objects that the figures are holding in the photo using the Lasso tool. Then merge the photograph and illustration (highlight both layers and hit Cmd/Ctrl+E).

11 PAPER TEXTURE FOR OBJECTS

Duplicate the Paper texture layer and place it underneath the figures. Highlight the area around the figures with the Magic Wand tool (W) and then go to Select> Modify>Expand and enter 1px so that the selection is underneath the illustration line. Hit Delete on the Paper texture layer.

12 BREAK UP THE UMBRELLA

Duplicate the Paper texture layer under the umbrella. On the Figure layer, highlight every other triangle with Magic Wand. Choose Select>Modify> Expand and enter 1px. Hit Delete on the second paper layer. Hit Image>Adjustments>Hue/Saturation; Lightness down, Saturation up.

13 APPLY A WARM HUE

Highlight the area of the figures by holding down the Cmd/Ctrl keys and then clicking on the layer icon. Create a new layer underneath and then go to Edit>Fill (or Shift+F5) with your desired colour (example: #ffbab1). Now set the Figures layer to Multiply blend mode.

14 USE EXTRA ELEMENTS

The extra guitar is simply a scanned illustration that has been coloured the same way as the guitar and umbrella. Duplicate the paper texture, highlight the area around the guitar, expand it by 1px and then finally hit Delete on the paper texture.

QUICK TIP
LASSO TOOL TIPS

If you're using the Lasso tool to cut around a figure's hair or grass on a mountain top, then you can add a feather to your Lasso selection before you delete the background. You could also duplicate your neatly cut photograph and add a Gaussian Blur to the layer underneath. Once you've cut out your selected area from your photo, go to Layer>Matting>Defringe by 1px. This is a really helpful little tool and makes all of the tiny bits of excess colour that you might have missed around the edges disappear like magic!

Original

15 INCLUDE SEAGULLS

Cut the seagulls out from the original photograph and paste them onto the artwork. Hide this layer and then highlight the seagulls by holding Cmd/Ctrl and clicking on the layer icon. Now create a new layer and Edit>Fill (or Shift+F5) with your desired tone.

16 TIDY UP AND FINISH!

You can then make the mountains little a bit more red by selecting the Mountains Final layer and then heading to Image>Adjustments>Hue/ Saturation and taking the Hue down to –10.

Originals

CREATE A VINTAGE COLLAGE

SOURCE FILES ✓
AVAILABLE ON THE FREE DISC

PHOTOSHOP

LEARN THE TECHNIQUES BEHIND CREATING YOUR OWN VINTAGE DESIGN, TAKING YOU BACK IN TIME ON A NOSTALGIC JOURNEY

There is a lot of enjoyment in creating a mash-up collage. If you want to provide a flashback to another era while exercising creativity, a collage made up of vintage elements is a versatile way to do just that.

A good collage should have a well thought-out composition with a sense of experimentation. It is a trendy way to construct whimsical and quirky juxtapositions of objects such as posters, album covers, stamps and portraits. Unlike photographic compositions, the variety and contrast of imagery in a vintage collage gives a unique, cutout

look – the aim is to be abstract and creative. This tutorial will show you how to adjust your images for a collage, with some handy filters to give your image a vintage appeal using handwritten texts, illustrations, textures, patterns and more. You will learn how to adjust colour and contrast as well as working with blend modes for best results.

As a finishing touch we will call upon filters to mimic old-fashioned film grain. These techniques can be applied to images that you can easily source yourself, such as old postcards, making this look as though it's from of the Fifties.

MAKE PATTERNS AND USE PHOTOS
CREATE PATTERNS FROM SCRATCH AND INCORPORATE EXISTING IMAGES

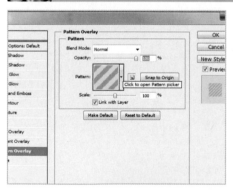

01 PATTERN MAKING
Open 'background. jpg'. Create a new layer and draw a rectangle with the Rectangular Marquee tool. Hit Opt/Alt+Backspace and then fill with a colour of your choice. Double-click on the layer in order to open Layer Styles and select Pattern Overlay. Load the pattern file 'stripe pattern'.

02 COMPILE THE COMPOSITE
Open up the model, car, stamps, hibiscus, palms, flowers, bird, letter, halftone, and pin-up girl images. Paste them into the file on separate layers. To keep things organised, be sure to name the layers as you go.

03 BLEND YOUR IMAGES
Add a layer mask to the Grass layer. With a soft black brush, cover the edges to make it spotty and soft. Repeat this process for the girl in the foreground to hide the edges of her hair.

04 ADD SUBTLE SHADOWS
Create a layer above the Grass layer. With a black soft round brush, paint a shadow under the car. Reduce the opacity of the shadow to 55% and pin it to the Grass layer. Repeat to create shadows for the pin-up girl, hibiscus flower, letter, and stamps.

05 ORGANISE

Select the Halftone layer. Hit Cmd/Ctrl+U and move Lightness to 100. To stay organised, put the letter, palms, halftone, and striped bar in a group. Name the group Background Elements. Put the Grass layer, Car, Pin-up girl, and their shadow layers in a group named Car.

06 GROUPING

Repeat step five to make a group using stamps, the model and the hibiscus. Call this group Foreground. Take a moment to rearrange the layers as shown for better organisation. Change the name of layers or groups by right-clicking in the Layers palette and selecting Layer Properties.

QUICK TIP
ALTERNATIVE GRAIN EFFECT

There are several ways to achieve a grain effect. An alternative to the Noise filter is to add the film grain texture. Go to Filter>Artistic>Film Grain. Here you can choose grain size, sensitivity and intensity. Size ranges from 0-20, but anything over 5 tends to become too pixelated. This filter works best with Intensity kept at a low value, and the highlight value can vary depending on the tonal range of the image.

07 ADD MORE ELEMENTS

Open the pattern palm images, and paste as shown. Repeat for 'line art flower.jpg'. Turn the blend mode of each line art flower to Multiply, so the texture of the background shows through.

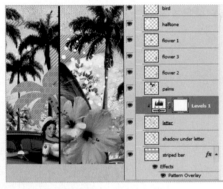

08 LETTER ADJUSTMENTS

The letter in the background looks too washed-out and faded. Select the Letter layer and go to Layer>New Adjustment Layer>Levels, and clip it to the Letter layer. Move the black slider to 90 to deepen the darker colors and make the image more noticeable.

09 PIN-UP ADJUSTMENTS

Repeat step eight for the pin-up girl. Drag the black slider to 48, and the white slider to 227. Essentially, this brightens the lighter tones and darkens the darker tones, increasing the overall contrast of the image.

10 COLOUR VARIATION

Create a new layer on top of the stack. With a large soft brush, cover the layer with red, orange, yellow, and a little blue and green. Turn the blend mode to Color and reduce Opacity to 50%.

11 ADD ADJUSTMENT LAYERS

Go to Layer>New Adjustment Layer>Hue/ Saturation. Do not clip it to the layer below. Move the Hue slider to -10, and the Saturation slider to -40.

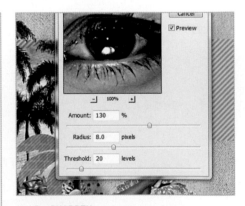

12 SHARPEN

Make a merged copy by hitting Cmd/Ctrl+A, go to Edit>Copy Merged, and then Cmd/Ctrl+V to paste. Go to Filter>Sharpen>Unsharp Mask. For Amount, enter 130% and enter 8px for Radius and for Threshold enter 20.

13 APPLY IMAGE

With the merged layer still selected go to Image>Apply Image. Set the blend mode to Multiply and check the Mask option box. Set Opacity to 60%. You can check and uncheck the Preview box to see the effect this will have on your image.

14 CREATE VINTAGE-STYLE GRAIN

Create a new layer. Go to Filter>Render>Clouds. Then go to Filter>Noise>Add Noise. Leave the settings at default, but check the Monochromatic option box and hit OK. Turn the Noise layer blend mode to Soft Light and reduce the Opacity to 50%.

15 ADD A GRUNGE BORDER

Make a new layer. Select white as your Foreground colour. Select the Brush tool and from the Options bar at the top of the screen load the 'Torn_Paper_Edges' brushes. At 100% Opacity, create a border. Stretch and resize the brush strokes to fit the length and width of the image.

QUICK TIP
SMALL ALTERATIONS RESULTING IN BIG CHANGES

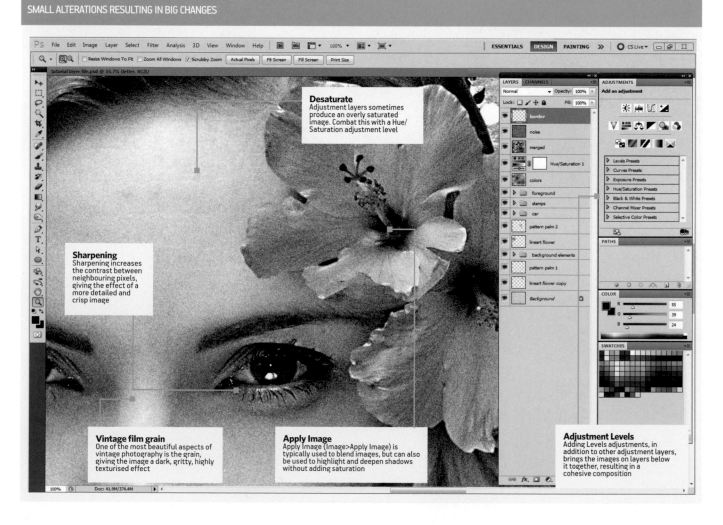

Desaturate
Adjustment layers sometimes produce an overly saturated image. Combat this with a Hue/Saturation adjustment level

Sharpening
Sharpening increases the contrast between neighbouring pixels, giving the effect of a more detailed and crisp image

Vintage film grain
One of the most beautiful aspects of vintage photography is the grain, giving the image a dark, gritty, highly texturised effect

Apply Image
Apply Image (Image>Apply Image) is typically used to blend images, but can also be used to highlight and deepen shadows without adding saturation

Adjustment Levels
Adding Levels adjustments, in addition to other adjustment layers, brings the images on layers below it together, resulting in a cohesive composition

Alexandrine
(Psittacula Eupatria)

Alexandrine Parakeet is native to south Asia. A bold red bill sits in contrast with vivid green plumage. Often confused with their smaller cousin, the Indian Ringneck parrot, they can be identified by brilliant scarlet-patched wings.

Original

USE BLEND MODES AND BRUSHES

PHOTOSHOP

TURN YOUR PHOTOS INTO MIXED-MEDIA MASTERPIECES BY BLENDING DIFFERENT PHOTOS AND TEXTURES WITH BLEND MODES AND BRUSH WORK

Compelling images are easy to achieve with effective use of blend modes, light effects, custom brushes, and a little bit of imagination. In Photoshop, the possibilities for altering an image know no bounds. When it comes to achieving the 'wow' factor in photomanipulations, chances are that blend modes play a key role. Blend modes give us different ways for a layer to interact with the layers underneath. When used in conjunction with layer masks, they quickly produce amazing effects that are pleasantly simple and fun.

Starting off with a quality photograph, we will first do some essential repairs and make some additions to the image in order to create a basic composition.

You will learn how to achieve a unique painted effect with some dripping, splatter brushes; alter colour and contrast with a variety of blend modes; and then enhance your image with a few artistic filters.

The beauty of this technique is in its chaotic nature. The idea here is to experiment and be messy (digitally, that is!) Select your brush colours at random and when painting, don't worry about what blend mode you should be using. The solution is to just try them all.

As usual, we've supplied an array of splatter brushes and photos (including this parrot!) with your resource pack so you can dive straight into the steps here and create your own beautiful bird.

TURN YOUR IMAGES INTO SOMETHING SPECIAL
USING A RANGE OF TECHNIQUES AND MEDIA YOU CAN TRANSFORM YOUR SHOTS INTO PIECES OF ART

01 PLACE YOUR IMAGES
Open 'bgtexture.jpg' and paste the parrot on top. Hide the branch by clicking the Add Layer Mask icon at the bottom of the Layers palette and painting on it with a black brush. Paste 'perch.png' into the document under the parrot layer.

02 ADD BACKGROUND COLOUR
Make a layer above the Background layer. Fill it with a soft orange to green gradient. Go to Filter>Blur>Gaussian Blur and set the Radius to 250px. Change the layer's blend mode to Color.

03 ADD FEATHERS
Select the Lasso tool and make a selection of the upper wing. Hit Cmd/Ctrl+J, and position the feathers over the tail. Then go to Edit>Transform> Warp to elongate them so that they look like tail feathers. Hit Enter to commit the transformation to the image.

04 REPAIR THE TAIL
Go to Layer>Layer Mask>Reveal All. Paint away any rough edges with a black brush. Add the Hue/Saturation adjustment layer and clip it to the new tail layer (Layer> Create Clipping Mask). Move the Hue to -20 and the Saturation to +10.

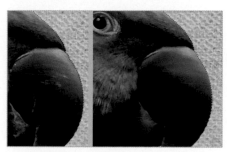

05 SMUDGE TO BLEND
Click on the parrot layer and select all pixels by holding Cmd/Ctrl and clicking the thumbnail. Zoom in on the beak and select the Smudge tool. Set the tool's Strength to 30%, Hardness to 0 and Size to 60px. Carefully smudge out the cracks.

06 BOOST LIGHT AND SHADOW
Set a new layer's blend mode to Overlay and place it above the parrot. Use a white brush at 40% Opacity. Visualize the direction of your light source, and accentuate the bird's highlights and shadows. Repeat this for the perch layer.

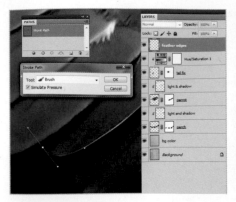

07 FEATHER EDGES

Create a new layer on top. With the Pen tool, trace the outline of a feather. Select a 2px white brush with 100% Opacity. In the Paths palette, Ctrl/right-click the work path and select Stroke Path. Choose Brush and tick Simulate Pressure.

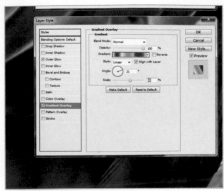

08 GLOWING FEATHERS

Repeat the previous step for all feathers and choose Layer>Layer Style>Outer Glow. Set the blend mode to Normal; Opacity at 100% and Size at 6px. Add a rainbow-coloured Gradient Overlay with Normal mode. Adjust until satisfied.

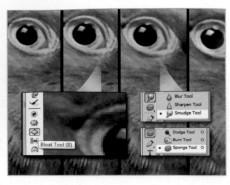

09 ENHANCE THE EYE

Select the parrot layer and choose Filter>Liquify. Zoom in on the eye and select the Bloat tool. Click the pupil to enlarge. Hit OK. Use the Smudge tool to reduce noise, the Sponge tool to reduce redness and with a small white brush, accentuate the highlights.

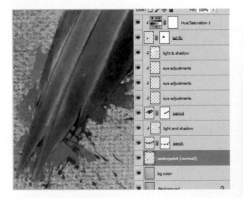

10 BEGIN PAINTING

Load up all the splatter brushes on your resource disc. Use the Eyedropper tool to select colours around the edges of the bird. Paint on a layer underneath the bird. Vary brushes and size, colours and opacity settings. Apply some of the custom paint brushes (by snakstock.deviant.com) around the edges.

11 MAKE A SPLASH

On a new layer above the parrot, add large splashes to key areas. We need to make sure the new splashes blend into the image more. To do this add a new layer mask (see step 4) and use a large, normal brush tip with 100% Hardness to brush away out of place splash marks.

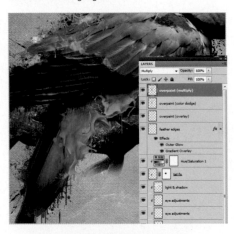

12 PAINT WITH RECKLESS ABANDON

Continue using splatters around the edges of the bird on new layers at the top of the stack. Vary the layers' blend modes to Normal, Overlay and Multiply. Experiment with brush sizes, orientation, colours and opacities. Save layers as you go.

13 PAINT THE TREE

Follow the same process for the perch. The more you switch up colours, brushes, opacities, and modes, the better the results. Have your swatches palette out, and choose your hues randomly.

14 USE ADJUSTMENT LEVELS

Take a moment. Are you happy with the colours? Go to Layer>New Adjustment Layer>Hue/Saturation. Move the Hue slider to +30 and Saturation to +10. Mask out areas of the adjustment layer where the original colours can shine through.

15 CREATE GLOWING EDGES

Hit Cmd/Ctrl+A, and go to Edit>Copy Merged. This makes a copy of everything. Go to Edit>Paste so that the merged layer is on top. Go to Filter>Stylize>Glowing Edges>OK and then turn the blend mode to Screen and set the Opacity to 50%.

16 ADD A SOFT BLUR
Paste another merged layer on top of the stack. Go to Filter>Blur>Gaussian Blur. Enter a value of 40px for the blur and hit OK. Then turn the blend mode to Soft Light and reduce Opacity to 50%.

17 SWITCH UP YOUR COLOURS
Create a new layer. With a large, fuzzy, round brush at 100% Opacity, paint the layer with random colours. Hit Cmd/Ctrl+F to give the colour blobs a Gaussian Blur and blend them together. Turn the blend mode to Soft Light.

18 DARKEN EDGES
Use the Copy Merged and Paste commands for the merged layer on top. Go to Filter>Stylize> Glowing Edges and hit OK. Turn the layer's mode to Subtract and reduce Opacity to 60%.

19 ADD LIGHT AND SHADOW
Create a new layer. Turn blend mode to Overlay and set 70% Opacity. With a large round fuzzy brush, darken edges and corners of the image with black. Darken shadows where needed. With white, add highlights to areas of the branch, eye, feathers, and the bird's shoulder.

20 ZOOM IN ON THE DETAILS
Take some time to look over the composition. Use the Clone Stamp tool to get rid of splashes that seem too dark, or that have blended poorly. If needed, add another Hue/Saturation adjustment layer, or change the colour in a certain area with a different paint.

21 MAKE A MERGED LAYER
Repeat the command Copy Merged and paste this on to a new layer. Make a final Hue/Saturation adjustment layer and move the Saturation slider to -30 to reduce the impact of colour.

22 SHARPEN IMAGE
Go to Filter>Sharpen>Sharpen More. Duplicate the layer and then go to Filter>Other>High Pass. Set Radius at 30px and turn the layer's blend mode to Soft Light, setting its Opacity to 50%.

QUICK TIP
ADD PERSONALISED TEXT IN TO MAKE THE ART MORE… PERSONAL!

01 SELECT TYPE TOOL
Keep the mouse button pressed to see options from the pop-up menu. Choose Horizontal Type tool, which lets you type from left to right.

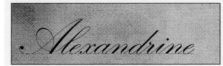

03 CHOOSE FONT AND ALIGN
A new layer is automatically created for your text. Type into the text box. Choose a script font, centre alignment and add a title.

02 CREATE TEXT BOX
Click where you want to add text. Drag to create a text box and drag the squares around the edge to adjust box size. Add a title and subtitle.

04 GO A STEP FURTHER
Click outside the text box to see how text appears. Click the lower right of the screen with the Type tool to add a description of the image.

3D ART

CREATE PHOTOREALISTIC PIECES OF ART AND EXPLORE THE WORLD OF 3D WITH THESE CREATIVE TECHNIQUES

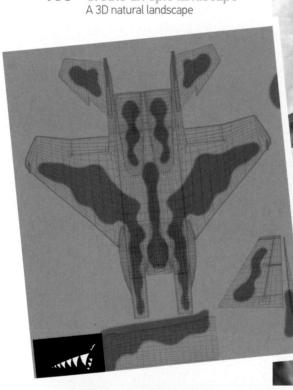

150

First Stage

Second Stage

Third Stage

Fourth Stage

156

160

144

MAYA

PHOTOSHOP

MUDBOX

KNALD

MAKE A REALISTIC 3D HUMAN

USE A VARIETY OF 3D SOFTWARE TO MAKE A REALISTIC PIECE OF ARTWORK THAT COULD BE MISTAKEN FOR A PHOTOGRAPH

Over the next few pages you'll be able to follow the steps and techniques used to create this image. First, we'll gather some reference and define the project to ensure a quicker and more organised workflow. We'll cover modelling in Maya, as well as sculpting and texturing within Mudbox using stencils and projections. Discover a free piece of scanning software that can be used on a smartphone for capturing 3D data

and using it in the final image. We'll cover creating and styling hair using Shave and a Haircut and the workflow for converting to Maya Hair. You'll also learn precisely how to create the eyes here, and the texture used. When we have everything modelled and textured we'll then create realistic V-Ray shaders for the skin, hair and eyes, and you'll get to know the lighting setup and render settings used for the final piece.

DEFINE YOUR CONCEPT
THE LEVEL OF PLANNING YOU DO CAN MAKE OR BREAK YOUR PROJECT

01 DECIDE ON AN IDEA
When working on their own projects, some 3D artists have a tendency to create a concept on the fly, rather than spending quality time deciding or defining exactly what the final image will look like. Without a clear goal, it's impossible to know what assets need to be created and when. At times this can lead to incomplete projects and/or an unrefined final image due to lack of planning. With this in mind, a decision was made here to create a realistic red-headed female wrapped in a red blanket and looking into the camera. Due to this process it was clear which assets were needed, such as a face, hair, eyelashes and blanket. With the idea defined, let's gather some reference to better guide us through the process.

02 GATHER REFERENCE
A lot of online references were gathered for hair colours, facial expressions and specific poses of the face that looked appealing. There was no intention for the model to fully match the references found, but rather they were used as inspiration and a general guideline to follow. Another big reference and help can be to use someone you know. Here, we took a few photos of the lady looking into the camera as a reference of the general look and angle we wanted to achieve. It was also very helpful to see how the blanket would look in the picture and how to make it.

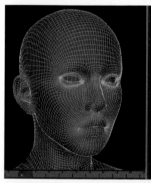
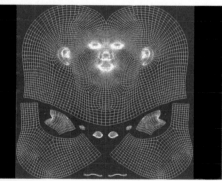

03 BLOCK OUT MESHES AND UVS
With your reference gathered, start blocking out the base meshes in Maya prior to sculpting. The basic head mesh here had already been created, and is being reused. Spend time ensuring that the head reacts well to sculpting and also deforms properly when adding facial expressions. Now lay out the UVs to ensure no overlapping and proper distribution of UV space among the polygons. You can test how the UVs respond by applying a basic checker texture in Maya. We can worry about creating the blanket later on, as we'll be creating it using a 3D scanning approach. With your head mesh ready with UVs, let's export that and the blocked-out blanket geo as an OBJ to bring into Mudbox.

QUICK TIP
BREAK IT DOWN TO BITE-SIZE PIECES

It can take quite a bit of time to build a head you're happy with and with nice UVs. Don't feel pressured to rush into creating a large, complete project right away. At times, 3D artists take on far too much as a first project, and end up sacrificing quality in order to complete a piece. Begin small and work on easier projects while concentrating on fundamentals. Practise anatomy and hone in on your skills in between bigger projects.

SCULPT THE HEAD IN MUDBOX
START FORMING AND TEXTURING THE HEAD

04 ADD EXPRESSION AND POSE

With our base head exported, open it up in Mudbox. Spend quite a bit of time ensuring all the proportions of the face are correct and look at as many references as possible. As we are creating this character from the imagination, it will be important to ensure it looks natural and that all proportions are accurate. Get the face in a proper neutral state where the expression is blank but natural when looking ahead. Place a bone in Mudbox on a sculpt layer, rotate the head to the angle that matches the reference and continue refining the shape. Add the expression that you want to convey in the face, largely using the Grab and Sculpt brushes. At this stage we are ready to add all the pores and wrinkles.

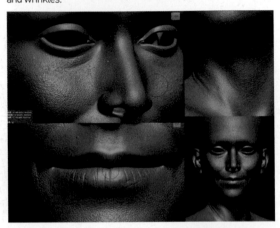

07 TEXTURE THE FACE FOR TEXTURING

It is useful to rely on photo references for projections. Begin using the Paint brush and blocking out very basic colours to show where you want blush, lip colour and eye shadow present. From there, create new layers and use photographs of Oldriska from 3D.sk as texture reference for projecting her skin and freckles. Do not be too concerned with the top of the head, ears or back of the head, as none of these will show in the final render. Ensure that the freckles pop as well, so use the Burn brush afterwards in order to really punch them out when it comes to rendering. Project a faint colour for the eyebrows to use later as a template with Shave and a Haircut. When done, save the finished texture as Colour, bring it into Photoshop and then create a slightly desaturated blue with less contrast. Save this out as Subsurface.

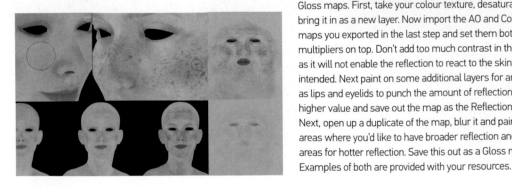

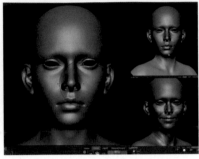

05 CREATE PORES AND WRINKLES

When creating the pores and fine wrinkles, we will need to subdivide the model to a high enough division to accept the sculpting information, for example, five in this case. Next, create a layer called Pores and select the Pores stencil that comes with the Stencil brush in Mudbox. From here you can use the Sculpt brush and start applying it to the entire head. With the pores complete, create a new layer called Wrinkles and, using the Knife brush, start defining the lips, the areas under the eyes and other areas that may have visible wrinkles. For the final touch, make a Bumps layer and use more of the provided stencils in Mudbox, applying each to the model to get the look we're aiming for.

06 SCAN AND RETOPOLOGISE THE BLANKET

For the blanket, try using the free 123D Catch software by Autodesk on your smartphone. Perhaps ask your model to wrap the blanket around her in the proper pose, and then use the software to capture 360-degree images of her before using the program to create a very basic 3D mesh. This method worked extremely well in this case. From here, retopologise the model, scale it and further sculpt and manipulate the geometry to fit with the head mesh in Mudbox.

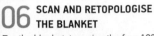

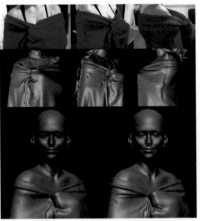

08 USE KNALD FOR REFLECTION

For the Reflection and Gloss maps, a newer piece of software was used called Knald (www.knaldtech.com). Among other features, Knald enables you to take maps and generate them into others. To start, save out a hi-res version of your head from Mudbox and then a lower subdivision (2 or 3 should be fine) without the pores and wrinkles present. Next, use XNormal or Mudbox to extract a normal map at 4,096 x 4,096. With the map baked, let's open Knald and play with the settings so there is enough detail present in the maps. We can then save out both an AO map and a Concavity map at 16-bit TIF format.

09 COMPLETE THE REFLECTION MAPS

Open Photoshop and start to build the Reflection and Gloss maps. First, take your colour texture, desaturate it and bring it in as a new layer. Now import the AO and Concavity maps you exported in the last step and set them both as multipliers on top. Don't add too much contrast in these maps as it will not enable the reflection to react to the skin as intended. Next paint on some additional layers for areas such as lips and eyelids to punch the amount of reflection with a higher value and save out the map as the Reflection map. Next, open up a duplicate of the map, blur it and paint dark areas where you'd like to have broader reflection and brighter areas for hotter reflection. Save this out as a Gloss map. Examples of both are provided with your resources.

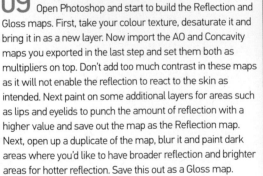

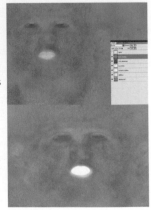

ADD REALISM TO THE HAIR AND EYES
CREATE THE HAIR WITH SHAVE AND A HAIRCUT AND THE EYES WITH REALISTIC TEXTURES

QUICK TIP
STYLING THE HAIR

When styling the hair it's important to take your time. Occasionally do quick test renders to see how the hairs are clumping together in order to get an idea of how it may look later on. Two separate passes of hair were created for this project – one for the majority of the hair and the other for individual strands that fall in front of her face. By creating additional hair selections you can control them later on with Maya Hair. Turn off the Shave and a Haircut Hair Visibility tab and just focus on the strands, as that's what you will ultimately be using. For the eyelashes, use the same approach as that of the eyebrows.

10 STYLE THE HAIR
To create the hair, import the lowest subdivision of your head mesh into Maya and extract a cap for the area you want to spawn hairs from. Duplicate the head mesh then select the faces that will act as our hair cap and use the Extract tool in Maya. Select the newly extracted mesh and using Shave and a Haircut select Create New Hair. With our new hair created, let's update the collision mesh by selecting the hair and shift-selecting our original head using Shave>Edit Current>Update Collision Mesh. The Shave Brush tool was used here by hand to style the hair to achieve the desired look. Once happy with the results, use Convert> Guides to Curves and then save them out for later to be used with Maya Hair.

11 SHAPE THE EYEBROWS
For the eyebrows, import your low-res head mesh into a new scene and apply your Colour texture to it to act as a guide for styling the eyebrows. We'll want to create curves to act as our eyebrows later that sit on top of the head mesh. To do this, let's make our head live by selecting it and then the magnet icon in Maya. With our head live, use the EP Curve tool and draw the specific eyebrows you want. Take your time with this and ensure that parts are elevated above the mesh by moving the curves after you've created them. With the adjustments made we can save these out as an eyebrow group for later.

12 MODEL AND TEXTURE THE EYES
When modelling the eyes, it's beneficial to use a simple but effective approach. Try breaking down the eyes into three separate parts: the lens, sclera and pupil. For the lens, create a sphere and ensure there is a bulge outwards such as in a real eyeball. For the sclera, it is a concave sphere with the centre hole cut out for the pupil. The pupil itself is just a standard plane that sits directly behind the sclera and is completely black. The sclera is the only piece that you should texture with a colour map that you can find provided with your resources. Next you will discover the specific materials to use.

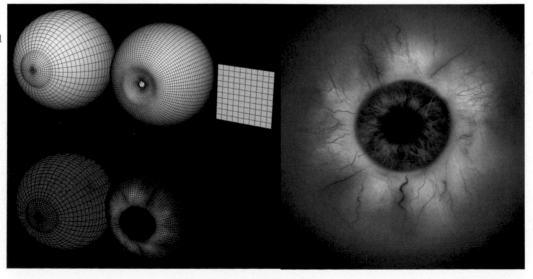

SHADERS AND LIGHTING
SHADER CREATION FOR THE SKIN, HAIR, EYES AND LIGHTING

13 LIGHTING SETUP
Bring in the highest-res OBJs of the head and blanket. Ensure Visible In Reflections and Visible in Refractions is selected for both meshes under your Render Stats Attribute. For lighting create a V-Ray Dome light and select an HDR image to be placed into the Dome Tex slot at maximum res. For the HDR image, use Newport Loft, available for free from hdrlabs.com. Set your Subdivs to around 24 for better sampling, and play with Intensity to find what works best for you. Create three basic poly planes and apply a basic lambert of a colour you want to illuminate your mesh. Create an off-white colour. Place them in areas where you would like to see some illumination on the character.

14 RENDER SETUP
Some of the major takeaways for the render settings are the Adaptive DMC settings, each of which was cranked to 6 here. This makes a huge difference in the quality of the hair rendering. For the Reflection Texture, use the HDR image from the dome light and set the GI Texture to a warm colour rather than texture. For the global illumination ensure it's turned on to take advantage of the planes you created. For Primary Bounce use Brute Force, and for Secondary Bounce use Light Cache. Have a go at using a multipliers setting of .7 but you can experiment.

15 LAYERED SKIN SHADER WITH REFLECTION
For the skin shader, start by creating the layered V-Ray shader VRay Blend Mtl. Create the skin material by selecting a V-Ray Fast SSS2 shader and plugging it in to Base Material. Plug your Colour texture in to the Overall Color slot and your Subsurface texture into the Sub-Surface Color slot. A dark red was used here for the scatter colour, and the Scatter radius was changed to .650 (depending on the size of your head mesh). Next let's create the reflection shader by creating a VRayMtl and slotting it into Coat Material 0. Input your Reflection map into your Amount under reflection, and your Gloss map into your Highlight Glossiness slot. You can see the specific settings that were used for the shader in the screenshots supplied with your resources.

16 CREATE THE EYE SHADER
For the eye shader, a VRayMtl was created for the lens mesh and a VRayFastSSS2 for the sclera. We want the lens to have only reflection and refraction, and the sclera to have a bit of subsurface scattering. The Reflection Color was turned on on the lens to just above black and the amount set at .740. Adjust both depending on the amount of reflection you want in your final image. Refraction Color was turned to white and set to 1.0. Refraction IOR was best set to 1.60. There was also a slight fractal bump map on the lens but it was barely noticeable. For the sclera, put the eye texture into the Overall Color.

RENDER AND COMPOSITE
ADD THE FINAL ELEMENTS AND BRING THE IMAGE TOGETHER

17 THE HAIR SHADER

When rendering the hair, it's best to take the curves we created earlier and apply them to a Maya Hair system. First let's create our hair system by creating a basic polygon cube and selecting Hair>Create Hair. Next, select your curves group and go to Hair>Assign Hair System> hairSystemShape1. This will apply your hair system to your hair curves. Play with the specific settings for how you want the hair to look. To select a V-Ray Hair shader, select your hair system, go to the top and select Attributes>V-Ray>Hair Shader. Now select VRayMtlHair3. You can see the settings used in the screenshots supplied with the resources.

QUICK TIP
DON'T FORGET THE EYELASHES AND EYEBROWS

For the eyebrows, use the same method for creating the hair. Start with the curves, create a new hair system and then apply it. For the shader, you can rely on a duplicate of the hair shader with darker values. For the eyebrows, create a new hair system but use the default material that comes with Maya Hair at almost a black value with slight transparency. Hair takes time to render correctly so don't get discouraged if it's not perfect right away.

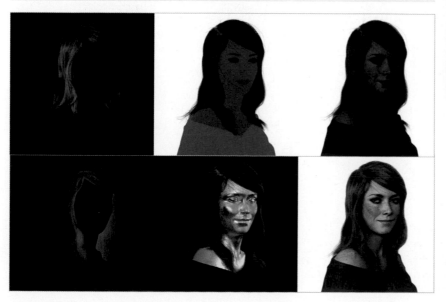

18 RENDER ELEMENTS

With everything ready to go, start rendering with V-Ray. Turn on Multiple Render Elements under Render Settings. Here you are able to choose what layers you prefer to render separately and therefore have the ability to adjust in composition later on. You can see the multiple layers that were rendered separately in the screenshot supplied with the resources.

19 QUICK PHOTOSHOP COMP

All the hard work you've put in has finally paid off and now it's time to play around with some colours and values. At this stage, you can do some minor touch-ups and colour adjustments. Play with some overlays using your render elements. There is no right and wrong way of touching up your photos. Ideally you will have done most of your hard work before rendering, so you won't have to worry about adding too much at this stage. For this project, you could try darkening the lashes and playing around with the levels to find the exact look you're after.

BUILD A DRAMATIC SCENE

BLENDER

GIMP

PHOTOSHOP

LEARN HOW TO BUILD A DRAMATIC SCENE FEATURING A REALISTIC FIGHTER JET BEING HOTLY PURSUED BY THE ENEMY

Here you'll learn how to model a fighter jet from scratch, then construct a dramatic scene featuring a dogfight high above the clouds. Throughout we'll be using Blender for modelling and rendering the 3D elements, GIMP for painting textures and Photoshop for the final composite. We'll cover blocking out the model from references, before creating the details with a mix of retopology and modelling methods.

Next we'll move to making materials for the fighter jet, with a view to rendering a final image with Blender's Cycles renderer. We'll focus on mixing procedural techniques with hand-painted maps while using Blender's node materials.

After finishing up the jet itself we'll move on to creating the final image, adding two pursuing jets into the background along with other exciting features such as explosions, contrails and clouds.

BEGIN MODELLING
BLOCK OUT THE FIGHTER JET WITH SIMPLE PLACEHOLDER GEOMETRY

01 START SIMPLE
Begin with basic primitives, such as cylinders, spheres and cubes, to input modifications (extruding and scaling to capture the overall shape of each major component of the model). This gives an early idea of where the challenges will lie when building the model and also acts as a starting point for creating more-complex meshes.

03 SHAPE THE WINGS
You'll need to find some reference for the cross-section of a fighter jet's wing to get the aerofoil shape right. Model these with curves, convert them to meshes, then space them out and loft them together with the Bridge Two Edge Loops operator in Edit mode. This provides us with a wing shape that we can then use as a guide to construct the wings. Apply the same process to produce the horizontal stabilisers (the rear wings) and the rudders.

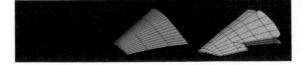

02 BUILD THE FUSELAGE
With the model blocked out, you are then able to start from the front and begin shaping the fuselage (the main body of the jet). Use the blocked-in model as a guide alongside your reference. Keep the poly count relatively low at this stage, as we'll be applying a Subdivision Surface modifier later. It's best to use a Mirror modifier to model symmetrically. After finishing the fuselage, move on to the air intakes. These are relatively box-like in shape, so start out with a cube, then gradually manipulate it into shape. Now insert edge loops and extrusions to produce geometry that will maintain its sharp edges when subdivided.

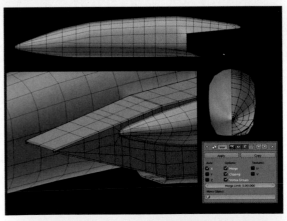

QUICK TIP
SNAPPING SURFACES

Throughout the modelling process, make use of Blender's surface-snapping tools to create new topology over the surface of existing objects. For example, when modelling the wing as shown in Step 3, you can turn on Snap with the magnet icon in the header of the 3D viewport, then set the Snap Target to Face and turn on Snap Projection. These options make it much easier to model surfaces with holes and other details in them. You can also keep the overall surface smoother by using a simpler shape for the guide.

Closest

DETAIL AND TEXTURE
NOW THE MAIN FORMS ARE ESTABLISHED, WE CAN START TO LAYER ON DETAILS

04 MODEL THE MISSILES
Adding details to the jet will mostly consist of examining reference material and modelling elements, such as individual panels on the body of the jet, the interior of the cockpit and the exterior areas of the jet engine at the rear. Of course, no fighter jet is complete without an arsenal of explosive weaponry strapped to it's belly, so try building three different kinds of missile based on real-world references, using the same techniques as those to build the fighter jet itself. These are mainly cylinders with some simple geometry added on for the fins, with a few extra details here and there.

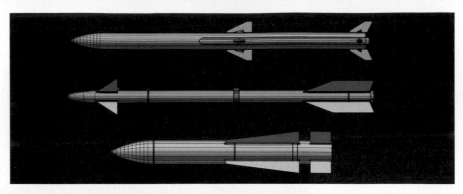

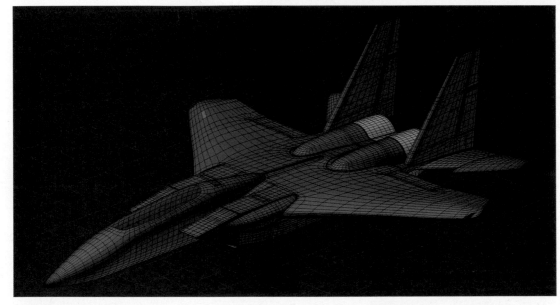

05 UV UNWRAPPING
It's now time to UV unwrap your jet's elements. Thankfully, Blender has a great set of tools for UV unwrapping, so start by adding seams around the main sections of the fuselage. These include the nose, as well as the upper and lower surfaces of the wings. You also need to unwrap the different parts of the underside of the jet. You can use Blender's default Unwrap operator to unwrap these pieces and pack them into a single UV grid. You will find that this grid will be very helpful later on when you begin to bake your textures.

06 MULTIPLE UV MAPS
Because we'll want to add decals to the model later, at this stage it's helpful to create a couple of extra UV sets. In addition to a standard unwrap, which gives each piece of the model it's own unique bit of UV space, we can create two other UV co-ordinate sets. Project large chunks of the model from key angles for the first (mainly from the top or the side). This provides a very simple UV set that we can use to paint broad textures, such as the large camouflage pattern on the wings and the shark's mouth design on the nose cone. Try projecting specific sections of the model from the most relevant Orthographic perspective – the top for the upper surface of the wings, the bottom for the belly of the jet and the left or right for the sides of the rudders. This provides a UV map that we can use for painting decals and other details, such as panelling on the model, without worrying too much about them becoming distorted.

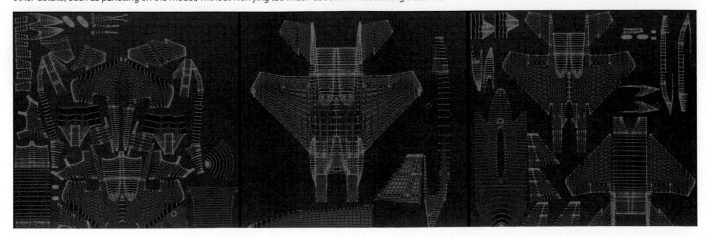

07 BAKE TEXTURES

Once we have the fighter jet unwrapped, we can add an Ambient Occlusion map for the whole model using the baking tools in Blender's Render tab (note: you have to set the renderer to Blender Internal for this, as Cycles doesn't currently support texture-baking). Now bake your AO map to the first UV set you created.

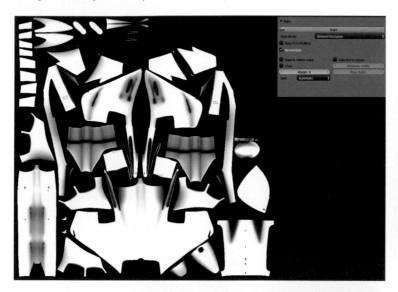

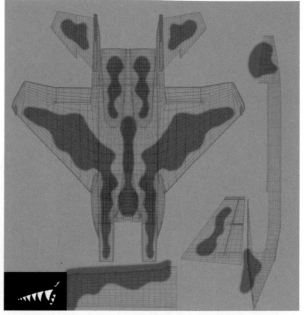

09 ATTACH DECALS TO THE JET

Now paint the decals for the jet on a separate texture with an Alpha channel, then build a couple of military-style designs as well as some random pieces of text and numbers. Place these appropriately on the wings, rudders and the fuselage of the jet.

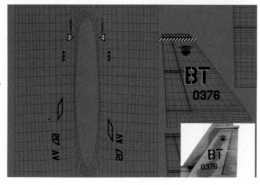

10 MAKE GRUNGE AND SCRATCH TEXTURES

Now build up a few different seamless textures for dirt and scratches to be used in various materials covering the jet. To make a texture seamless, first offset it in GIMP and place the boundaries of the image in the middle of the canvas. Select the seams and use the Resynthesise filter to fill them with a continuous texture. This should produce a smooth result.

08 PAINT A CAMOUFLAGE PATTERN

Here we've gathered various textures for the fighter jet as separate images, which can be combined in Blender when making materials. Begin by defining an overall base colour for each part of the jet with a camouflage pattern and, for extra character, also paint in the shark's mouth design for the nose cone of the jet on this texture. To act as a guide, export the UV layout created as an image, use the UVs>Export UV Layout operator in Blender's UV Image Editor and open this up as a layer in GIMP.

QUICK TIP
DRAWING TEXTURES IN BLENDER

To create the impression of complex panels and rivets over the surface of the jet, partly use a Displacement map. Rather than laboriously painting this in GIMP, model the outlines of the panels with curves in Blender. Use the exported UV co-ordinates created earlier as a guide and lay out the scene from a top-down perspective. Use an Orthographic camera to render a texture that perfectly matches up with the jet's UV co-ordinates. This could later be combined with other textures.

REALISTIC SURFACES
APPLY BLENDER'S NODE MATERIALS READY FOR RENDERING

11 CONSTRUCT A DIFFUSE SHADER
Initially make a Diffuse shader for the body of the fighter jet, then take the Diffuse BSDF shader and begin incorporating your textures. Combine these with Color Mix nodes before plugging them in to the Diffuse Shader node. Join the camouflage texture with the decals texture, and then add in some further details using the seamless grunge textures. Because the different textures use various UV co-ordinate sets, you can include some Attribute nodes (into which you can enter the name of the UV set you wish to use). Plug the Vector Output of these into the Vector Input of the image textures to let them know the correct UV co-ordinates to use. For the seamless textures, use the Image Texture node's blended box-mapping feature to apply the textures without the need for UV co-ordinates.

12 APPLY GLOSSY REFLECTIONS
Now you can combine the Diffuse shader with a couple of Glossy BSDF shader nodes using Mix Shader nodes. You can also reuse some of your textures to affect the Color and Roughness inputs for the Glossy shaders, to provide a bit of variation in the glossy reflections. Apply two Glossy shaders: one for broad soft highlights over the shape of the jet and the other to give some sharp reflections on top. This isn't physically correct, but it gives extra control over the look of your material. Use a couple of Layer Weight nodes to control the mixing of the shaders.

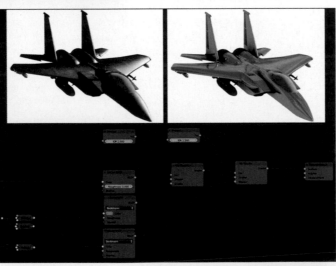

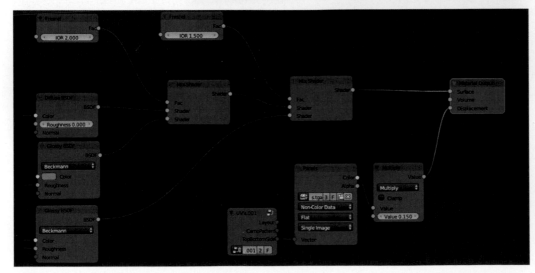

QUICK TIP
THE CYCLES RENDER PREVIEW

The new Cycles render engine has a fantastic live preview for getting instant feedback on your materials and lighting. You can enable this in the 3D viewport if you have the renderer set to Cycles and it will constantly update with a rendered preview. It's beneficial to use this when creating materials in order to get an idea of how they look under some simple lighting, then again later when making the final scene to tweak lights, World settings and render options. It's best to split off a smaller 3D viewport in your window layout and use this as your preview render while you work in another 3D viewport. This will give you a rendered preview that updates quickly, all while keeping it simple to select and edit an object in your main 3D viewport.

> "You can also reuse some of your textures to affect the Color and Roughness inputs for the Glossy shaders, in order to provide a bit of variation in the glossy reflections"

13 DISPLACE ELEMENTS
The Cycles renderer supports a couple of methods for defining surface texture for your materials. Here we opted to plug the panels texture into the Displacement Input of the Material Output node. This provides some fake displacement for the material and highlights the panels that were drawn in. We also used a Multiply Math node to tone down the intensity of this displacement.

DEVELOP THE SCENE
BUILD A DRAMATIC ENVIRONMENT

14 LINK THE JET INTO A NEW BLEND FILE

To create the final image, start a new BLEND file to work on lighting and to render the jet in. To link the jet into this new file, assign all of the objects making up the jet into a single group, then link this group into the new BLEND file. This enables us to go back and modify the jet in it's original file and have the final scene update automatically when we reload it. It also enables us to create a couple of duplicates of the jet to act as the other fighters in the scene.

15 BUILD UP SMOKE TRAILS

To add some extra intensity to the image, you can include some smoke trails created with Blender's smoke-simulator tools. These have to be rendered with Blender's older render engine – Blender Internal – which supports volumetric materials. Render these effects in separate scenes, then link in objects like the jet to act as masks (using the Mask Layers options when rendering).

POST-PRODUCTION
REFINE THE LIGHTING AND RENDER SETTINGS

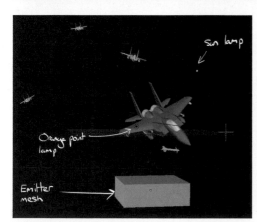

16 POSITION THE LIGHTS

The lighting in this scene is pretty simple. We used an HDR sky map to provide some global illumination lighting and a sun lamp for the main directional lighting. We also added a large flat cube below the jet (out of shot on final image) and assigned a light-blue Emission material to it. This provides some lighting from below to mimic reflected light from the clouds. You can also try adding a bright-orange point light on the damaged wing, just where the smoke is supposed to be pouring out, to create an orange glow on that side of the jet.

17 RENDERING AND FINAL COMPOSITION

This final composite was completed in Photoshop. GIMP is preferred for painting textures, but Photoshop has flexible layer-management for making multilayered images. We rendered out each of the elements for the image as separate passes, while completing a small amount of compositing in Blender. We then opened all the passes as layers in Photoshop. At this point you can add aerial perspective (fading distant objects), as well as some extra motion blur. You can also tweak the colours of the various cloud and smoke layers.

CREATE REALISTIC OBJECTS

ZBRUSH

MAYA

MENTAL RAY

PHOTOSHOP

ACHIEVE REALISTIC TEXTURES, MATERIALS AND LIGHTING FOR A TASTY DIGITAL DISH

This tutorial will be divided into several sections; the first will look at gathering references and briefly discuss the modelling stages. Since the main drive of this guide is texturing and rendering, we will look at these in a little bit more detail before moving to the compositing stage.

One of the main challenges of this project was to ensure the right mood was captured for the scene. If you look at food photography, you will find that the camera focus plays a big role in close-up shots –

particularly in dreamy bright scenes where you have lots of light pouring in or light can be distinguished from other properties.

In terms of software, Maya was used for scene setup, ZBrush for sculpting, mental ray for rendering and Photoshop for texturing and postproduction. However, the ideas and workflow covered in this tutorial can also be applied to other packages.

Follow along and feel free to use the resources provided or your own in order to create photorealistic food.

BUILD A CONCEPT
FIND EXAMPLES TO INFORM YOUR WORK'S REALISM

01 GATHER REFERENCES
The first thing you always need to do is gather references for your work. Without them you are relying on your imagination. When it comes to creating something that is photorealistic, you need to have those references to ensure you capture everything correctly. The risk is always getting something wrong and because you are dealing with an object that people are used to seeing, the errors jump out immediately. Photorealism isn't a forgiving form!

03 START TO MODEL
The modelling stage is a pretty straightforward process. Hard surface objects are created in Maya whereas natural ones are sculpted in ZBrush. For the strawberry, you could create a few seed brushes in ZBrush, which are included on the disc. You can use these brushes to stamp seeds onto the surface of the strawberry on a different layer and they can save a lot of time.

02 SEARCH FOR DETAIL
Since we are trying to make the piece look as convincing as possible, it's useful to find a lot of fruit-related references. Try to observe any surface qualities you can find of strawberries, seed orientations, peaches, scatterings of light and so on. From there, roughly plan the pipeline.

LET THE LIGHTS IN
GET THE RIGHT TONALITY AND A SUITABLE MOOD

04 SET UP THE SCENE
Because this image was meant to be a stillframe, you don't need to make the most of the Decimation Master plug-in thanks to the help of a normal map. Nonetheless some objects, for example the cake sponge, only have both normal and displacement maps. In some conditions you may experience viewport slowdown after importing some high-res geometries. To overcome such issues you can always export high-res geometries as a MI (render assembly) file format and treat it as a render proxy.

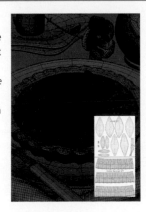

05 EDIT LIGHTING
Before you actually begin texturing models, create a temporary lighting setup to get the overall mood for the scene, because it renders faster and more efficiently. The first thing to manage is setting up the scene, meaning applying all the normal or displacement maps if applicable. All objects are given mia_material_X_ passes as no other shader can beat them in accurate behaviour. Try to keep the lighting setup on a separate render layer which has a grey material (mia_material) override in order to adjust lighting later more easily.

06 USE THE LINEAR WORKFLOW

After setting up the scene, don't overlook LWF (linear workflow). In recent versions of Maya there are LWF features but it's challenging to get them working the way they should. Assign a lens shader to the camera and a gammaCorrect node to any textures or colour swatches (RGB channels). Regarding shaders and lights, even blackbody or cie_d nodes produce RGB values rather than Kelvin Color Temperatures so they need to be gamma corrected if they're connected to the colour input of any node.

ADD TEXTURES
COMPLETE YOUR LIGHTING, MOVE TO MATERIALS AND SHADING

07 TURN ON THE LIGHTS

The scene has an IBL node with a suitable HDRI image for the environment and a blurred version of it for final gather. Base the camera angle upon the IBL node orientation in the scene. Create two key Area Lights in places where they can be regarded as light sources in the HDRI image. Match them with the light sources in the image, as with close-up positions where you have so much white reflection the viewer expects to see some diffuse contributions.

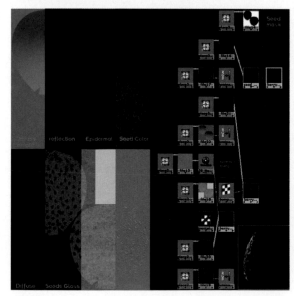

09 BEGIN TEXTURING AND SHADING

Most models were textured in Photoshop; the rest ZBrush. Maps prepared were mainly colour, gloss, reflection, bump and normal. For the strawberry, create a mask separating its seeds and later use it to separate the seed shader from the rest of it using the mix8.Layer shader (www.creativecrash.com/maya/downloads/shaders/c/mix8-layer-for-mentalray). So it consists of one shader for the flesh; one for seeds. The mia_material shader for the flesh had an SSS shader plugged into its additional colour.

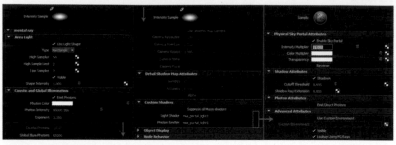

08 EDIT ENVIRONMENT EFFECTS

Portal lights are connected to Area Lights to focus FG rays. Don't check Custom Environment, so the program will sample the environment colour that the camera sees by default unless it's given a different environment look-up. These lights also emit photons, as it's a close-up interior shot, to provide even more decent light bounces.

10 CAKE SPONGE AND PEACHES

Many cake pieces had an SSS shader plugged in to make them more convincing. The cake sponge has epidermal and subdermal maps, dictating it to get more saturated and reddish the more light leaks inside. Each of the four types of peach slices around the centre has its own textures to add variations to the rendered image. Each peach slice has shell and flesh. Use mix8.Layer to separate the two. Both flesh and shell have their own SSS shader setup.

QUICK TIP
CREATE ADDITIONAL LAYER

To create the other layer of geometry around the peaches, combine all medium resolution peaches together and sculpt the layer in a way that it could represent a water shell around them. To handle objects that need some sort of surrounding, repeating pattern, use Radial Symmetry. Later when satisfied with the look add another layer and deform the object to suit the piece. This method usually saves a lot of headaches, not to mention time.

RENDER SETUP
FINALISE THE LOOK DEVELOPMENT AND RENDER

11 Add jam shading
Now to explore the jam shading. Jam is a refractive/ translucent type of material, so it lets light through but only to a certain extent. Activate Use Max Distance under Advanced Refractions and gave a darker red colour to gradually fall into the material. Also use translucency to make it seem more believable. In addition to jam shading, to obtain some variations in its dryness or wetness create a glossiness map and add it to the shader.

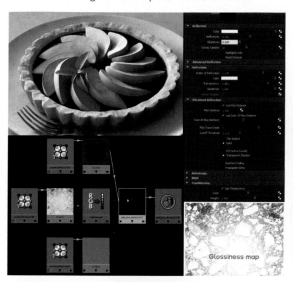

Glossiness map

12 Render pass options
To have maximum control over the look of the final image render it in passes in a single EXR file. Separate the SSS pass to front, middle and back to have maximum control over it. When you are trying to get a realistic 3D image, check the 32-bit Full Float output otherwise you will not be able to get nice burnt highlights in postproduction owing to the fact that hot spots in 8-bit or even 16-bit images can't be tweaked to bleed into another colour without crushing down the shadows.

Diffuse   Indirect   Composited SSS

Incandescence   Refraction   Reflection

Specular   AO   ID

13 Avoid shortcuts
You can achieve burnt highlights by either not following the LWF, with the help of lens shader (that doesn't grant you the freedom you have in post) or tweaking light and material attributes too much. As a result it's best to render out 32-bit images. We see those highlights in so many situations during our day, it's best to have them in our work as well. Simply play with the image levels and experiment.

QUICK TIP
OBSERVATIONS

It's necessary to observe objects in reality as much as you can and work from their surface properties for inspiration. Notice how dirt in different climates changes and where scratches occur on varying surfaces. This way you are able to extend your knowledge to create new stuff yet have it look convincing and real because it draws from genuine sources.

14 Begin post work
Having the passes, go to NUKE to do a simple composite because Photoshop is poor at handling 32-bit EXR files. After that send it to Photoshop to complete the final touches. You can bring the image to life in postproduction. Try to capture the desired mood as much as possible. This doesn't have a specific formula, just try anything that works for you, come back to it after a day, flip it and fix the flaws you find. The composited image is brought into Photoshop as an 8/16-bit image to be retouched further.

First Stage

Second Stage

Third Stage

Fourth Stage

CONTINUATION OF COMPOSITING IN PHOTOSHOP

Gradient is added here to intensify light!

15 Go to postproduction
The main jobs are sharpening, colour correcting, adding DOF with the help of a zDepth pass, placing some chromatic abberations, including grains, refining a few shapes, painting out a few flaws and so on. To intensify the light brightness that's coming from left, screen a gradient to the whole image.

CREATE AN EPIC LANDSCAPE

VUE

PHOTOSHOP

USE VUE TO PRODUCE AN EPIC LANDSCAPE OF AN OLD RUIN IN A NATURAL, PICTURESQUE ENVIRONMENT, AND THEN MAKE YOUR FINISHING TOUCHES IN PHOTOSHOP

SOURCE FILES ✓
AVAILABLE ON THE FREE DISC

The theme of this tutorial is based on a lush, rocky environment from a bird's-eye view, as you can see. The image depicts the discovery of forgotten places.

This tutorial will illustrate the key steps to building an epic landscape. From planning to rendering and post-production, you will learn all of the techniques used to create this piece. We'll describe how terrain is generated as well as how to set up multi-layer material distribution, achieve realistic lighting, optimise materials for greater believability and shorter render times.

Throughout the tutorial you'll notice that we'll be using commercial products to build the environment. Don't worry; the tutorial focuses on methods that can be applied to any kind of content you have in your library. For example, grass from AsileFX is a personal choice here, but Vue ships with several kinds of grasses you can use without having to purchase extra items. We'll focus on EcoSystem manipulation, atmosphere and lighting settings, render setups, optimisation, material tweaking and so on. All of this is important when it comes to building scenes in Vue, regardless of what content is used.

INITIAL STEPS, TERRAIN AND MATERIALS
SET THE FOUNDATIONS OF THIS LARGE-SCALE ENVIRONMENT

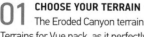

01 CHOOSE YOUR TERRAIN

The Eroded Canyon terrain was chosen from the (D&D Creations) Canyon Terrains for Vue pack, as it perfectly fits the scene (available online at **http://tinyurl. com/canyonvue**). This detailed terrain has a curvy riverbed and steep, highly eroded cliffs. The shape is based on a procedural terrain created in Vue using the terrain fractal with Canyon and Strata filters. The erosion was added using the World Machine 2 terrain generator (**www.world-machine.com**). You can find the terrain supplied with the disc. With the terrain loaded, find a spot with a cliff wall that looks iconic enough to be in focus with the ruins. You can then add the ruin components (a model purchased from **Renderosity.com**) next to the wall and adjust the camera angle to suit.

02 CONTROL MATERIAL DISTRIBUTION

The terrain has three layers of material: the riverbed is a wet, sandy area; the cliff walls are sandstone; the flat surfaces have a green, mossy material. Before loading, set the material distribution, and highlight the materials with different colours, so you can see and control the distribution. Set the terrain's material to Mixed Material: material 1 becomes the riverbed; material 2 becomes the rest of the terrain. Set Distribution dependent on Altitude (100%) only and set the Mixing Proportions to 72%.

03 ASSIGN YOUR PROPORTIONS

Select the second material and change it into a Mixed Material; its second material becomes the moss layer. This time the material distribution is dependent on Slope (100%) only. The Mixing proportions are set to 31%. After setting up the distribution, load materials: a darker sand from the RealSand pack, our own sandstone material (supplied) and Grass 'n' Rocks from Mark Lawson's Cliffhangers product. Find his products on Cornucopia3D: www.cornucopia3d.com/ purchase.php?item_id=11447.

ADD SOME VEGETATION
THE NEXT FEW STEPS WILL FOCUS ON ECOSYSTEMS MANIPULATION

04 ADD A MURKY RIVER
Let's quickly discuss some tricks for handling water in Vue. After loading water into the scene, tweak the material to make it look more like a river you'd find in a canyon. Check out some reference photos for examples of this, as there really is a distinction to be made. Try using a physical water model with a darker-brown Absorption colour and a light-brownish Scattering colour in order to help it fit the environment. The Depth where the light can reach in the water is set to 6.2 metres. Increase the Highlight Intensity to 84% and Highlight Size to 80%. To finish, change Highlighting to 81% Anisotropic.

05 OVERGROWN CLIFF
Set up the EcoSystem of the cliff in the middle. On the cliff wall (sandstone) use three layers of ground-covered EcoSystem: a layer of long grass from AsileFX Grasses (www.asilefx.net), a layer of hanging roots from AsileFX, plus a layer of small field-grass plants. Due to the scale of the terrain, even Dynamic Population isn't an option, so apply the EcoSystem Painter on the cliffs to distribute the foliage manually. Set the Direction to 100% Perpendicular and due to the steepness of the cliff enable 360-degree Population.

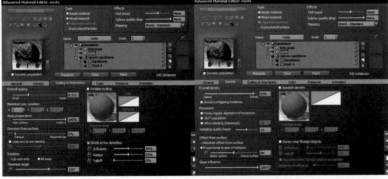

06 POPULATE THE RUINS
The goal of the grassy groundcover EcoSystem is to help the cliff and ruins blend together. This is an effective way to unify the whole scene and draw the viewer's eye around all of the details. On the ruins, make sure you use a similar EcoSystem: a layer of the same long grass plus a layer of hanging roots. The grass layer's direction from the surface is set to Perpendicular, while the roots are set to Vertical. The Density of the grass is set to 100%, while for the ruins it is set to 93%. Before populating, make sure that you set the Slope Influence to 100%.

07 INSERT BUSHES
Add the bushes layer to mossy material. In this EcoSystem use three shrubs from Xfrog (http://xfrog.com). To achieve realistic distribution, tick Variable Density and load the grainy fractal. To save resources, use Dynamic EcoSystem Population. On the leaves, set Highlight colour to white, increase Highlight Intensity and make it duller. In Effects, set Backlight to 100%. To speed up rendering reset the Bump map and disable Caustics.

LIGHTING AND ATMOSPHERE
TAKE A FEW STEPS TO SHED REALISTIC LIGHTING AND ATMOSPHERIC EFFECTS

08 GLOBAL RADIOSITY
Now it's time to add some atmosphere using the Light tab. The first step is to enable Global Radiosity, with Indirect Skylighting and Optimize for Outdoor Rendering ticked. Set a low Gain value of 0.4 and a very dark-greenish Bias colour (RGB 21, 25, 23). To get effective contrasts, set Light Balance towards Sunlight (90%). The ambient light comes entirely from the sky, providing a realistic and rich ambience.

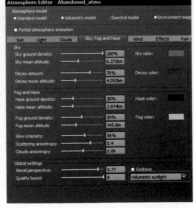

09 ATMOSPHERIC EFFECTS
In the Sky, Fog and Haze tab of the Atmosphere Editor, enable the Volumetric Sunlight option to achieve realistic lighting. With higher Haze (30%) and Fog (50%) levels generate subtle rays where the terrain blocks the sunlight. Set a dark Haze tone, as particles in our atmosphere are dark. The Glow Intensity is set to 56%, Scattering Anisotropy to 0.4 and Aerial Perspective value to 5.77 to give more depth to the scene. Finally, Quality Boost is set to +8 to avoid noise.

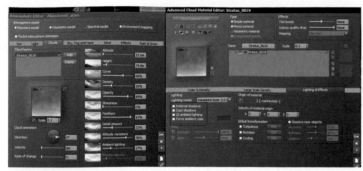

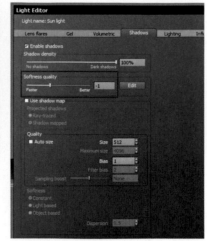

10 ADD SOME LOW FOG

Add a stratus cloud from AsileFX's Spectral v2 Clouds – Low Altitude pack. Set the Altitude to 27m and the Height to 75m. Increase the Detail amount and Altitude variations, and set Density to 29%. In the cloud's Material Editor set Volumetric colour to white.

11 PREPARE RENDER

After tweaking the atmosphere to a point where it can be considered ready, take steps to speed up the rendering process without any virtual quality loss. In the Atmosphere Editor reduce the Lighting Quality to -0.5, then open the cloud's Material Editor and in the Lighting & Effects tab disable all four options. In the Light Editor reduce the Shadows Softness Quality to -1.

RENDERING AND POST-PRODUCTION
WE CAN NOW TAKE OUR FINAL STEPS TO FINISH UP THE WORK

12 RENDER SETTINGS

After going through the usual optimisation steps – ensuring the lighting is how we want it and so on – the scene is ready to be rendered. In the Render Options select User Settings and disable Depth of Field, as this isn't something we need for this project. Set the Advanced Effects Quality to 40%. You may think this is low, but with the right atmospheric settings it's enough. Try your own way, too, and see what works.

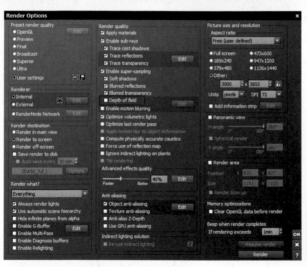

13 ANTI-ALIASING AND RENDERING

Since the scene needs to be rendered for print in a large resolution, use a soft Anti-Aliasing method, with Min 3 and Max 9 Subrays per pixel. With these settings we save a lot of detail and, due to the low Subray count, the rendering process is quicker. With these settings applied we don't need Texture Filtering, so disable it. The scene was rendered in a little less than 19 hours at a resolution of 3,000 x 3,800 pixels. A single machine was used with an i7-2600k CPU and 16GB DDR3 RAM.

14 POST-PRODUCTION

When a render is done, always load the image into Photoshop for a little post work. With this project we adjust the contrast, make the highlights more powerful with Levels adjustment layers and further enhance the image with Curves. To help the vegetation look more realistic, slightly saturate the green and yellow tones on the leaves.

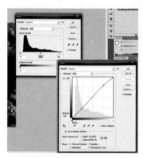

15 FILTER

Forge tweaks If you want to give a really nice boost to your renders, Filter Forge (www.filterforge.com) is a perfect choice. The Dreamy filter is a great one, because it provides more control over the highlights, contrast and colours. We don't want the highlights too strong in this project, because that way we'll lose details in the background. However, we still want to make the atmosphere more powerful to give a real impact and complement the piece. To do this, set Highlight Coverage to 9, Highlight Strength to 57, Highlight Radius to 100 and Dreamy Colors to 35. This gives a bit more contrast and vibrancy to the overall effect.

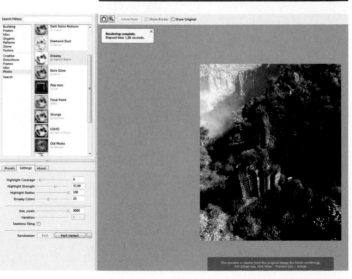

PHOTO EDITING

170

USE YOUR PHOTOGRAPHS
AS A BASE FOR YOUR
DIGITAL-ART PROJECTS
AND MAKE INCREDIBLE
CREATIVE EDITS

188

182

174

178

166

Original

TURN PHOTOS TO SKETCHES

GO A STEP FURTHER THAN BASIC FILTERS TO ACHIEVE AN IMPRESSIVE SKETCH EFFECT AND LEARN EFFECTIVE EDITING SKILLS ON THE WAY

Using sketch filters is a good place to start when trying to re-create a hand-drawn look in portraits, but with a few extra layers and a little bit of time you can create a really vivid and professional result. The style reflects a thick sketch, emphasising the hand-drawn, rough nature of a graphite pencil – a realism that will leave your friends wondering if you did actually draw it! Instead of spending years and years honing your drawing skills, getting high-quality paper and pencils

you will soon be creating digital art masterpieces effortlessly with new-found skills.

You could call it cheating, but it's better to think of it more like using your initiative. The main focus here will be on working with layer masks and using artistic license to manipulate the contours of the portrait, accentuating the shadows in a lovely two-toned digital painting. If you have a graphics tablet to hand then it will be invaluable, otherwise a mouse will work fine.

SKETCH OUT YOUR PHOTO
ADD LAYERS TO YOUR SKETCH FILTERS FOR IMPRESSIVE RESULTS

01 PREPARE YOUR PORTRAIT
Open 'model.jpg' in Photoshop and, using the Heal tool (J), neaten up your image – focus on things that you wouldn't include if you were drawing a portrait, like blemishes, scratches, dust, etc.

02 GET RID OF THE COLOUR
Duplicate the Background (Cmd/Ctrl+J) and desaturate (Cmd/Ctrl+Shift+U). For a better texture, hit Filters>Noise>Add Noise, set to Amount: 12%, Distribution: Gaussian, Monochromatic.

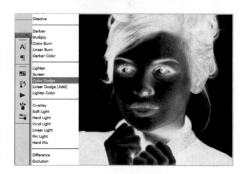

03 GET A HIGH-CONTRAST BASE
Duplicate your black and white layer by pressing Cmd/Ctrl+J and invert it by pressing Cmd/Ctrl+I. Set the blend mode to Color Dodge. Your canvas will go white, which is normal.

04 ADD GAUSSIAN BLUR
With the inverted layer selected, go to Filter> Gaussian Blur and set the Radius between 150-250px. Create a new group through the Folder icon an the bottom of your Layers palette called Base Image, and then drag these two layers into the group.

05 PREPARE FOR SKETCHING
Add a new layer by pressing Cmd/ Ctrl+Shift+N; call it Paper and drag it beneath your existing layers to stop any colour coming through. Now duplicate your original black and white layer then drag it to the top, outside the group. Call it Texture.

06 LOAD DRY MEDIA BRUSHES
Set the blend mode to Multiply and add a layer mask through Layer>Layer Mask>Hide All. Now select the Brush tool, expand the Brush Preset window and click on the arrow on the right-hand side of the panel. Select Dry Media Brushes.

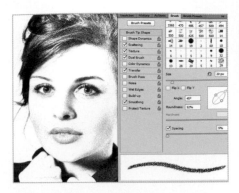

07 SETTING UP THE BRUSH

The brushes appear at the bottom of your Brush Preset Picker. Choose Small Pastel on Charcoal Paper and open the Brush palette. Drag the adjustment circle into an oval using the anchors on the sides to stretch, then rotate to a diagonal.

08 EXTRA BRUSH CONTROL

Select Shape Dynamics and set the Size Jitter to 100%, Angle Jitter to 2% and Minimum Diameter around 10-20%. All other settings can be left at their defaults. Elements users: just increase Spacing by 5%.

09 ADD IN THE DETAIL

Using your custom brush, paint just the main shadows on your Texture layer mask in white. Use varying opacities of 5-35% and alter your brush size using [and] to give it a more realistic hand-drawn look.

10 START WITH BASIC SHADOWS

Keep it simple for now. This layer is only the second layer to keep the Noise texture in the shading, so strokes here can be quite big and messy, focusing on larger areas. Midtones, highlights and shadows are to be added soon.

11 BOOST THE CONTRAST

To quickly increase the contrast, Ctrl/right-click and duplicate the Base Image group, then Ctrl/right-click on the copy and select Merge Group. Drag this layer to the top, set the blend mode to Overlay and the Opacity to 50%.

12 UTILISE GLOWING EDGES

Go back into your Base Image group and duplicate the black and white layer via Cmd/Ctrl+J. Drag it to the top and call it Brighter. Now go to Filter>Filter Gallery>Stylize>Glowing Edges, and set Edge Width: 1, Edge Brightness: 20, Smoothness: 7.

QUICK TIP
KEEP IT REAL – PAY ATTENTION TO DETAIL

Always bear in mind that your intention with this tutorial is to make your image appear to be genuinely hand-drawn. Don't neglect the 'paper' background, and be sure to add larger, softer tones to give the impression that the greys have been blended using smudges, or have been rubbed by hand while drawing. Also, the majority of people will tend to draw with strokes going diagonally from the top-right to the bottom-left – try to keep this consistency throughout the image by using only a few strokes that run in the opposite direction in order to emulate a realistic drawing style.

13 ADD IMPORTANT HIGHLIGHTS AND MIDTONES
Hit OK. Invert the Brightness layer by pressing Cmd/Ctrl+I and set the blend mode to Screen. Add a layer mask through Layer>Layer Mask>Hide All. Go back to the still-customised brush tool; begin to paint bright areas with a low-Opacity brush.

14 GET THE BALANCE
Remember that we are emulating a hand-drawn style. Effectively, this layer is the equivalent of using an eraser, or of not drawing at all. Avoid drawing bright lines in order to create shapes, and use the highlights simply to enhance the shadows.

15 REMOVE DETAIL FOR REALISM
To keep it looking like a drawing, remove the edges of the brightest side in order to make it fade into the paper. Select the Base Image group and then go to Layer>Layer Mask>Reveal All. Now all you need to do is draw in black at a low Opacity over some of the edges.

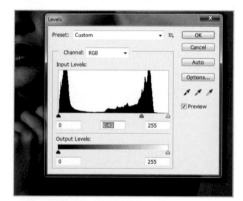

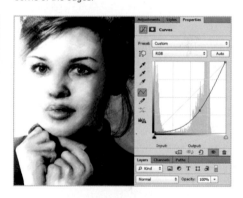

16 PREPARE FOR MAIN TONES
Duplicate the original colour layer and desaturate. Drag to the top and name it Smoother; this layer will be for the main tones without the Noise texture. Hit Cmd/Ctrl+L and make the Midtones darker.

17 ADD ESSENTIAL TONING
Add a Hide All Layer Mask to this layer, select the Brush tool (B) and begin to paint in white more details and shadows onto the image at a low Opacity. With this layer, concentrate on smaller, rougher strokes and focus on edges and features.

18 KEEP ADDING SHADOWS
Spend a bit of time getting the texture and look right on this layer. Then, you can add even more shadows using a Curves adjustment layer (by dragging the centre of the curve down) and also the same layer mask technique. Imagine yourself actually shading the photo.

QUICK TIP
ROUGH IT UP, NEAT, PERFECT STROKES LEAD TO IMPERFECT IMAGES

Be careful to avoid harsh edges within the image; these will give it away as a photograph. Instead, be sure to utilise the manual black and white strokes to give the impression that the edges have been hand-drawn – so keep it slightly shaky, imperfect and a bit more tonal. Don't forget to zoom in while doing details like this: what might look good at 20% may look very amateurish at 100%. Hold the Spacebar to move around the image while working.

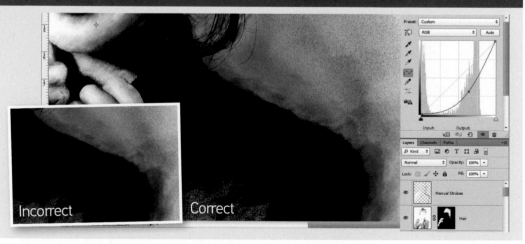

Original

MAKE ART WITH LAYERS

HARNESS THE REAL POWER OF LAYER MASKS TO TURN YOUR PHOTO INTO A COMPELLING IMAGE

Eye-catching images can be created from almost any photo with the right use of layer blend modes, brushes, shapes, stock photos and lighting effects.

In Photoshop, an image can be altered with new layers, where each layer adds a special effect. Each new layer is a separate image that can have an effect on all the previous layers, like an acetate sheet, so you can gradually build up an increasingly pleasing image one change at time, one layer at a time. For example, you can add shapes to the background to create a bespoke feel for your image and then, in a subsequent layer, you can change the colour of your shapes to match, contrast or complement your image, as you prefer.

The following tutorial will show you how to create special effects, and once you have learned the techniques you can let your imagination run wild. You can play and experiment with boring stock photos and turn them into stunning artwork.

Download the supplied resources from your disc to re-create this yourself – we've included all the images and brushes you'll need, as well as a special cosmic lights pack courtesy of www.psdbox.com.

CREATING THE EFFECT
GO A STEP FURTHER WITH YOUR OWN ADDED IMAGES AND ELEMENTS

Make this piece unique with your own added images. We tried flowers and beach scenes using layer masks to cut and position them. Place new images on separate layers with the blend mode set to Overlay and varying opacities. Add texture for interest and a Levels adjustment for a warm magenta hue. For a final touch, duplicate all layers and merge them into one. Apply a Halftone Pattern filter to that filter with blue as the Foreground colour and magenta as the Background. Again, use a layer mask to erase areas to suit, adjusting the opacity as you go.

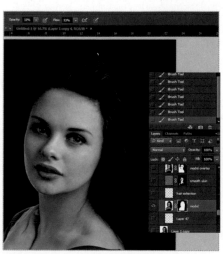

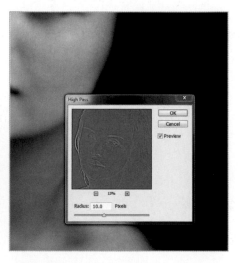

01 CUT THE MODEL OUT
Place the model on top of 'background.jpg'. Go to Select>Color Range, use the '+' Eyedropper tool and click OK. You can use Magic Wand tool (A) in Photoshop Elements. Now go to Layer>Layer Mask> Hide Selection. You will see that the background has disappeared. That is how you create a layer mask.

02 REFINE THE MASK
Use a black soft-edged brush set at 30% Opacity and with Flow set at 50% to erase the unwanted remnant of hair that are still visible in the background. Set the brush's Size to 200px for the best effect.

03 RETOUCH THE MODEL
Go to Layer>Duplicate Layer, click on the layer mask, hit Cmd/Ctrl+I and set the blend mode to Vivid Light. Go to Filter>Other>High Pass and set Radius to 10. Select Filter>Blur>Gaussian Blur, set Radius to 2, then mask out the eyes, lips and hair.

04 DESATURATE THE IMAGE

Hit Cmd/Ctrl+Opt/Alt+Shift +E to duplicate the entire image, then Cmd/Ctrl+U to bring up Hue/ Saturation. Set Saturation to -100, set the blend mode to Soft Light and the Opacity to 72%. Go to Layer>Layer Mask>Reveal All. Now brush out the hair, eyes and lips with a soft black brush.

05 INTRODUCE SOME SHADOWS AND HIGHLIGHTS

Go to Layer>New>Layer, hit Shift+F5 to bring up the Fill dialog, select 50% grey and apply. Set the Overlay blend mode and paint some shadow with a soft black brush at 200px and 5% Opacity. Use a white brush at 70px and 5% Opacity for highlights.

06 ENHANCE THE EYES

Add a new layer and brush in any colour you like for the eye make-up. Set the blend mode to Color with an Opacity of 50%. Go to Layer>New Adjustment Layer>Curves, click and hold on the line and then drag it up to Input: 81, Output: 160.

07 REFINE YOUR EDITS

Click on the mask and then hit Cmd/Ctrl+I to invert the mask to black. Paint onto the eye area with a soft-edged brush to bring the Curves effect back in. Reduce the layer's Opacity if necessary to get a better, more natural result.

08 LIGHTEN THE HAIR

Import the 'light.jpg' image and set the blend mode to Screen. Go to Edit>Transform> Warp and warp the layer into the desired shape, then hit Return. Place the warped light onto the model's hair, then hit Cmd/Ctrl+U and play with the Hue slider to change the colour. Try to add more variation.

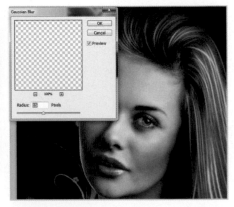

09 INCLUDE SOME SWIRLS

Download some custom brushes; http:// aka-joe.deviantart.com has some great ones. Use one on a new layer, then transform your swirls and place where desired. Duplicate the layer, add a Gaussian Blur and set Radius to 10 for a nice glow.

10 GRAPHIC SHAPE

Create a new layer underneath the hair light layers and trace the model's clothes using the Polygonal Lasso tool (L). Fill this with white and go to Layer>Layer Mask>Reveal Selection. Now remove the part where the arm was supposed to be, using a soft-edged brush at 30% Opacity.

11 USE MORE GRADIENTS

Duplicate the layer and go to Select>Load Selection to create a selection marquee. Choose black from the Swatches palette, Radial Gradient from the Gradient palette and set Opacity to 30%. Now click and drag from right to left.

12 RED SHAPE

Make another shape in a new layer and fill it with red. Set this to 44% Opacity, then mask out the arm area and paint the right side of the arm with a soft black brush set to 20% Opacity to soften it. Now duplicate the layer and set the blend mode to Vivid Light.

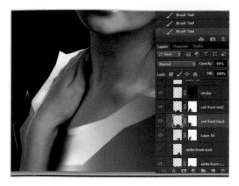

13 APPLY A WHITE STROKE
Duplicate the layer, go to Select>Load Selection. Now go to Edit>Stroke. Set the Width to 11px, Color to White and Location to Inside. Change the blend mode to Screen, create a layer mask and then mask out the unwanted area.

14 INCLUDE MORE GRAPHICS
Experiment with different shapes and place them behind the model. Don't limit yourself to just the blend modes mentioned so far – explore the whole range. Also experiment with masks, lightly brushing out areas so the image doesn't look flat.

15 TURN UP THE LIGHTS
Go back to the top layer and create a new layer. Paint a subtle white glow using the Radial Gradient tool (G) with 20% Opacity. Choose White to Transparent and then put the glow at the bottom of the canvas.

16 INJECT SOME SPARKLE
Make a new layer, load the supplied Sparkle brush and paint in some sparkles. Change the Size of the brush for each sparkle to simulate the random, visual nature of sparkles. Scatter these sparkles around the canvas.

17 GET A COLOURFUL BACKGROUND
Create a new layer and grab a soft brush with 30% Opacity. Pick the colour you want to use and then paint where you like; we used magenta, white and yellow. Bring the layer's Opacity down to 54%, then click and hold it to drag it down and place it above the background layer.

18 USE MORE COLOUR
Now repeat Step 17, this time placing the new layer below the white lights layer created in Step 15. Paint in magenta and yellow, and then change the blend mode to Color. You can add several different layers to build colour depth, if desired.

19 INSERT LIGHT STREAKS
Import 'color-spectrum.jpg' to the top layer and change its blend mode to Screen. Place the image in the top-right corner, then duplicate the layer and place that somewhere else. Vary the size to avoid uniformity, and also include further streaks and place them around the canvas.

21 ADD A HIGH PASS FILTER
After adjusting the brightness to suit, duplicate the entire image to a new layer, by clicking on topmost layer. Hit Cmd/Ctrl+Opt/Alt+Shift+E, go to Filter>Other>High Pass and set Radius to 2.8. Set the blend mode to Soft Light to sharpen the image.

22 MORE CONTRAST
Hit Cmd/Ctrl+Opt/Alt+Shift+E to duplicate the entire image to a new layer one more time, as in the previous step, but this time don't use High Pass. Instead, change the blend mode to Soft Light and then set the Opacity to 30%... and you're done!

COMPOSE TEXTURED PORTRAITS

PHOTOSHOP

SOURCE FILES ✓
AVAILABLE ON THE FREE DISC

CREATE A FUN, COLOURFUL IMAGE USING ONLY TWO PHOTOS AND A HOST OF FILTERS, BLEND MODES AND MASKS

Starting with a few photos, we can come up with a lively, textured piece of artwork by utilising Photoshop's filters and tools.

Using a dandelion as a backdrop, we'll introduce a model photo and go bonkers with filters. The Texture filters will enable us to introduce roughness and depth without the need for texture photos. We'll use blend modes and layer masks to mix each filtered reinvention of the original photos with the evolving composite.

You will see the incredible value of merging layers together as a flattened stamp, in order to apply overall sharpening and to fill in some decorative circles as a final touch. After completing the tutorial, you may want to try it again with your own photos – just use the steps and filter values as a rough guide, and check out the alternate image we came up with for further ideas. Experiment with other effects and filters. Your only obligation is to stick with the 'two photo' restriction.

Any users of Photoshop versions lacking Smart Objects are able to simply apply filters directly to layers instead. In addition to this, Vibrance can be replaced with Hue/Saturation, if needed. With Photoshop's tools as faithful allies, though, you are bound to surprise yourself with what you can achieve.

INJECT SOME FUN INTO YOUR PORTRAITS
MAKE THE MOST OF FILTERS, BLEND MODES AND MASKS

01 DANDELION DROP
Open the supplied 'Dandelion.jpg'. To vary our colours, let's punch out a transparent hole. Add a layer mask via the Layers palette icon. Use a soft, round brush at 80% Opacity to paint out over to the right.

02 MOSAIC TILES FILTER
File>Place the supplied 'Model.jpg'. Go to Filter>Texture>Mosaic Tiles. Set Tile Size: 52, Grout Width: 7 and Lighten Grout: 7. Add a layer mask, paint a little black in the bottom right and set to Vivid Light.

03 FACIAL RESTORATION
Duplicate the Model layer via Cmd/Ctrl+J. Drag the layer's Smart Filter to the Trash. Fill the mask with black to hide everything, switch your Foreground to white, then paint to reveal the unaltered face.

04 EERIE COLOURS
In the Layers palette, hit the Create New Fill/ Adjustment Layer button and choose Solid Color. Input #c4ac81, set the blend mode to Difference and drop the Opacity to 90%. It's an interesting effect, but the image is now a tad dismal. We'll correct it.

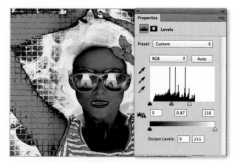

05 LIGHTEN UP
Add a Levels adjustment layer using the same button in the Layers palette. Drag the Midtone and Highlight sliders to the left to brighten the image. Notice we still need to restore the skin tone and lighten colours from the original photo.

06 RESTORE LIGHTER COLOUR
Opt/Alt-click and drag the Model layer above the Levels adjustment layer. Now Ctrl/ right-click on its mask and choose Delete Layer Mask. Set the blend mode to Lighter Color.

07 A BIT OF COOL
Duplicate the layer again with Cmd/Ctrl+J. Set the blend mode to Hue to add some cool colouring. Add a layer mask, switch the Foreground colour to black, then paint out areas surrounding the model.

08 STAINED GLASS FILTER
Duplicate the layer once more then set its blend mode to Color Burn and Opacity to 80%. Go to Filter>Texture>Stained Glass. Set Cell Size: 19, Border Thickness: 4 and Light Intensity: 3. Click OK and paint black onto a new mask at the top, reducing the impact in areas.

09 EVEN MORE BURN
Duplicate the layer, bump the Opacity back up to 100% and then fill the mask with black. After that, set your Foreground colour to white and then lightly paint some of the central area back into the image.

10 MERGE LAYERS
Press Cmd/Ctrl+Opt/Alt+Shift+E in order to create a merged copy, then Ctrl/right-click and choose Convert to Smart Object. Next, go to Filter>Texture>Stained Glass. Set Cell Size: 19, Border Thickness: 4 and Light Intensity: 3, and then set it to Hard Light.

11 DUPLICATE AND BLEND
Duplicate the layer and drag the Smart Filter to the Trash. Set the blend mode to Multiply and layer Opacity to 50%. Now paint with black onto the mask to reduce some of the darkened areas.

12 LOOKING SHARP!
Merge your layers again and convert to a Smart Object. Now apply Filter>Sharpen>Unsharp Mask. Set the Amount to 80% and the Radius to 5.5px. Click OK and, with a black brush, paint over any areas that you don't want sharpened.

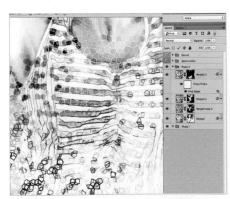

13 ADD AN ILLUSTRATIVE TOUCH
Merge your layers and convert to a Smart Object again. This time, head over to Filter>Stylize>Find Edges. Now add a layer mask, fill it with black, then paint over some of the areas with white at 80-100% Opacity in order to add some illustrative flair to your growing mosaic artwork.

14 VIBRANCE CONTROL
Pick Vibrance from the Adjustment layer list in the Layers palette. Drop Vibrance to -50. Paint black in the mask to restore some colour. Add another Vibrance adjustment, this time with Vibrance: 30 and Saturation: 20, then tweak with the mask.

15 CIRCLING SHAPES
Merge and convert to a Smart Object, then tick the eye icon to hide the layer. On a new layer, use the Ellipse tool (set to Shape in the Options bar) to create a circle, holding Shift as you drag. Add a slight Drop Shadow via Layer>Layer Style.

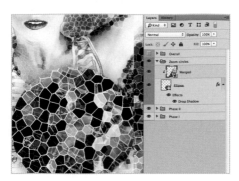

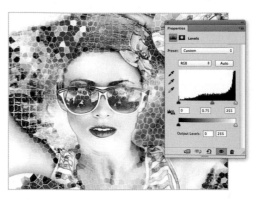

16 ZOOM EFFECT

Turn the visibility back on for the merged layer. Opt/Alt-click between the circle and merged layers to clip them. Use Free Transform (Cmd/Ctrl+T) in order to scale and position the merged layer. Enlarge and zoom in on an interesting area of the effect.

17 THREE'S COMPANY

Now create two more circles of differing sizes. Apply Drop Shadows. Duplicate the merged layer twice, then position and clip with the other two circles. Free Transform the merged layers to scale and rotate, or even try warping them.

18 LEVELS TO FINISH

We'll finalise with a Levels adjustment. Use the sliders to fine-tune contrast, then paint black on the adjustment's mask over areas that don't benefit from the adjustment. You can even add another Levels adjustment for extra tonal control.

QUICK TIP
VARY SHAPES AND COLOUR SETTINGS FOR A MORE SUBTLE RESULT

This tutorial is just one of many possibilities. Every step can be modified, replaced or discarded – it's all up to you! Here we have used the same model and tried a lighter approach. The Mosaic Tiles and Stained Glass filters were used, but with different settings. As a counterpoint to the inverted triangle (formed by the model's arms), we have created some upward-pointing triangles, with a few of them facing down for variation.

Go ahead and use the same photograph (or your own) to create a new outcome. Use the Texture filters or try some from other categories, such as Artistic and Stylize. When it is time to blend layers, cycle through the various blend modes (Shift and +/-) until you get the right mix.

Experiment
By means of trial and error, you can edit the settings at the Mosaic Tiles stage to achieve a lighter outcome

Retro shapes
Vary the shapes for a different effect and copy/paste your main image for a 'magnifying glass' result

Keep it themed
Replicate shapes to continue the theme throughout and use similarly-toned colours to highlight them

Photo editing

Create a panorama
Our first steps are to use Photomerge to seamlessly stitch images into a panorama. The result is then cropped and tidied up before any visual effects are then added

Original

New skyline
The original sky isn't dramatic enough, so we bring in a new one and blend it into the scene using layer masks

SOURCE FILES ✓
AVAILABLE ON THE FREE DISC

PHOTOSHOP

MAKE STUNNING PANORAMAS

TURN SO-SO CITY SCENES INTO ATMOSPHERIC ENVIRONMENTS USING FILTERS, ADJUSTMENT LAYERS AND SOME NIFTY TRICKS

Panoramic images are dramatic in their own right. However, sometimes they are crying out for a bit more atmosphere. Here we will show how you can get creative with panoramas.

First, we will look at creating a panoramic using Photomerge. We have provided you with the start images, but you can skip this step as we have also supplied the ready-made panorama. Once the image is stitched together, we neaten it up by filling in any holes left by the Photomerge process.

When the groundwork is done, effects can be added. We are going to replace the sky using layer masks. We are then going to darken the rest of the image so it all fits in. From here, we can paint in a little light to shine through the dark. We finish with a little weather – some mist and rain to set it all off.

Rain and mist
As a final step we add some rain using filters, and mist using a soft brush in order to help bring the image together

Remove unwanted objects
Our original image has a lamppost running right down the middle, so we use the Content Aware Fill and Clone Stamp options to remove it

Moody effects and toning
We darken the image before adding a blue tint to go from day to night, before bringing some light back into the streetlamps

STRETCH YOUR SHOTS
TAKE YOUR LANDSCAPE IMAGES AND MAKE THEM MORE ATMOSPHERIC

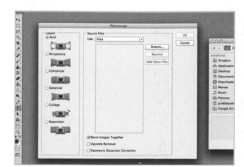

01 CREATE THE PANORAMIC
Collect the images for the panoramic. Go to File>Automate>Photomerge (in Elements it's Enhance>Photomerge>Photomerge Panorama). Then you just need to hit Browse under Source Files, choose the panoramic images, select Auto and then OK.

02 TIDY THE PANORAMIC
Photoshop will create a panorama. Grab the Crop tool to remove the blank areas at the edges. For the remaining blank areas, select with the Magic Wand tool, then use Edit>Fill>Content Aware.

03 THE ELEMENTS METHOD
In Elements, once Photomerge has finished, you will be asked if you want to automatically fill in the blank areas. This does the same job as Content Aware in Photoshop. Select Yes and then crop out the required composition.

If you want to try this on your own photos, you will need a tripod or level surface. Set your camera up at one edge of your scene and take the first photo. Move it along a bit, overlapping with the first photo's edge, and take the next. Continue until you have a minimum of three images (but more is better) taking in the whole of the scene that you want to capture. The overlap is very important, as this will help Photoshop figure out how the images should be stitched together.

04 TIDY UP THE IMAGE
To remove unwanted objects, duplicate the Background layer. Select the whole of the lamppost using your favourite selection tool. We used the Pen tool, but you can get pretty good results with the Magic Wand. Next go to Edit>Fill>Content Aware.

05 REFINE THE REMOVAL
Content Aware Fill does a decent job (also see the Remove Objects in Elements boxout). Select the Clone Stamp and zoom in. Use Opt/Alt-click to select a source area and clone away imperfections.

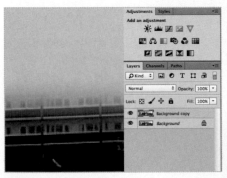

06 AND REPEAT...
It takes quite a bit of time to achieve a good result. Once the lamppost is removed, do the same on any other unwanted object. We are getting rid of the A-board in the bottom-left corner and one of the uglier buildings.

07 SELECT THE SKY
Duplicate the Background copy layer and use the Magic Wand tool to select as much of the sky as possible. Adapt the Tolerance value to suit. Go to Select>Inverse and hit the Add Layer Mask button at the bottom of the Layers palette.

08 BRING IN A NEW SKY
Open the sky image. Copy and paste it into the panorama and place it underneath the layer with the mask. Align to the right. Paste the sky in a second time, but rotate it 180 degrees and place it on the left-hand side to fill the whole sky.

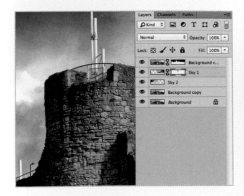

09 BLEND THE SKY
Add a layer mask to the top sky layer, then select a 50% Opacity brush with black paint. Carefully paint over the join of the two sky layers to blend them together. Now, go back to the top Background layer and select the layer mask there.

10 MORE SKY WORK
Set the black brush back to 100% Opacity. Zoom right into the sky line, and then paint on the mask where the original sky shows through to help blend in the new sky perfectly. This will take a bit of time to get right.

11 ADD SOME ATMOSPHERE
The rest of the image is too bright now. Hold down Cmd/Ctrl and then simply click on the layer mask on the top Background layer to create a selection of everything bar the sky. Add a Levels adjustment layer.

12 CONTROL THE LEVELS
Take the left-hand Levels control and pull it to the right to darken the shadows in the image. Do the same with the middle control to darken the midtones. You can go for any value you like; ours is 74, 0.76, 255 for the values from left to right.

13 TONE THE IMAGE
Give the image a slight blue tone to make it more dramatic. Add a Hue/Saturation adjustment layer at the top of the layers. Tick Colorize and make Hue: 201 and Saturation: 37. Change the Opacity of the layer to 55%.

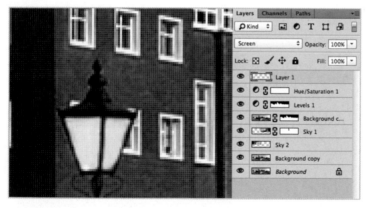

14 TURN ON THE LIGHTS
Add a new blank layer, setting its blending mode to Screen and Opacity to 80%. Select a small, soft-edged brush and choose an orange/yellow shade. Zoom in on the lamppost to the right of the church, and carefully paint into the glass.

15 DODGE THE LIGHT
Create a merged layer at the top of the stack (Cmd/Ctrl+Opt/Alt+Shift+E). Select the Dodge tool, set to Highlights and 50% Exposure. Paint over your streetlights and areas that would be hit by the light.

16 LET IT RAIN
Add a new layer and fill with black. Go to Filter>Noise>Add Noise, tick Monochromatic and add a lot of noise (250). Use Levels to emphasise tone, then apply Filter>Blur>Motion Blur to get the rain effect, changing the Angle to around -50%.

17 FINAL MIST
Set the Rain layer to Screen and lower the opacity. Create one last blank layer and select a large soft brush filled with white set to 20% Opacity. Paint in some mist along the bottom of the image and change the layer blending mode to Overlay.

QUICK TIP
REMOVE OBJECTS IN ELEMENTS

Photoshop Elements does have some Content Aware features, but it doesn't yet have the option to fill an area with the technology at your request. Therefore, when it comes to removing objects from the panoramic, you will need to try other methods. The most accurate is to simply use the Clone Stamp tool very methodically. However, you can get a good start with the Healing Brush tool which fills the area using information from a source point. It's not perfect, especially on bigger objects, but used in conjunction with the Clone Stamp tool, you can get decent results.

CREATE MATTE ARTWORK

CREATE REALISTIC DIGITAL MATTE ARTWORK USING PHOTOGRAPHIC REFERENCES AND DIGITAL PAINTING

PHOTOSHOP

SOURCE FILES ✓
WWW.SXC.HU
WWW.CGTEXTURES.COM

Digital matte painting is achieved by combining digital painting with photography to achieve photorealism. Today, this process is widely used within the film industry to create fantasy settings or landscapes which would otherwise be impossible to shoot. In this tutorial, you will learn how to edit, manipulate and paint over photographic imagery and tailor them to a specific need in order to create your own fantasy matte painting.

Once this has been completed, you will have a better understanding of how to use and manipulate photographs to your advantage in several different ways, and how to combine them with digital painting techniques to get the most out every piece. Achieving photorealism does not happen overnight, so use this information as a starting point to build upon. Once a firm grasp has been made, there are little to no limits as to what can be done with these techniques.

This tutorial will require some prior knowledge of layer masks and how to apply them via selection, quick masks and painting and erasing. Other knowledge includes colour grading and correcting, clipping masks, basic brush and toolbar settings, Transform tools, and some usage of the Clone Stamp tool.

Photo editing

REALISTIC EDITING TECHNIQUES
DISCOVER HOW TO CREATE MATTE ARTWORK THAT LOOKS BELIEVABLE

01 SETTING UP
The first thing that needs to be done is to create a new document and place the photographic plate. Go to File>New and set the image size to 3000 x 1136px. Download image ID 1252246 from **www.sxc.hu** and place it into the scene. Use the Transform tools to adjust and tilt the layer. Name the layer 'Plate'.

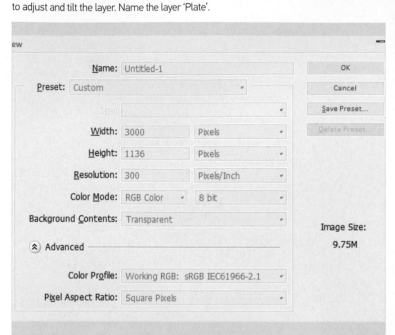

02 THE PLATE
Now to paint over parts of the layer that aren't needed. Select a soft round brush and with a dark green colour (not too saturated), paint over the water portion of the plate. Create a new layer and place it under the Plate layer. Use the Eyedropper tool to select a dark blue colour from the sky and using the Brush tool, paint in a small portion of the sky. Merge this layer with the Plate layer.

> The goal is to create realism, but going too far or too short will break that. Giving an even balance to everything is absolutely essential

03 REPLACING THE SKY
Now it's time to import the new sky. Since the old one is dull and doesn't tailor to the scene's needs, it needs to be replaced with one that is able to fill the void. Go to **www.cgtextures.com** and download image ID 35830, then place it into the scene as seen in the example image. Depending on its size, it might need to be scaled down. Use the Transformation tools (Ctrl/Cmd+T) to adjust the scaling and tilt.

QUICK TIP
LET YOUR PHOTOS DO THE WORK

It's tempting to paint as much as you can, but unless you're working in a high resolution, the best way to obtain photorealism is to let the photographs do most of the work. As your painting skills increase, so too will your knowledge of how to use those references.

04 PLACING EXTRA CLOUDS
Download the additional cloud image from **www.sxc.hu/profile/ukunurk** (the large cloud is in the centre, while the smaller one is on the left). Extract and paste them into the scene file. Scale and place them as shown in the image. Select the Brush tool and a nice cloudy brush, then paint dark and light tones on the larger cloud to create a more dramatic effect. The entire cloud does not need to be painted, so only paint as much as is necessary, as shown above.

05 BUILDING THE BASE

Now start building up the base where the main mountain will be. Take the Brush tool and a good tree-shaped brush (with some Scatter) and paint a mountain similar to the example image. Colour doesn't matter, as you'll be overlaying it with texture later. At this point it's a good idea to map out how the light will hit the mountain, which will be useful when texturing later on. Paint lighter tones to simulate where light will be.

07 LIGHTING THE MOUNTAIN

Grab the Brush tool and select a tree-shaped brush or something equivalent. Change the colour to a light yellow (not too saturated) and begin painting in the highlights on the mountain. Pay attention to where the sun is coming from in the base plate: right to left. If needed, lower the opacity and fill of the brush. This will lower the density of the brush stroke to allow a slower build up and make painting more forgiving and natural.

08 BUILDING THE BACKGROUND

There are several different ways to create the mountain shapes. One is to create a selection and fill it with a colour, and another is to use the Brush tool and paint it. Use whatever is most comfortable. The goal is to create realism, but going too far or too short will break that. Giving an even balance to everything is essential. Download image ID 78057 from **www.cgtextures.com** and paste it into the scene. Clip it to the base layer and position and scale it as needed. Create a new layer, clip it and paint highlights and shadows onto the mountains.

06 TEXTURING THE MOUNTAIN

Search for images 1273649 and 1252247 on **sxc.hu**. Extract and paste them into the scene. Using the Transformation tools, set them into place as you see in the example. Use the Clone Stamp tool and begin cloning parts of the textures to cover the painted areas. Make certain that there are no repeating patterns. Clone parts of the tree texture over to the front of the mountain to make it match the example. If necessary, paint extra detail into the rock to make it look more rigid.

09 ADDING WATERFALLS

Download image 1337592 from **sxc.hu** and paste it into the scene. Use the Transformation tools to adjust and tilt the image appropriately. Use a layer mask to hide the top, bottom and side areas. With the Brush tool and a dark cool blue, paint a shadow on the top half of the waterfall, just above the rocks. This will act as the cast shadow from the castle. On the lower half, paint in the remaining highlights and shadows. Remember what direction the sunlight is coming from. The other waterfalls were painted with a chalk brush.

11 ADDING TEXTURE

Go to CGTextures and search for image ID 82231. Click on the image and choose any of the ones that appear. Then repeat for ID 82144 and choose the image on the far right. Extract and paste them into the scene. Place them above the FG mtn base layer you just created and clip them to the layer. The textures will now only appear where the base layer is. Position the textures into place and use the Transformation tools if needed. Unclip the layers from the base if there is difficulty positioning them, and then re-clip them. The goal here is get as much balance between rock and grass as possible.

10 CREATING FOREGROUND MOUNTAINS

Much like in the background, you can create the foreground mountains by making a selection and filling that with a colour, painting, or any other method. The main idea behind these mountains is to lead the viewer's eye up towards the castle (main focal point). By pointing them upwards, it would create an implied line that leads to this focal point. Once the mountain bases are created, they will be used as a clipping mask for the textures. Name this layer 'FG mtn base'.

Paint along the edge where the light meets the shadow to create a crisp line

Use multiple dark colours to paint extra cracks in the mountain rock

Colour pick from the texture and adjust it to a lighter tone for the highlights

The edges should not be too bright or the mountain will appear flat

12 PAINTING AND LIGHTING

Use the Eyedropper to grab a selection of grass and stone colours from the texture and store them in the Swatches tab. Get your brush and use these colours to paint extra grass and rock to create added detail. Once done, create a new layer and clip it to the base layer. Get a light yellow-orange colour (not too saturated) and paint highlights onto the front side of the mountains. Paint shadows using a dark blue colour on the other side so that they don't appear flat.

QUICK TIP
USE LAYER MASKS

Layer masks are a great way to edit non-destructively. They can hide and show parts of a layer at any time due to the contents of the layer itself never being erased, but only hidden. If needed, they can always be merged with the layer to lower the file size.

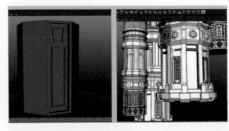

13 PLACING THE TREES

Download the trees 35864 from CGTextures and 841073 from **www.sxc.hu**. Extract and paste them into the scene. Go to Layer>Matting>Defringe, set it to 2px and hit OK. Use the Transformation tools to scale and position them according to the example image. Create two new layers, set them to Overlay and clip each to their respective tree layer. Grab the Brush tool and with a light yellow-orange colour, lightly paint in highlights on the trees. With a dark cool blue, paint shadows on a separate layer (set to Normal blending mode).

14 CREATING THE CASTLE

The 3D model of the castle was created in Autodesk Maya. It was box-modelled from a cylinder and primarily extruded and bevelled to give the desired look and feel. Other objects were created from spheres and spline elements. Texturing consisted of Substance materials within Maya and rendered with V-Ray. Before rendering, the main castle was duplicated, scaled, rotated and reordered several times to create a denser look for the final matte painting.

15 IMPORTING THE CASTLE

Once the castle has been created either by 3D modelling or piecing together photographic references, paste it into the scene and make it a group if it contains multiple layers. Adjust its position and tilt using the Transform tools. Create a layer mask for the castle layer. Select the Brush tool and with the colour black, paint near the bottom of the castle to hide this part. Be sure to paint on the layer mask and not the layer itself. Use tree-shaped brushes if possible for added detail.

16 LIGHTING THE CASTLE

Even though the castle itself has been previously lit, it could still benefit from some dramatic lighting and increased intensity. With the Brush tool, a soft round brush and a dark cool blue, lightly paint a shadow at the top of the castle. This will decrease the focus brought to this area and increase the focal point. Next, pick a light yellow-orange (not too saturated). Create a new layer and set it to Overlay/Soft Light. Now lightly paint in stronger highlights on the castle to simulate harsh sunlight. If needed, paint additional shadows on the other sides.

17 CONSTRUCTING THE ARCH

Use the Elliptical Shape tool to draw a circle. Copy it, make the duplicate smaller and place it in the centre of the larger circle. Cmd/Ctrl-click on the smaller circle to make a selection and delete it from the larger circle. Delete the small circle and the lower half of the original. Duplicate it, scale it down and place it under the arch. Set its Opacity at 70%. Group these together and position them in between the background mountains.

18 ADDING THE TEXTURE

Download **http://farm3.staticflickr.com/228 2/2179154776_65a486debe_o.jpg**, clip it to the arch base layer and set it to Overlay. Set Opacity at 70%. Hit Cmd/Ctrl+T to activate the Transform tools. Ctrl/right-click and select Warp. Now adjust the texture to the shape of the arch. Hit Enter to apply the warp. With the texture adjusted, feel free to erase the remainder of it that is not being used. If needed, desaturate the texture by hitting Cmd/Ctrl+Shift+U.

19 LIGHTING AND EXTRAS

Create a new layer above the arch group and clip it to it. Select a soft round brush at about 200-400px and change its colour to a light yellow (not too saturated). Lightly paint a highlight near the middle of the arch to simulate the sun lighting it. The triangle was achieved by painting with a hard brush. Inner Shadow, Drop Shadow and Inner Glow were used as layer styles to create the outer bevels.

> " The main castle was duplicated, scaled, rotated and reordered several times to create a denser look "

20 FINISHING DETAIL

Like the Arch, use the Elliptical Shape tool and draw out a circle. This will be the rainbow. Copy it, make the duplicate smaller and place it in the centre of the larger circle. Cmd/Ctrl-click on the smaller circle to make a selection and delete this portion from the larger circle. Now apply a Rainbow Gradient Layer Style to the larger circle and Gaussian Blur it 10-40px. For the low-lying clouds, select the Brush tool and get a soft cloud-shaped brush. Using real clouds as a reference, paint them along the bottoms of the mountains.

21 COLOUR GRADING

Go to 'Photo Filter', change the colour to a greenish cyan and set the Density at 32%. Create a new Color Balance and change the following; Shadows: Magenta/Green +1, Yellow/Blue +4, Midtones: Cyan/Red +16, Highlights: Cyan/Red +1, Yellow/Blue -16. Create a Gradient Map and set the left side to black and the right to white. Now change its layer Opacity to 40%. This is a good base to work from, so feel free to make changes and experiment.

USE BRUSHES FOR SURREAL COMPOSITES

LEARN HOW TO USE SIMPLE TECHNIQUES TO CREATE A COMPLEX COMPOSITION, COMBINING IMAGES AND BRUSHES

In this tutorial we'll demonstrate how to use a variety of images and brushes to create a stunning composition. We'll start with the basics, creating a gradient background and then we'll enhance the images using the lighting and colour adjustments. Another great technique used in this tutorial is adding shadows and highlights with the Dodge and Burn tools. We'll also be calling upon custom brushes to apply over the image to add a dramatic effect. To supply the final flourish, we will pay a visit to the layer styles. We created this in Photoshop Elements, but if you happen to be using Photoshop CC you have more professional features to go even further. When creating the water drops, for example, add an Inner Shadow and also modify the contours, trying different settings to create a more realistic effect. One of the secrets of a great composition is to use good quality images. You will find all the images and brushes to work with in the supplied files.

TAKE YOUR COMPOSITION OUT OF THE REAL WORLD
USE STRAIGHTFORWARD TECHNIQUES TO MAKE A PHOTOMANIPULATION

01 SET UP THE FILE
Go to File>New>Blank File or hit Cmd/Ctrl+N. Name it Storm in a Tea Cup, setting the Width to 230mm and Height to 300mm. Set the Resolution to 300 then click OK.

02 MAKE A GRADIENT BACKGROUND
Grab the Gradient tool (G) and click Edit to open the Gradient Editor. Create a new gradient using the colours #000000 and #5a5a5a, set it to Linear and then click OK.

> We created this surreal composite using Photoshop Elements, which just goes to show what can be produced if you use simple techniques wisely. If you happen to be using Photoshop CC you have even more professional features to go further

03 PLACE THE IMAGE
Go to File>Place, find the 'Teacup.jpeg' file and hit Place. Grab the Quick Selection tool (A) and, using a hard brush, select the background. Right-click on the Smart Object thumbnail and choose Simplify Layer (CC users choose Rasterize Layer), and then press backspace.

04 REFINE YOUR SELECTION
Go to Select>Refine Edge, check Smart Radius, change Radius to 0.2px, Smooth to 35, Feather to 1px, Contrast to 0%, Shift Edge to -25%, and Decontaminate Colors to 50%. Click OK.

05 RELOCATE THE IMAGE
Hit Cmd/Ctrl+T to open the Free Transform tool. Drag the image down to the bottom of the canvas, and check the Constrain Proportions box, set the Width to 150% and then rotate the image around 2 degrees.

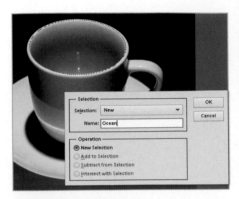

06 SAVE THE SELECTION
Grab the Elliptical Marque tool (M), set Feather to 0 pixels, and select the top part of the cup. Go to Select>Transform Selection and use the handles to adjust. Go to Select>Save Selection, name it Ocean, choose New Selection, and click OK.

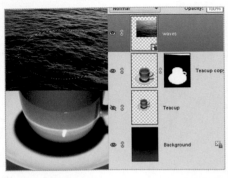

07 INSERT IMAGE
Head to File>Place and select 'Waves.jpeg'. Right-click the Smart Object thumbnail and choose Simplify Layer (CC users choose Rasterize). Go to Select>Load Selection, on Source dropdown menu choose Ocean, check the Invert box and click OK. Hit backspace on your keyboard.

08 CUT TO FIT
Press Cmd/Ctrll+D to deselect the image. Grab the Move tool (V) and drag the waves image down to create the idea of depth. Go to Select>Load Selection and choose the Ocean selection again, check the Invert box, click OK and press the backspace key on your keyboard.

09 CREATE THE WAVES
Right-click on the Waves layer and then choose Duplicate Layer. Grab the Smudge tool (R) set the Size to 125 pixels and the Strength to 50%. Drag the Smudge tool around the edges to create some waves.

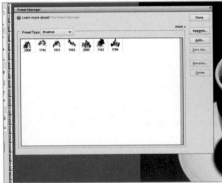

10 ADD BRUSHES
Now let's load some brushes. Go to Edit>Preset Manager (CC users go to Edit> Preset>Preset Manager), click Append, and locate 'Teacup storm.abr' from the supplied files. Click Load and then Done.

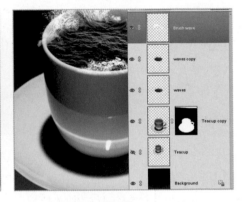

11 ENHANCE THE WAVES
Create a new layer. Grab the Brush tool (B) and open the Brush Preset Picker. Choose the Splash brushes, resize and paint some splashes over the image. Use the Brush Settings to change the angle and the Eraser tool (E) to rub out the image.

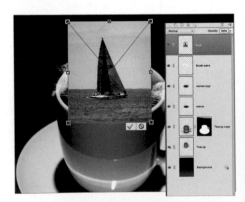

12 PLACE THE BOAT
Head to File>Place and add 'boat.jpeg'. Right-click on the Smart Object thumbnail and choose Simplify (CC users choose Rasterize). Check the Constrain Proportions box and resize the image around 25%. Grab the Quick Selection tool (A), select and delete the sky.

13 ERASER TOOL
Grab the Move tool (V) and drag the boat to the centre. Now grab the Eraser tool (E), choose a soft brush and a small size, and rub out the ocean part of the image.

14 DODGE TOOL
Now grab the Dodge tool (O), set the Range to Highlights, the size to 200 pixels and Exposure to 20%. Paint over the boat image, overexposing a little at the top of the main mast.

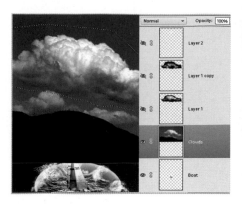

15 ADD CLOUDS
Go to File>Place and pick 'Clouds.jpeg'. Right-click on the Smart Object thumbnail and choose Simplify Layer (CC users choose Rasterize). Grab the Polygonal Lasso tool (L), set the Feather to 10px, and select around the cloud. Go to Select>Inverse and press backspace.

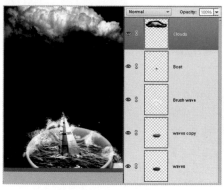

16 ADJUST LIGHTING
Click Cmd/Ctrll+T to open the Free Transform tool. Rotate the image to -10 Degrees. Now click Cmd/Ctrll+U to open Hue/Saturation, set the Saturation to -100. Hit Cmd/Ctrll+L to open the Levels, and set the Input Levels to 78, 1.00, and 255, click OK.

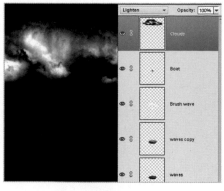

17 DODGE AND BURN
Change the blending mode of the Clouds layer to Lighten. Grab the Burn tool (O), set the Range to Highlights, Size: 500, Exposure: 40%, and paint over to underexpose around the cloud. Select the Dodge tool and, using a smaller brush, paint to overexpose some areas.

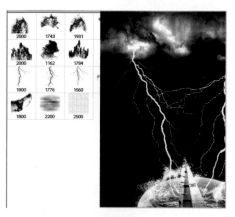

18 BRING THE STORM
Create a new layer name and name it Lightning. Now select the Brush tool (B) and open the Brush Preset Picker. Choose any of the Lightning brushes, resize and paint over the cloud image.

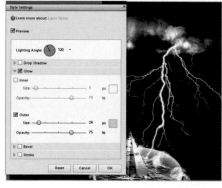

19 LAYER STYLE
Let's add a glow effect on the lightning layer. Go to Layer>Layer Style>Style Settings. Click on Glow and check the Outer box, set the Size to 24px, click on the Color box, pick a light blue colour, set the Opacity to 75%, and click OK.

20 RAINSTORM
Create a new layer, name it Rain. Grab the Brush tool (B), open the Brush Preset Picker and choose the rain brush to paint over the image. Press Cmd/Ctrll+T to rotate and resize the image and use the Eraser tool (E) to rub out the borders.

21 ADD SHADOWS
Create a new layer, name it Shadow and place over the Background layer. Grab the Elliptical Marquee tool (M), set Feather to 25px and create a selection that is almost the same size as the teacup plate. Fill with black colour, and change the layer opacity to 60%.

QUICK TIP
APPLY THE LAYER STYLES TO CREATE REALISTIC WATER DROPS ON THE IMAGE

Use the Layer Styles window to create a variety of effects. Create a new layer and name it Water Drops. Go to Layer>Layer Style>Style Settings. Set the Lighting Angle to 45° Check Drop Shadow, set the Size: 3px, Distance: 1px and Opacity: 60%. Now check the Bevel, set the Size: 15px, Direction: Up, and then click OK. Change the blend mode to Multiply and the Opacity to 60%. Grab the Brush tool, pick a bush with a hardness of around 50% and start painting the water drops around the border and over the teacup plate.

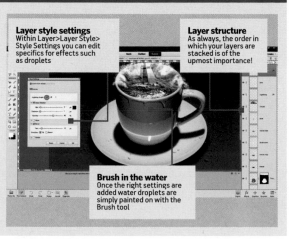

Layer style settings
Within Layer>Layer Style>Style Settings you can edit specifics for effects such as droplets

Layer structure
As always, the order in which your layers are stacked is of the upmost importance!

Brush in the water
Once the right settings are added water droplets are simply painted on with the Brush tool

Special trial offer

Enjoyed this book?

Exclusive offer for new

Try
3 issues
for just
£5*

About the mag

How Photoshop Creative can help

Inspirational techniques
Each issue is packed with tutorials showing you how to do everything in Photoshop

CD packed with resources
Every month enjoy a free CD full of resources

Join the community
Become part of the **Photoshop Creative** community with competitions, galleries and more

subscribers to...
Photoshop® creative™

Try three issues for £5 in the UK*
or just $7.85 per issue in the USA**
(saving 49% off the newsstand price)

For amazing offers please visit
www.imaginesubs.co.uk/pcr

Quote code ZGGZINE

Or telephone UK 0844 848 8415 overseas +44 (0)1795 592 871

ON THE DISC

Windows ⊞   Mac X

YOUR FREE CD OFFERS VIDEO TUTORIALS, PROJECT FILES AND MORE TO ACCOMPANY THIS BOOK

Tutorials
Access the tutorial files here and follow along with the tutorials in the bookazine or use them in other projects

Video Tuition
Create a digital painting effect and design a female android in Photoshop by following these video tutorials

Resources
Whether it's Photoshop brushes, textures or models, enhance your projects with these resources

Back Issues
Check out magazines that will further aid your digital-art projects, no matter what level you're working at

TUTORIAL FILES
FOLLOW ALONG STEP-BY-STEP

You are able to follow many of the tutorials in the bookazine step-by-step and even use the same images that we used. All you need to do is download the tutorial files and away you go. If you've seen something you like that could be used in other projects, there's nothing stopping you from doing this either.

VIDEO TUITION
WATCH AND LEARN FOR A CLEAR UNDERSTANDING

Sometimes it can be useful to see exactly how things are created, and a video tutorial is just the ticket. Learn how to create a digital painting effect on your portraits with the help of Andrei Oprinca in his hour-long video tutorial. Also, discover how to design a female android in a two-part video tutorial from Digital-Tutors.